Dress, Law and Naked Truth

The WISH List

(Warwick Interdisciplinary Studies in the Humanities)

**Series editors: Jonathan Bate, Stella Bruzzi, Thomas Docherty and
Margot Finn**

In the twenty-first century, the traditional disciplinary boundaries of higher education are dissolving at remarkable speed. The last decade has seen the flourishing of scores of new interdisciplinary research centres at universities around the world, and there has also been a move towards a more interdisciplinary teaching.

The WISH List is a collaboration between Bloomsbury Academic and the University of Warwick, a university that has been, from it foundations, at the forefront of interdisciplinary innovation in academia. The series aims to establish a framework for innovative forms of interdisciplinary publishing within the humanities, between the humanities and social sciences and even between the humanities and the hard sciences.

Also in *The WISH List*:

Reading and Rhetoric in Montaigne and Shakespeare
Peter Mack
ISBN 9781849660617 (Hardback); ISBN 9781849660600 (e-book)

*Raising Milton's Ghost: John Milton and the Sublime of Terror
in the Early Romantic Period*
Joseph Crawford
ISBN 9781849663328 (Hardback); ISBN 9781849664196 (e-book)

The Public Value of the Humanities
Edited by Jonathan Bate
ISBN 9781849664714 (Hardback); ISBN 9781849660624 (Paperback);
ISBN 9781849660631 (e-book)

Open Space Learning: A Study in Transdisciplinary Pedagogy
Nicholas Monk, Carol Chillington Rutter, Jonothan Neelands, Jonathan Heron
ISBN 9781849660549 (Hardback); ISBN 9781849660556 (e-book)

Confessions: The Philosophy of Transparency
Thomas Docherty
ISBN 9781849660556 (Hardback); ISBN 9781849666794 (e-book)

Forthcoming:

Critical Practice: Theorists and Creativity
Martin McQuillan
ISBN 9781780930350 (Hardback); ISBN 9781780930343 (Paperback);
ISBN 9781780931012 (e-book)

The Constitution of English Literature: Ideology, State and Nation
Michael Gardiner
ISBN 9781780930367 (Hardback); ISBN 9781780931098 (e-book)

Joseph Cornell versus Cinema
Michael Piggot
ISBN 9781780934150 (Hardback); ISBN 9781472503534 (e-book)

Dress, Law and Naked Truth

A Cultural Study of Fashion and Form

GARY WATT

B L O O M S B U R Y

LONDON · NEW DELHI · NEW YORK · SYDNEY

Bloomsbury Academic
An imprint of Bloomsbury Publishing Plc

50 Bedford Square	1385 Broadway
London	New York
WC1B 3DP	NY 10018
UK	USA

www.bloomsbury.com

Bloomsbury is a registered trade mark of Bloomsbury Publishing Plc

First published 2013

© Gary Watt, 2013

British Library Cataloguing-in-Publication Data
A catalogue record for this book is available from the British Library.

ISBN: HB: 978-1-4725-0042-7
ePub: 978-1-4725-0043-4
ePDF: 978-1-4725-0045-8

Library of Congress Cataloging-in-Publication Data
A catalog record for this book is available from the Library of Congress.

Typeset by Newgen Knowledge Works (P) Ltd., Chennai, India
Printed and bound in Great Britain

To my brother
Steven Watt
'bullet-proof'

Contents

Figures

Series Editor's Foreword

Dress and the law are fundamental structuring devices for our global societies: dispensing with either has been seen in literature, art and theory as an indicator of anarchy, moral collapse, even totally unrealizable liberal utopianism. One end of the spectrum – the call to orderliness – is exemplified by the closing line of Joe Orton's satirical farce set in a dysfunctional private lunatic asylum *What the Butler Saw*: 'I'm glad you don't despise tradition. Let us put our clothes on and face the world.'[1] Epitomizing the other is the manifestly more visionary but far less practical final chapter of British psychoanalyst John Carl Flügel's 1930 study *The Psychology of Clothes*, in which he calls for dress to be abandoned and nakedness to be embraced, encouraging his readers to

> contemplate the possibility that dress is, after all, destined to be but an episode in the history of humanity, and that man (and perhaps before him woman) will one day go about his business secure in the control both of his own body and of his wider physical environment, disdaining the sartorial crutches on which he perilously supported himself during the earlier tottering stages of his march towards a higher culture.[2]

The abandonment of our 'sartorial crutches' is as much a utopian, lawless fantasy now as it was in 1930, as Gary Watt intimates when, at the outset of *Dress, Law and Naked Truth* he cites the story of Stephen Gough, the 'naked rambler', who was arrested while attempting to walk the length of the UK naked apart from his shoes. However inaccurate a prediction of future attitudes to nakedness, Flügel's endpoint provides both an interesting challenge to the repressive conformity of either the representatives of law and order in Orton's final play or those affronted by Gough's self-exposure.

As Watt intimates when he says 'dress always represents order and control', law and dress are ostensibly used to set boundaries, establish rules or offer routes to conformity by suppressing subversive tendencies, whether social

---

1   Joe Orton, 'What the Butler Saw' (1969) in *The Complete Plays* (London: Eyre Methuen, 1976), pp.361–448, 448.
2   John Carl Flügel, *Psychology of Clothes* (1930) (London: The Hogarth Press, 1950), p.238.

or individual. However, 'control' – somewhat paradoxically – can also be exercised subversively, as when interactions with the law and or uses of dress and clothes provide ways for individuals to announce their individuality or unconformity. An illuminating and entertaining example is the iconic trial at the Old Bailey in 1971 of the editors of *Oz Magazine*, the longest obscenity trial in British legal history. Richard Neville, Jim Anderson and Felix Dennis posed outside the courtroom in naughty schoolboy costumes and strode into Court 2 barefoot and in flares, their attire and long hippie hair loudly proclaiming their anti-establishmentarianism and embodying the 'turn on, tune in, drop out' counterculture, which Justice Michael Argyle had such trouble comprehending.

Law and dress define us; they can form a barrier between civility and chaos and help keep bestiality and primitivism at bay. It was Aristotle who said: 'At his best, man is the noblest of all animals; separated from law and justice he is the worst.'[3] This is rather categorical, but where would we be without our unspoken laws and sense of morality? As Immanuel Kant idiosyncratically put it, 'Two things awe me most, the starry sky above me, and the moral law within me'.[4] And so, where also would we be without our attachment to dress? Clothes are discarded at several crucial junctures in Pier Paolo Pasolini's irreligious allegory *Teorema*, in which enlightenment comes to all members of an upper-bourgeois Milanese household following their serial seductions at the hands of an anonymous 'visitor', played by Terence Stamp. Right at the end of the film, the head of the household Paolo (played by Massimo Girotti) divests himself of all his clothes (and arguably also his conventionality, his heterosexuality and perhaps even his 'mortal coil') on the concourse of Milan station before running, with hands aloft, naked and screaming into a bleak, uncompromising volcanic wilderness. The puddle of clothes Paolo leaves behind (in Milan, after all, the centre of the Italian fashion industry) is perhaps the second skin that made him acceptable to the world but also accepting of it.

Law and dress facilitate mutual understanding and public interaction. The *WISH List* has always sought to enable and extend interdisciplinary

3   Aristotle, *Politics*, Book I, chapter 2.
4   Immanuel Kant, *Critique of Practical Reason* (*Kritik der praktischen Vernunft*) (1788) *Gesammelte Schriften* Deutsche Akademie der Wissenschaften zu Berlin (Berlin: G. Reimer, 1910–55), pp.1–163, 161.

dialogue within the Humanities, and in his discursive rumination on the interlaced cultural histories of dress and law, Gary Watt has embraced this ethos. Starting from the premise that 'dress is law and law is dress', Watt not only analyses the crucial intersections between law and dress but also ultimately mounts a brilliant and erudite argument for multidisciplinary study itself.

Stella Bruzzi, University of Warwick. March 2013

Author's Preface

Encounters between dress and the law appear almost daily in the news media. On 21 March 2012, *The Guardian* reported the case of a Muslim woman who, on the point of being sworn in to a jury in a criminal trial, confirmed her preference to continue wearing a 'veil' (*niqab*) and was therefore required by the judge to stand down.[1] Three days later, the same newspaper reported the story of Stephen Gough, the so-called naked rambler, who, in an attempt to walk the length of Great Britain wearing no clothes apart from shoes, was arrested in Scotland and subsequently imprisoned. The author of that article noted that Mr Gough, a former Royal Marine, had already 'effectively been in custody for nearly six years for refusing to get dressed'.[2] Is the sight of the undressed human form inherently alarming or disturbing? Is it harmful? Whom does it harm? Most of us, no matter how modest, will see ourselves naked on an almost daily basis. Is such exposure self-harming? If it is not, in what sense is public exposure harmful to others? These are questions worth asking, and I will offer my own responses before the end of this book.

In his 1859 essay *On Liberty*, John Stuart Mill argued that 'the only purpose for which power can be rightfully exercised over any member of a civilized community, against his will, is to prevent harm to others' and that '[o]ver himself, over his own body and mind, the individual is sovereign'.[3] If we were to accept, for the sake of argument, that Stephen Gough's persistent public exposure of his naked human form is not harmful in itself, one of two consequences must follow: either the authorities' response to his persistent public nudity is right for reasons other than harm, in which case Mill's harm principle is wrong; or Mill is right and the authorities are wrong. Whether Mill is right or wrong, most people will hopefully accept that the exercise of our freedoms (including the freedom to dress or undress as we choose) comes with a responsibility to have regard for the reasonable feelings of others. This is the responsibility that we describe as 'showing respect'. Just because an obligation to respect others cannot be enforced in court does not mean that it cannot have a customary force equivalent to law. One of the lessons that we will ultimately learn from the present study is about the

---

1   Owen Bowcott, 'When a Veiled Woman Had to Leave Court', *The Guardian* (Features), 21 March 2012.
2   Neil Forsyth, 'Losing Streak', *The Guardian* (Weekend), 24 March 2012.
3   Chapter I, para 9.

limits of laws that are established by the juridical system as laws 'properly-so-called'. It is only within the practically limited world of juridical laws that we must suffer the nonsense suggestion that an individual's social obligations extend only so far as another has a right to enforce them. Ironically, the courtroom provides one of the few contexts in which the logic of the harm principle is suspended. If conduct (such as appearing naked before a judge) is deemed to be a 'contempt of court', it is punishable by way of fine or imprisonment as if a crime had been committed even though no harm has been done to any individual. The basis of a finding of contempt of court is lack of respect for the legal process and for the juridical (not the private) person of the judge.[4]

Why is it that dress is 'a thing of consequence in the polite world'?[5] Why do we wear uniforms to police the political State? Why are certain modes of dress and undress provocative to civil authorities? Why is dress more provocative in some contexts – such as the courtroom, the immigration border, the public street – than in others? There are ready responses to all these questions, and they usually revolve around such pragmatic concerns as identification and security. In this book, I want to offer a more philosophical response. I will argue that guardians of good government have a vested interest in the supervision of superficialities; that their authority as gatekeepers at the border between the civil and the uncivil is materially substantiated in surface appearance. Forms of dress, as with forms of architecture, are not mere metaphors for the power and authority of the political State; they instantiate the power and authority of the political State. To put it another way, we can say that dress is not a 'mere' metaphor for the power of State, but a 'meaningful' metaphor for the power of State. Consider the metaphor of the rising sun. In terms of abstract scientific reality the sun does not in fact rise, but for most of us for most purposes this does not matter. What matters, in the sense of being meaningful to us, is that in our shared perception the sun appears to rise. The metaphor of the rising sun is inaccurate in a cosmological sense, but materially true according to other senses (including human senses) that matter. With that in mind, let me briefly state the thesis of this book. It is that dress is law and law is dress. It might be objected that I am speaking metaphorically, but the metaphor is no less real and meaningful

---

4   See Chapter Four at p.128.
5   Philip Stanhope, 4th Earl of Chesterfield (letter to his son, London, 30 December 1748).

than the metaphor of the rising sun. Actually, the assertion that dress is law and law is dress is even more meaningfully true than the metaphor of the rising sun, because law, like dress (and unlike the solar star), is to a great extent an artificial human construction. The statement 'dress is law' might be metaphorical, but it is nonetheless real, because there is no better way to appreciate the nature of dress in political society.

My philosophy of dress as law and law as dress will explain the reaction of legal authorities to dress of certain types in certain contexts. It will also elucidate the related phenomenon of State dress: police and military uniforms, judicial robes and so forth. In addition, it will offer a new appreciation of the universal human instinct to dress; the struggle to fit the individual to social forms; and the relationship between truth and human inquiry. So far as the latter is concerned, my argument, in a nutshell, is that the collective human endeavour to know truth is not an endeavour of discovery but an endeavour of fabricating satisfactory surface appearance. Consider the nutshell: if we are content with the beautiful appearance of the shell, we might prefer to keep it intact rather than break it in search of contents. If we give it a moment's thought, we might wonder if there is a sound kernel of truth within, but we will not go searching for it if we are satisfied with the appearance of the shell. Focusing on such practical examples as the legal endeavour to establish truth by means of evidence, I will show that the project of power in polite society is not to reveal and *dis*-cover underlying truth, but rather to establish satisfactory superficialities. A proof of this is the fact that the law conceives the human in polite (i.e. 'political') society to be an actor hidden behind a mask of public performance. The very notion that our social relations are mediated through legal 'personality' is an artificial construct made in terms of the metaphorical materiality of the mask (*persona*) that was worn by actors in public dramas in the ancient world.[6] The law struggles to hear and to see the nuances of our inner being, and so it prefers to deal with the abstract superficiality of legal personality. Even corporations have legal personality and it is only with reluctance that the courts will occasionally lift the so-called corporate veil to reveal the underlying reality of a corporate entity.[7] Another

---

6   Peter Goodrich, *Languages of Law: From Logics of Memory to Nomadic Masks* (London: Weidenfeld and Nicolson, 1992); Connal Parsley, 'The Mask and Agamben: The Transitional Juridical Technics of Legal Relation' *Law Text Culture* 14.1 (2001), pp.12–39 (citing Giorgio Agamben *Nudità* [Rome: Nottetempo, 2009], p.71).

7   See Chapter Four at p.80.

proof is the language of proof itself. I will demonstrate that the civil project is to establish impenetrable proofs much as one might fabricate waterproof or bulletproof clothes. The civil project of truth-seeking is not to expose that which lies below surface appearances but rather to establish superficial forms with such solidity that they are able to deflect practically any suspicion that there might be a better truth below the surface.

In a letter written to Goethe in 1831, Thomas Carlyle complained that the world of London was 'dancing a Tarantula Dance of Political Reform, and has no ear left for Literature'.[8] The same complaint might be raised today within the legal academy. The dominance of the 'social science' paradigm – sometimes beholden to political manifesto or restricted to an empiricist mindset – too often obscures the (perhaps disconcerting) fact that the creation and enforcement of laws is a human artifice or performance. The present study proceeds on the assumption that if one wants to test the possibility that law and dress are the same artistic or artificial cultural phenomenon, one will learn as much from artists and cultural commentators as from university scholars. In this regard, many of the greatest insights are to be found in the work of individuals who have an especially imagistic or visual imagination. Among them are certain creative artists who have a genius gift of being able to discern human meaning and human motives within the dress, display and artificial theatre of life.

The central chapters of this book are arranged in broadly chronological order – ranging from prehistory and the ancient, to the early modern, to the modernity of the nineteenth century and the present day. The aim is to offer an analytical appreciation of perennial connections and tensions between dress and law. Whereas the particular shapes of dress and law shift constantly, their performance of power *in limine* ('at the threshold') of civil society has remained constantly present throughout human political history. Since humans first started to dress thoughts in language and to dress brute force in published laws, we have been able to draw certain constant inferences from the habit of dressing the human body. One such is the social desire to create normative order. I agree with Roland Barthes where he writes:

> The crucial methodological caution is to be slow to equate superstructure (dress) with infrastructure (history). Meaningful epistemology moves us

---

8   13 August 1831.

more and more to study the socio-historical totality as a system of forms and functions: for dress (as for language) the forms and functions are normative in nature; they demonstrate society's power to create itself.[9]

In Chapter One, I introduce my argument that 'dress is law and law is dress'. The remaining chapters can be outlined, in terms of content and their place in the general chronology of the book, as described next.

Chapter Two, 'Foundations of the State of Dress', engages with the prehistory and early history of dress, especially as it is revealed through cultural accounts of human origins (including *The Epic of Gilgamesh* and *The Book of Genesis*) and through the etymology of the dress lexicon. Moving on to examine dress as a mode of political performance in antiquity, this chapter demonstrates that dress, no less than law, may be regarded as a maker of the civil world. As Thomas Carlyle observed, we inhabit an *Orbis Vestitus*.[10] This chapter will reveal that the foundations of the idea of the civil State include three mutually correspondent cultural orders: the orders of dress, architecture and law. A fourth order, which joins the other three even as they are joined to each other, is the order of language. It will be apparent from all this talk of 'order' that there is nothing postmodern in the cultural foundations of the civil State.

Chapter Three, 'Shakespeare on Proof and Fabricated Truth', demonstrates that law and dress are partners in a project of fabricating persuasive 'shows of truth' in the form of satisfactory proofs.[11] Focusing on legal and cultural developments in early modern England, especially as elucidated by Shakespeare's dramatic works, we will see how artificial forms of truth relate to the notion that there is a better truth to be revealed under superficial appearances.

Chapter Four, 'The Face the Law Makes', shows how the face of civil authority in polite society has been fashioned and reinforced throughout history by forces of uniformity and conformity harnessed to forms of official

---

9   'Histoire et sociologie du vêtement: quelques observations méthodologiques' *Annales: Économies, Sociétés, Civilisations* 12.3 (1957), pp.430–41, 441 (my translation).

10   Thomas Carlyle, *Sartor Resartus: The Life and Opinions of Herr Teufelsdröckh* (Boston: James Munroe and Co, 1836), Book I, chapter 5. (Originally published in serial form in *Fraser's Magazine* [November 1833–August 1834].) Throughout the present study, quotations are taken from the Oxford World's Classics edition: Kerry McSweeney and Peter Sabor (eds) (Oxford: OUP, 1987).

11   A version of this argument was first presented at the conference *La Preuve* ('Proof and Evidence') organized by Jean-Pierre Schandeler and Nathalie Vienne-Guerrin at the *Institut de recherche sur la Renaissance, l'âge Classique et les Lumières* (Université Montpellier III, June 2010).

and professional dress. This chapter likens the dress-based modes that form the face of civil authority to the persuasive modes that constitute dramatic performance, focusing especially upon 'theatrical' performance by the legal profession in the mid-nineteenth century.

Chapter Five, 'Addressing the Naked and Unfolding the Veil', argues that in the polite society of a civil State, public nudity and public face-covering (including, in non-Islamic States, covering by means of the Islamic veil) will inevitably produce confrontation with the fabricated face of legal authority in certain situations. This chapter asks what is, and what should be, the response of civil authorities to extremely clothed and extremely unclothed modes of dress.

Chapter Six, 'Something More Comfortable: A Fitting Conclusion', addresses the other side of the question: it asks to what extent the individual in civil society is under a duty to compromise their freedom to self-fashion and to what extent any such duty ought to be enforceable in law.

Dress and law overlap in their functions and concerns in a way which, far from being fleeting and casually coincidental, actually has the capacity to elucidate the enduring significance of both law and dress. I argue that the territorial similarity between the 'jurisdiction of law' and the 'jurisdiction of dress' produces at least three related cultural effects. The first effect is a general preoccupation with outward appearance, which is most clearly demonstrated in legal concern for evidence and proof (this is the subject of Chapter Three, 'Shakespeare on Proof and Fabricated Truth'). The second effect is that the law appropriates the liminal layer of dress for the rhetorical or theatrical performance of regulatory power; an effect which has been demonstrated throughout history in the form of togas, gowns, judicial robes, police uniforms and so forth (this is the subject of Chapter Four, 'The Face the Law Makes'). The third effect is that the law demonstrates anxiety with regard to attempts by individuals to exercise performative power, through personal modes of dress and undress, in the liminal space of dress that the law takes to be a locus of its own dominion (this is the subject of Chapter Five, 'Addressing the Naked and Unfolding the Veil').

The reader will notice that every chapter begins with a quotation from the writings of Thomas Carlyle, most of them taken from *Sartor Resartus: The Life and Opinions of Herr Teufelsdröckh*.[12] *Sartor Resartus* ('The Tailor

---

12   Carlyle, *Sartor Resartus*.

Retailored') is an extraordinary genre-defying work.[13] It never retains any form long enough for us to pin it down as satire, novel, essay or extended sermon. Carlyle, a Scot, disguises his ideas in the words of an English editor who purports to present the discovered work of a German philosopher by the name of Diogenes Teufelsdröckh. Seen one way, *Sartor Resartus* is layered in multiple false forms, but considered holistically it presents a philosophy of clothes that is all the more integrated and persuasive precisely because it is all dressed up.

Thomas Carlyle has rightly been called the 'founder' of dress studies.[14] The subject of dress is nowadays taken very seriously, not only in the academic disciplines of costume, fashion and material studies, but also in the scholarly fields of anthropology, sociology, philosophy, politics, classics, gender studies, literary studies, theatre and performance studies, social psychology and in any number of subplots in these fields. A handful of legal academics have undertaken sustained and interesting engagement with the iconic and semiotic significance of dress and law and a few have even acknowledged the importance of Carlyle's *Sartor Resartus*.[15] Most jurists, in contrast, have been content to engage with various aspects (including 'human rights' aspects) of the legal regulation of dress. When legal scholars have occasionally engaged with that most obvious of overlaps between dress and law – the 'sumptuary laws' that have established dress codes down the ages – they have too often

13   See, generally, William J. F. Keenan, 'Introduction: *"Sartor Resartus"* Restored: Dress Studies in Carlylean Perspective', in William J. F. Keenan (ed.), *Dressed to Impress: Looking the Part* (Dress, Body, Culture) (Oxford and New York: Berg, 2001), pp.1–49; Michael Carter, *Fashion Classics from Carlyle to Barthes* (Oxford and New York: Berg, 2003), chapter 1.

14   Keenan, 'Introduction: *"Sartor Resartus"* Restored', p.4.

15   For example, Peter Goodrich, 'Signs Taken for Wonders: Community, Identity, and "A History of Sumptuary Law"' *Law & Social Inquiry* 23.3 (1998), pp.707–28; and also by Goodrich, 'Lex Laetans: Three Theses on the Unbearable Lightness of Legal Critique' *Law & Literature* 17 (2005), p.293; 'Satirical Legal Studies: From the Legists to the Lizard' *Michigan Law Review* 103 (2004), p.397; Paul Raffield, 'A Discredited Priesthood: The Failings of Common Lawyers and Their Representation in Seventeenth Century Satirical Drama' *Law & Literature* 17 (2005), p.365. Paul Raffield, *Images and Cultures of Law in Early Modern England: Justice and Political Power, 1558–1660* (Cambridge: CUP, 2004); Jeffrey Malkan 'Literary Formalism, Legal Formalism' *Cardozo Law Review* 19 (1998), p.1393; Christopher Tomlins, 'The Threepenny Constitution (and the Question of Justice)' *Alabama Law Review* 58 (2007), p.979; I. Bennett Capers, 'Cross Dressing and the Criminal' *Yale Journal of Law & the Humanities* 20 (2008), p.1; Nick Hull observes a kindred spirit between one of America's greatest law teachers, Karl Llewellyn, and Thomas Carlyle (who, according to at least one commentator was briefly a student of law: Carlisle Moore, '*Sartor Resartus* and the Problem of Carlyle's "Conversion"' *PMLA* 70 [1955], pp.662, 664, 669). Hull notes that Llewellyn occasionally wrote under the pseudonym 'Teufelsdröckh'. (Nick E. Hull, 'The Romantic Realist: Art, Literature and the Enduring Legacy of Karl Llewellyn's "Jurisprudence"' *The American Journal of Legal History* 40.2 (1996), pp.115–45.)

focused on the law and overlooked the clothes. Peter Goodrich argues that we should pay attention to the jurisprudence of the dress itself:

> The lesson of sumptuary law is in large part that far from seeking to make clothes transparent, the task of legal scholarship is to attend to the detail of dress and the other forms of appearance of legal and political power.[16]

The present study is the first attempt by a legal scholar to engage with the body of dress scholarship and to offer an integrated philosophy of dress and law. A visitor to the field of dress studies is confronted with a truly daunting volume of scholarly work and must be resigned to the fact that no individual could possibly read it all. The Hilers's 1939 *Bibliography of Costume* lists around 8,000 scholarly works on various aspects of fashion and dress.[17] If one were to produce a similarly comprehensive book today, and if it were to list works in non-Latin alphabets and the recent proliferation of academic journal articles, it would break the bookshelf. Dress is nowadays so ubiquitous in scholarship, media and the arts that the present study might have been expanded with examples to ten times its size. I have tailored my materials to a rather tighter fit in the hope that the reader will more clearly see the shape of my thought within them. The scholar of dress studies will observe that I refer to many early writers on the subject, including such luminaries as Thomas Carlyle, James Laver and Quentin Bell. I do not neglect more recent writers, but if some of my choices seem old-fashioned, it is because the ideas of writers who were working before dress scholarship was established as a discipline are sometimes especially amenable to inter-disciplinary connection with other areas of thought, including law.

The end of this beginning seems an appropriate place to express my thanks to Stella Bruzzi, author of *Undressing Cinema*,[18] who chaired the public lecture in which I offered some early explorations on the theme of dress and law, and to Leif Dahlberg who published those first thoughts in an edited collection on the subject of law and the image.[19] As one of the supervising

---

16   Goodrich, 'Signs Taken', p.724.

17   Hilaire and Meyer Hiler, *Bibliography of Costume* (New York: Benjamin Blom, 1939).

18   Stella Bruzzi, *Undressing Cinema: Clothing and Identity in the Movies* (London: Routledge, 1997).

19   Leif Dahlberg (ed.), *Visualizing Law and Authority: Essays on Legal Aesthetics* (Berlin and New York: De Gruyter, 2012).

editors of the 'WISH List' series, Professor Bruzzi deserves special thanks for encouraging me to develop my ideas in book form. I am also grateful to Caroline Wintersgill, Mark Richardson and to the other staff at Bloomsbury Academic for bringing this book to print. Most of all, I am grateful, as ever, to my family for their constant encouragement and support.

CHAPTER ONE

Dress is Law

*[A]ll Forms whereby Spirit manifests itself to sense, whether
outwardly or in the imagination, are Clothes . . . the Pomp and
Authority of Law . . . are properly a Vesture and Raiment.*[1]

A principal form 'whereby Spirit manifests itself to sense' is the form of
words. In one of his *Letters to His Son*, Philip Stanhope, the 4th Earl of
Chesterfield, called words 'the dress of thoughts'.[2] We might readily accept
that law goes dressed in the form of words, but will we also accept that law
goes dressed in dress? Moreover, can we accept that dress *is* law and that
law *is* dress? The image of a thing is usually contrasted with the thing itself;
the image of a thing is said to be reflective, representative, reproductive or
mimetic of the thing, rather than identical to it. And yet the image of a thing
can sometimes be the most reliable knowledge we have of a thing. Sometimes
we lack capacity to see the thing itself because the thing itself is too profound
or too abstract or too remote. In such cases we might have to settle for a
flame-cast shadow on the wall of a cave[3] or an image reflected in a mirror.[4]
The idea of law in human society is so primal and pervasive, so innate and
inescapable, that we struggle in vain to perceive what law is apart from the
cultural forms in which it is expressed. Lawrence Rosen was surely right
when he observed that 'law is so deeply embedded in the particularities of
each culture that carving it out as a separate domain and only later making
note of its cultural connections distorts the nature of both law and culture'.[5]
Can we imagine a society without law? Perhaps. Can we imagine a society
without dress? Perhaps. Can we imagine a society with law which does not
have dress, or a society which has dress but has not law? It is almost certain

---

1   Thomas Carlyle, *Sartor Resartus: The Life and Opinions of Herr Teufelsdröckh* (1833–4) (Boston:
     James Munroe and Co., 1836), Book III, chapter 9.
2   London, 20 November 1753.
3   Plato, *The Republic*, Book VII.
4   1 Cor. 13.12. Biblical references are to the New International Version unless otherwise stated.
5   Lawrence Rosen, *Law as Culture: An Invitation* (Princeton, NJ: Princeton University Press, 2006),
     p.xii.

that no such society has ever existed, or will ever exist; for the same social and cultural forces which compel us to dress, compel us also to make and obey laws. If dress and law are essentially the same cultural phenomenon, as I contend, it will follow that when we better understand the nature of dress, we will better understand the nature of law. Clothing is an image of law, certainly, but it is one of those species of image that is not merely a reflection of the thing but as close as one can get to an expression of the identity of the thing. I will argue that the nature of law as a social and cultural idea is expressed as well in clothing as in any written text, so that clothing is a material substantiation of law's nature as social and cultural fact. Of course, I do not claim that dress codes and conventions are 'laws' as judges and jurists define them – they are not in that sense 'laws properly-so-called' – but I do contend that they operate in many cultures as rules with a normative force equivalent to the force of laws properly-so-called. Ask yourself when was the last time you felt compelled to alter your behaviour so as to comply with a law laid down by the legislature or by a judge. Ask yourself when was the last time you felt compelled to alter your behaviour to comply with a custom or convention of dress. An extraterrestrial visiting most human cultures on earth would be hard-pressed to know which normative body of rules – the juridical or the sartorial – should carry the label 'law'.

The dress of words cannot be ignored. It is in the layer of words that we find one of the most compelling proofs for my thesis that dress is culturally identical to law, for the etymological connection between law and dress is intimate, ancient and profound.[6] The very word 'dress' ultimately derives from *reg-*, which is precisely the same Proto-Indo-European (PIE) root that gives modern European languages and legal systems their most basic word-set for legal order (the set which includes 'rule', 'right', 'director', '*rex*', 'regulation' and so forth).[7] To dress is therefore to 'regulate' or to 'order'.[8] Leading scholars of PIE language and culture have observed that in the reconstructed PIE lexicon, 'much of the concept of "law" derives from that of "order" or "what is fitting"'.[9] The same is true of a great deal of our modern

6   Unless otherwise stated, etymologies are taken from R. K. Barnhart (ed.), *Chambers Dictionary of Etymology* (London: The H Wilson Company, 1988).
7   '*Costume de rigueur*', a French term for a strict dress code, makes the etymological point.
8   In Tudor England, the language of 'ordering' was synonymous with that of 'tailoring'. See Jane Ashelford, *The Art of Dress: Clothes and Society, 1500–1914* (London: National Trust, 1999), p.51.
9   James Patrick Mallory and Douglas Quentin Adams, *The Oxford Introduction to Proto-Indo-European and the Proto-Indo-European World* (Oxford: OUP, 2006), p.276.

language for clothing and dress. 'Raiment', for example, is the etymological twin of 'arrangement'.

The word 'vesture' (derived from the PIE root *wes-)[10] is obviously of significance to the notion that legal power is something that may be 'invested'. We see the ongoing significance of that notion in, for example, the investiture ceremony by which appointments are made to the Supreme Court of the United States of America. The legal notion of acquiring a 'vested' interest in an asset, such as land, might also be directly related to clothing. The historians Pollock and Maitland suggested an origin in the ancient ceremony of land transfer known as 'livery of seisin' which frequently required, among other things, that the donee should wear a war glove or gauntlet transferred to him by the donor. This glove, they record, is the *vestita manus* that will fight in defence of this land against all comers'.[11] Even the word 'investment' can be understood to indicate a fund or asset that is clothed in care. This is supported by the fact that a trust fund which trustees are required to give up on demand, and which they are therefore under no duty to 'invest' (prudent investment being incompatible with short-term planning), is said to be held under a 'bare' trust.[12]

The PIE lexicon was probably formed around the period 4500–4000 BC, and had already undergone major dispersal by around 2300–1600 BC, which is approximately when the speakers of Greek are thought to have first arrived in the territory of Greece.[13] The origin of the word 'costume' may not be as old as that, but it is another word that is intimately associated with law, for 'costume' and 'custom' are etymologically the same word. Law is something which it is our custom to follow and to which we become accustomed. Long-standing systems of law such as that which prevails in the jurisdiction of England and Wales invariably have their origins in (and still bear the vestige of) practices that are properly described as 'customary'.[14] A name frequently associated with the local laws of France, before the

10   Ibid., p.231.
11   Frederick Pollock and Frederic William Maitland, *The History of English Law before the Time of Edward I: Volume II*, 2nd edn (Cambridge: Cambridge University Press, 1898), p.85.
12   Gary Watt, *Trusts and Equity*, 5th edn (Oxford: OUP, 2012), p.403.
13   Martin E. Huld, 'Indo-Europeans', in Michael Gagarin and Elaine Fantham (eds), *The Oxford Encyclopedia of Ancient Greece & Rome*, Vol. 4 (Oxford: OUP, 2010), pp.63–5.
14   See, generally, Amanda Perreau-Saussine and James Bernard Murphy (eds), *The Nature of Customary Law* (Cambridge: Cambridge University Press, 2007).

introduction of the Napoleonic *Code Civil*, was '*coutumes*'.[15] The word 'habit' is also suggestive of law and dress. The word derives from the Latin *habitus*, and in turn from *habere* ('to have' and 'to hold'), and this is derived from the PIE root **ghēbh-* ('to take'). It might be assumed, therefore, that a habit is something we take hold of, but far more accurate, surely, is the sense that a habit is something that takes hold of us. Law and dress are connected by habit in that sense. As Michael de Certau has written: 'There is no law that is not inscribed on bodies. Every law has a hold on the body'.[16] (Habit in the sense of something that takes hold of us and something to which we become accustomed, also calls to mind Bourdieu's sociological concept of *habitus*.[17]) Finally, even the word 'law' itself denotes a layer (from the PIE root **legh-* 'to lie').[18] A Swedish word for law is 'lag'. The same word in English means to clad. Lawyers have sometimes been portrayed as liars who pull the wool over our eyes or as loquacious advocates who 'lay it on thick'. There is at least an etymological truth in the caricature.

In cold countries, and also for the conduct of certain perilous activities, clothing performs the practical function of conferring physical protection,[19] but when clothing is not required for protection, why do we wear it? An English barrister once claimed that the tax-deductable expenses of her professional self-employment should include the cost of purchasing her court attire. There is no doubt that a barrister, as a courtroom advocate, has to be appropriately dressed; indeed it has been said that '[w]ithout gown and bands, the barrister is officially 'invisible' to the judge in court'.[20] The House of Lords nevertheless rejected her claim because, in addition to satisfying her professional needs, her clothes were considered to confer 'warmth and decency'.[21]

The notion of 'decency', which informs such criminal offences as 'indecent exposure' and 'public indecency',[22] is not merely a matter of law; it is

15   For example, David Hoüard, *Traités Sur Les Coutumes Anglo-Normandes* (Rouen: Le Boucher, 1776).

16   Michel de Certeau, *The Practice of Everyday Life* (trans. Steven F. Rendall) (Berkeley: University of California Press, 2002), p.139.

17   Pierre Bourdieu, *Outline of a Theory of Practice* (*Esquisse d'une théorie de la pratique*, 1972) (Cambridge: CUP, 1977).

18   Mallory and Adams, *The Oxford Introduction*, p.277.

19   The Yaghan people of Tierra del Fuego, who used to live naked despite very cold temperatures, are often cited as an exception.

20   James Parkyns Derriman, *Pageantry of the Law* (London: Eyre & Spottiswoode, 1955), p.38.

21   *Mallalieu v. Drummond* [1983] 2 AC 861, 875 (House of Lords).

22   Modern legislation in the jurisdiction of England and Wales has abandoned the language of decency (Sexual Offences Act 2003 s.66), but it still survives in some other jurisdictions.

something made by law and culture. It is an almost universal feature of human societies to have a code or convention for the dressing or adornment of bare human flesh. This, if one reflects upon it, is a remarkable thing. Few animals adorn themselves artificially, and arguably none does so for reasons of dress, but adult humans invariably do. In his book *Social Conventions,* Andrei Marmor reminds us that the social convention of dress does not always take the form of clothing:

> Suppose that the reasons, or needs, functions, etc., for having dress code norms in our society are P. . . . Now, it shouldn't be difficult to imagine a different society where P is instantiated by a different kind of social practice, for instance, that people paint their faces in various colors in comparable circumstances.[23]

Clothing is obviously a major component of dress, but so too is artificial bodily modification ranging from shaving to scarification. When we accept that dress is not limited to cloth cladding of the sort that is usual in human societies in cold climates, we can proceed to observe that dress and adornment are as pervasive as laws. Not only do law and dress distinguish human civil society from animal modes of life, but also, within civil society, dress and adornment mediate between the bare human individual and the social group in a way that parallels law's function as a mediator between the individual and society. It is therefore plausible to argue that dress is not merely an image of law's functions of social communication and social regulation, but that it might occupy a cultural locus identical with law, so that dress becomes not merely correspondent with law but potentially cooperative and competitive with law.

The letter of the law requires us to dress in public places, but quite regardless of the letter of the law, the vast majority of adults go dressed in public because they acknowledge a strong social convention that compels them to dress. Indeed, it may be supposed that most people would more readily cross the line of a written law of the land (such as the prohibition against parking a car in a restricted zone) than to contravene an unwritten customary prohibition against public nudity. A few years ago, I gave a public lecture on law and dress. The formal invitation card contained the advice 'Dress Code: None',

---

23   Andrei Marmor, *Social Conventions* (Princeton, NJ: Princeton University Press, 2009), p.75.

but nobody turned up naked. Let us suppose that 'to dress' is culturally as fundamental as 'to obey law'. Let us conjecture that the cultural forces that compel us to dress are the same as those which compel us to make and obey laws. In such a world, might it be that the evident efforts of legislators and other officers of law to dominate the barrier of dress that exists between the ordered and the unordered, is not so much an effort to exert a power that they possess as an effort to harness a power that resides in the barrier itself?

At this point, it will be useful to elucidate some of the key terms that are used throughout this book (and which appear in its title). Namely, 'dress', 'law', 'naked', 'truth', 'culture' and 'fashion'. Each of these terms is thought-provoking and contestable. I cannot define what they mean, but I can begin to explain what I mean by them.

A number of authors agree on the following working definition of the 'dress' of an individual: 'the assemblage of body modifications . . . and body supplements . . . displayed by a person and worn at a particular moment in time'.[24] No definition is ever perfect, and on a strict reading of this definition the requirement that dress be 'worn' would seem to exclude the clean-shaven face from the category of dress, which would surely be an error. One can perhaps be said to wear a trimmed moustache or a groomed beard, but one cannot be said to wear facial hair that is not there at all (without prejudice to the possibility that all faces are, in a sense, 'put on'). Despite that pedantic reservation, the preceding definition of individual dress serves as a useful working definition of what dress *is*. What it does not profess to tell us is what dress *does*, and why it does it. In answer to the question 'what does dress do?', I would respond that it 'orders' or 'arranges us'. By this I mean that the process of dress creates an arrangement or 'raiment' out of our bodies and other material. It follows that dressing is a deliberate activity and one that has an intrinsic order to it. We might joke that we sometimes just 'throw stuff on', but that is never really true when we are talking about dress. Pure accidents happen, of course, and some of them (including, reputedly, the accident of setting a tailcoat on fire) have been the inspiration for modes of dress,[25] but until we deliberately exercise the will to adopt an accident

24 Joanne B. Eicher, Sandra L. Evenson and Hazel A. Lutz (eds), *The Visible Self: Global Perspectives of Dress, Culture, and Society*, 2nd edn (New York: Fairchild, 2000), p.4; Mary Ellen Roach-Higgins and Joanne B. Eicher, 'Dress and Identity' *Clothing and Textiles Research Journal* 10.4 (1992), pp.1–8.

25 Quentin Bell, *On Human Finery* (1947) (London: The Hogarth Press, 1976), p.96.

as a mode of dress, it remains an accident pure and simple. In answer to the question 'for what purpose does dress arrange us?', I would respond that we dress in order to project ourselves and to protect ourselves. The projective aspect (which has been observed in dress since at least as far back as Tertullian)[26] might be said to be outward-looking in the main and the protective aspect might be said to be inward-looking in the main, but there are surely times when we dress in order to project a sense of ourselves inwards to be appreciated by our own inner eye and other times (perhaps especially when we dress in uniform) when the protective aspect of dress is not directed inwardly to self-protection but outwardly to the protection of others. The practical purposes of dress are always directed towards one or more of decency, decoration and defence, and each of these purposes falls within one or other of the paradigm purposes of projection or protection. Decoration is perhaps mostly projection. Defence is mostly protection. Decency is both, inasmuch as it projects a sense of respect for civil order and it protects us from the accusation that we are disrespectful, uncivil or impolite. To summarize, I proceed on the understanding that dress is the ordering of bodily appearance for purposes of protection and projection.

One feature of our physical accoutrement which does not fit easily within the category of protection or projection (or within the subcategories of decency, decoration and defence) is the feature of bearing a load. Dress no doubt includes trousers with pockets and overtly decorative handbags, but not all cargo-carrying accoutrement is a form of dress. When we go shopping, it is a rare plastic carrier bag that will qualify as dress (a carrier bearing the name of a high-status store might just qualify). It is likewise a rare rucksack that will qualify as dress. I stated earlier that dress has a deliberate aspect. In the case of a commonplace carrier bag or rucksack, our deliberation is wholly directed towards the cargo-carrying function of the rucksack, and that thought leaves little or no room for deliberation of dress. It is no doubt for this reason that Stephen Gough, the so-called naked rambler, does not consider that his principles are in any way compromised by the expediency of carrying a backpack. More intriguing is the fact that he is willing to wear shoes, since footwear is undoubtedly an item of dress and a very significant one.[27] If we regard Mr Gough as undressed despite the fact that he wears

---

26   De pallio 3.7.1.
27   Giorgio Riello and Peter McNeil, *Shoes: A History from Sandals to Sneakers* (Oxford and New York: Berg, 2006).

shoes this might indicate that in dress, as in law, the *de minimis* principle applies; which is to say that in a cloth-based dress culture an individual is still deemed to be unclothed even if he or she sports a peripheral item of dress. Either that, or the conundrum of an unclothed man wearing shoes might simply be an illustration of the fact that strict definition is always inaccurate oversimplification.

If dress is difficult to define conclusively, it is no more possible to be definitive about the nature of law.[28] By 'law' I mean civil order on very many levels, from the most general level that distinguishes anarchic human association from ordered civil society to the very particular level of a judicial decree that is binding on the parties to a case. A species of law need not be a juridical law properly-so-called for it to operate and feel like law, and therefore to be meaningfully spoken of as law. A rule of dress can be of this sort. As Professor Hart wrote: 'there *is* a rule that a man must bare his head in church.'[29] The rule that we must go dressed in public is also a customary law in society regardless of whatever, for the time being, the judges or the statutes lay down as juridical law properly-so-called. It has been said that we are 'such creatures of fashion that we tend to accept its influence almost as a law of nature'.[30] It is even more true to say that as civil creatures, we are creatures of dress and obedient to the dress code. Laws that lay down rules for the regulation of behaviour are generally of two types, either they are prescriptive laws that require certain conduct or they are proscriptive laws that prohibit certain conduct. It has been observed that commentary on dress frequently employs the same dichotomy.[31] For example, the title of the popular television series *What Not to Wear* is in the proscriptive mode, whereas the title to John T. Molloy's famous book *Dress for Success* is in the prescriptive mode. Legal prescriptions and proscriptions have the capacity to be internalized over time, and the same is true of dress codes. This capacity of law and dress to convert the 'obligatory' into the 'desirable' accords with the function of ritual as Victor Turner describes it.[32]

'Naked' I take to mean an absence of dress. This might seem too trite to state, but ask yourself whether a dog or a bird is 'naked' and one instinctively

---

28   Herbert L. A. Hart, 'Definition and Theory in Jurisprudence' *LQR* 70 (1954), p.37.
29   Herbert L. A. Hart, *The Concept of Law* (Oxford: Clarendon Press, 1961), p.10.
30   Bell, *On Human Finery,* p.57.
31   Eicher, *Visible Self,* p.77.
32   Victor W. Turner, *The Forest of Symbols: Aspects of Ndembu Ritual* (Ithaca: Cornell University Press, 1967), p.30. (Turner applies Émile Durkheim's observations on the internalization of social norms.)

senses that such words are inappropriate to bare animal life because the presence of nakedness implies an absence of dress and it is not in the nature of animals to 'dress'. It cannot be denied that some animals modify their bodies, but appreciated from the perspective of the human cultural tradition of using dress as artistic and aspirational expression there is apparently nothing resembling artificial art in what animals do. The animal instinct to modify appearance, to the extent that it exists, never involves the sort of deliberation that would qualify it as 'dress'. This psychological and philosophical distinction between humans and other animals might be hard to establish as a biochemical fact, but it is readily recognizable as a cultural fact. Of course, the 'fact' of human distinction from the rest of zoological nature may be a creation of human linguistic constructs and of other anthropocentric aspects of the culture of human civil society, but as a culturally recognized fact it is self-evident and meaningful even if it can be accused of being self-defining and self-serving. Instead of describing animals as naked, it might be better to describe them as 'bare';[33] it might be even better to describe animal life as merely 'zoologically natural'. The cultural distinction between human nature and zoological nature in the matter of dress finds some support in the distinction that Kenneth Clark drew between the 'naked' and the 'nude' human form.[34] According to Clark's theory, the naked is merely the human form undressed, whereas the nude is the human form idealized in art. There is no equivalent to this distinction between 'nude' and 'naked' anywhere else in the animal kingdom. It should be noted that there is a curious connection between the numerous illustrations that accompany Clark's classic study *The Nude*. Namely that the vast majority of the so-called nude figures are actually in contact with material forms, for example fabricated metal or cloth. Where a figure is free of any material trappings, it will usually be associated with a tangible sense of architectural order – for example by means of a rigorously ordered hairstyle. One example from Clark's book – the famous 'Vitruvian Man' by Leonardo Da Vinci – is the epitome of the nude figure dressed or ordered in an architectural frame. In the Western tradition, the artistic ideal of human civilization is not the nude figure in splendid isolation but the nude in association with artificial frames or fabricated material.

33   Compare Giorgio Agamben, *Homo Sacer: Sovereign Power and Bare Life* (trans. Daniel Heller-Roazen) (Stanford: Stanford University Press, 1998).
34   Kenneth Clark, *The Nude: A Study in Ideal Form* (London: John Murray, 1956).

'Truth' is perhaps the most contestable word in this book. It may be the most contestable word in any book. The philological search for the meaning of the word 'truth' is hardly less perplexing than the philosophical search for the meaning of truth. By the end of this book, I hope that we will have acquired a new appreciation of the concept of truth as it is used in legally ordered society, but we cannot hope to render the word less contestable. The problem of speaking 'truth' is a function of language. Thomas Hobbes was right when he said that '"true" and "false" are attributes of speech, not of things'.[35] One cannot give meaning to the word 'truth' without employing metaphor, and the metaphor one employs determines the meaning of the word. There are many metaphors for truth and falsehood – 'the copy' and 'the reflection' to name just two – but consider how much of our language for truth and falsehood corresponds to, or coincides with, language for dress: 'reveal'; 'discover'; 'colour'; 'mask'; 'disguise'; 'veil'; 'put on a front'; 'spin a yarn'; 'unravel lies'; 'under cover'; 'keep it under your hat'; 'she has something up her sleeve'; 'he's a wolf in sheep's clothing'. At first sight, 'insincerity' depends upon a different material metaphor (it alludes to patching up a cracked ceramic object with wax – from the Latin *sin cerae* ['without wax']), but even here the implication is that the person who is trying to pass off broken pottery as having integrity will also dress the surface of the patched-up ceramic by painting or papering over the cracks. The philosopher William James suggested that truth is merely 'what works'.[36] One aspect of my argument is that juridical truth is established by means of artificial fabrication. This is not to say that juridical truth is a lie. It is, by its own terms, the truth, the whole truth and nothing but the truth. But it is not the only truth.

'Cultural' is a word that I am happy to leave to its etymological meaning. I take it to indicate something that grows in a society as a plant grows in a garden. It takes the form it does partly on account of conditions over which we have no control and partly on account of human art. Architecture, law, painting. These are all cultures, and part of culture.

So we come at last to the word 'fashion'. The first task is to distinguish fashion from dress. If dress is the line that distinguishes animal from civil,

---

35   *Leviathan* (1651) I.iv. On truth construction in legal language, see Michael Freeman and Fiona Smith (eds), *Law and Language*, Current Legal Issues, Vol. 15 (Oxford: OUP, 2013).

36   William James, *Pragmatism: A New Name for Some Old Ways of Thinking* (London: Longmans, Green and Co, 1907). James cites Schiller and Dewey in support of a similar view.

then fashion is variation in the shape of the line. The question 'why dress at all?' is of a different order to the question 'why dress this way?', although the concerns of both questions inevitably overlap. There is an element of order in the progress of fashion. Certain dress features, such as the rise and fall of skirt length, seem to display a pendulum or cyclical regularity over time.[37] The trends are not precise enough to predict what will be worn, say, ten years from now. The most we can say is that a degree of order will be discernable retrospectively. With that thought, we will now look back to the earliest foundations of civil order and civil dress.

37   See 'Laver's Law' on the progress of fashion (James Laver, *Taste and Fashion: from the French Revolution Until Today* [London: George Harrap, 1937]). Georg Simmel expressly compared the order of fashion to the order of law. Fashion, he says, is 'a social form of marvelous expediency, because, like the law, it affects only the externals of life, only those sides of life which are turned to society' ('Fashion' *International Quarterly* 10 (1904), pp.130–55, 148).

CHAPTER TWO

Foundations of the State of Dress

For neither in tailoring nor in legislating does man proceed by mere Accident, but the hand is ever guided on by mysterious operations of the mind. In all his Modes and habilatory endeavours an Architectural Idea will be found lurking; his Body and the Cloth are the site and materials whereon and whereby his beautified edifice, of a Person, is to be built.[1]

This quote from Carlyle prefaces all the major concerns of this chapter. The phrase 'mysterious operations of the mind' alludes to the innate human predisposition to dress. More recent writers on dress have concluded, to quote James Laver, that '[c]lothes are never a frivolity: they always mean something, and that something is to a large extent outside the control of our conscious minds'.[2] There is also something mysterious at work in the cultural impulse of the collective mind to form and follow fashion. Simmel wrote of fashion that 'in countless instances, not the slightest reason can be found for its creations from the standpoint of an objective, aesthetic or other expediency'.[3] In this chapter, we will consider the foundations of the mysterious 'force of habit' as they are accounted for in the prehistory and antiquity of human culture. Carlyle's 'Architectural Idea' alludes to the possibility that dress, like the architecture of buildings, is designed to bring order to human social life. I will argue that dress is indeed culturally equivalent to architecture and that architecture is culturally equivalent to law, so that we have in the 'Architectural Idea' further support for the thesis that dress is culturally equivalent to law. The quote from Carlyle concludes by identifying a significant place in which cultures (of dress, architecture, law)

---

1   Thomas Carlyle, *Sartor Resartus: The Life and Opinions of Herr Teufelsdröckh* (1833–4) (Boston: James Munroe and Co, 1836), Book I, chapter 5.

2   James Laver, *Modesty in Dress* (London: William Heinemann Ltd, 1969), p.14. Gilles Lipovetsky's *L'Empire de l'éphémère: la mode et son destin dans les sociétés modernes* (Paris: Gallimard, 1987) concludes: 'fashion has its reasons that fashion does not know'; (trans. Catherine Porter), *The Empire of Fashion: Dressing Modern Democracy* (Princeton, NJ: Princeton University Press, 2002), p.225.

3   Georg Simmel, 'Philosophie der Mode' (1905). English translation: 'The Philosophy of Fashion', in David Frisby and Mike Featherstone (eds), *Simmel on Culture* (London: Sage, 1997), p.189.

operate, and a significant purpose of their operation there. The place is the superficial zone of skin and coverings ('Body and the Cloth') and the purpose is to fabricate a public face or *persona*, what Carlyle calls the 'beautified edifice, of a Person'. We will see that the architectural area of the threshold equates to the dressed area of the human surface and that the architectural or dressed surface equates to the zone of legal regulation and judgment. It may seem a truism to say that '[d]ress lies at the margins of the body and marks the boundary between self and other, individual and society',[4] or as Elizabeth Wilson puts it, that '[d]ress is the frontier between the self and the not-self',[5] but the significance of such statements can hardly be overstated; for if they are true, then it will be no exaggeration to say that dress occupies the same territory as architecture and law, or to say that dress, no less than architecture and law, makes the social world as we know it.

There is something innate about the urge to dress. An apocryphal tale is told of male academics who were bathing naked on the River Cherwell in Oxford when they were surprised by women coming down the river. All the men instinctively covered themselves below the waist, except one who covered his head, saying 'I don't know about you, gentlemen, but in Oxford I, at least, am known by my face'.[6] Even the man who pretended to a degree of presence of mind acted instinctively to cover himself. Corresponding to the impulse to dress, there is an equally innate impulse to undress. At the conclusion of Shakespeare's *King Lear*, there is a profoundly pathetic moment when Lear laments the loss of his most beloved daughter Cordelia:

> Why should a dog, a horse, a rat have life,
> And thou no breath at all? Thou'lt come no more,
> Never, never, never, never, never!
> Pray you undo this button: thank you, sir.
> Do you see this? Look on her, look, her lips,
> Look there, look there! (5.3.323–8)[7]

---

4   Joanne Entwistle, 'The Dressed Body', in Joanne Entwistle and Elizabeth Wilson (eds), *Body Dressing* (Oxford and New York: Berg, 2001), p.37.

5   Elizabeth Wilson, *Adorned in Dreams: Fashion and Modernity* (1985), rev. edn (London: I B Tauris & Co Ltd, 2009), p.3.

6   Wendy Doniger, *The Bedtrick: Tales of Sex and Masquerade* (Chicago: University of Chicago Press, 2000), p.193.

7   All quotations from the works of William Shakespeare are taken from the 'RSC edition' (J. Bate and E. Rasmussen [eds], *The RSC Shakespeare: Complete Works* [London, Macmillan, 2007]) unless otherwise stated.

The gesture to undo a single button is so much significant precisely because it concerns so small a matter. Shakespeare has understood the human instinct to unbutton the artificial forms of polite culture in that moment when all the fabrications of civil order seem undone by death. Literature has testified to this instinct since earliest times. In *The Book of Job*, Job rends his clothes in grief.[8] In *The Epic of Gilgamesh*, the response of Gilgamesh to the death of his friend is to rip off his finery and cast it away as if it were 'something taboo'.[9]

As the instinct to undress is seen in moments of primal grief, so it is observable in moments of primitive joy. The rules of Association Football (soccer) prohibit players from removing their shirts during a match, but despite the near certainty of being punished, some players still strip off their tops in the exuberance of scoring an important goal. A classical precedent for this instinct to strip in moments of joy is the story of Archimedes who, having received a scientific revelation upon plunging himself into his bath, proceeded to run naked through the streets of ancient Syracuse shouting '*eureka!*' ('I have found it!'). That story is a pleasant illustration of the metaphoric principle that science progresses through discovery, but, just as the metaphor is of doubtful accuracy,[10] so it is doubtful that the event ever really took place. We can, however, be more confident that something very like it occurred one day in 1872 within the polite confines of the British Museum. According to witnesses, George Smith, a researcher in the Assyriology Department of the museum, suddenly 'jumped up and rushed about the room in a great state of excitement, and, to the astonishment of those present, began to undress himself'.[11] Smith's remarkable disrobing had been triggered by a few lines of Akkadian script that he had just read on a clay tablet unearthed some years earlier at the site of the royal library of ancient Nineveh. 'I am the first man to read that after two thousand years of oblivion', Smith rejoiced. This was his *eureka* moment, and, having made the discovery of a lifetime, his instinctive, primal reaction had been to dis-cover himself. The few lines of Akkadian pressed into the surface of that clay tablet constituted a fragment of *The Epic of Gilgamesh*; perhaps the first story

---

8   Job 1.20.
9   Andrew George, *The Epic of Gilgamesh* (Penguin Classics), rev. edn (London: Penguin Books, 2003), Tablet VIII, line 64. All quotations are from this edition unless otherwise stated.
10   See the discussion in Chapter Three at p.73.
11   E. A. Wallis Budge, *The Rise and Progress of Assyriology* (London: Clay & Sons, 1925), p.153.

ever set down by human hand. Even today, Smith's fragment remains the 'best-preserved manuscript of the story of the Deluge'.[12]

In *The Epic of Gilgamesh* and in other early accounts of human social life, we may hope to find the foundations for the social structures that we nowadays take for granted. We might especially hope to learn more about the nature of the wall of the city State or polis; the wall that establishes the very idea of political society. In his *Ars Poetica*, Horace encourages us to see the civil wall as a fabrication of human art. He describes how Amphion built the wall of Thebes not by brute strength but by the music of his lyre, and he associates the wall with the inscribed threshold of law: 'the wisdom of the olden days' was to 'draw a line between sacred and secular, public and private . . . to build towns and inscribe legal codes on wood'.[13] It is in the hope that we might unearth the wisdom of old that we now turn to the story that caused such a stir in the British Museum in 1872.

The Epic of Gilgamesh is the ancient Sumerian tale of the warrior king Gilgamesh (or Bilgames). It was first written down some 4,000 years ago and the Babylonian 'standard version' which was inscribed around 3,000 years ago is the most complete version to come down to us. It comprises 11 tablets plus a twelfth that can be considered an appendix to the main story. The 11 tablets are about 300 short lines in length, with a few nearer 200 lines in length. The epic grapples with perennial human concerns – here are love and loss, sex and violence, life and death, and here, most significant for us, are worlds of difference between well-dressed city dwellers and those who wander undressed in the wilderness beyond the city walls. What the ancient authors clearly saw, and what we have largely forgotten, is that to understand dress is to understand the difference between wilderness and civil society.

The 'standard version' of *The Epic of Gilgamesh* is more specifically named after its opening words: 'He who saw the Deep.' That description of King Gilgamesh might indicate any number of signal events in the life of the hero, but it is clear from the first line in full – 'He who saw the Deep, the country's foundation' – that the event which best accounts for the title is the hero's ferry journey to the far side of the Waters of Death and the conference he has there with Úta-napíshti, a Noah-like survivor of the Flood. In the course

<hr>

12   George, *The Epic of Gilgamesh*, p.xxiii.
13   Horace, *Ars Poetica* (trans. Niall Rudd), rev. edn (London: Penguin, 1987), pp.397–8, 399.

of that quest, Gilgamesh can be said to have delved down to the antediluvian origins of his people.

There really was an ancient city State of Uruk in the Mesopotamian region of Sumer. It was at its zenith around 5,000 years ago and might well have been the largest city on earth at the time. The earliest entry in James Laver's illustrated history of *Costume in Antiquity*,[14] is an illustration of the carved marble head of a woman of Uruk which is in the collection of the Iraq Museum, Baghdad. Dating to around 3000 BC, the head is now just a 'dressed' marble block, but it would originally have been dressed in more than stone. Recesses in the brow and the top of the skull indicate where the head would have been decorated with inlaid eyebrows and a wig. The artefact makes for interesting comparison with the carved head of a male figure (complete with a beard set in orderly, formal rows of tightly groomed hair), which is in the same museum collection and may be a depiction of a king of Uruk.[15] According to the Sumerian King List, an historical King Gilgamesh reigned for more than a hundred years sometime around 2500–2700 BC. Within two or three centuries of his reign, he appears to have been elevated to the status of deity and after a similar period of time he became the subject of a cult and shortly thereafter the hero of an oral poetic tradition. The earliest surviving written elements of a Sumerian Gilgamesh poem were set down around 4,000 years ago; about a thousand years before the Babylonian scholar-priest Sîn-liqe-uninni compiled *He Who Saw the Deep* in the standard Babylonian dialect of the Akkadian language. Like the vast majority of ancient cities, Uruk, which the epic describes as being the 'centre' of political power,[16] was enclosed within a high defensive wall.[17] In *He Who Saw the Deep*, the city is named 'Uruk-the-Sheepfold', which might be an allusion to the original function of the Uruk site but which no doubt became a symbolic denomination denoting sanctuary, domesticity and the essence of civilization. There is a tantalizing line at the start of the fourth stanza of the epic that presents the image of 'its wall like a strand of wool'.

---

14   (London: Thames and Hudson, 1964).

15   Compare, also, the orderly, architectural form of the judicial periwig described in Chapter Four.

16   Dominique Charpin, 'Rebîtum "centre"' *Nouvelles Assyriologiques Brèves et Utilitaires* 4.84 (1991), §112.

17   On the iconicity of the wall and other material features of the *Epic of Gilgamesh*, see Keith Dickson, 'The Wall of Uruk: Iconicities in *Gilgamesh*' *Journal of Ancient Near Eastern Religions* 9.1 (2009), pp. 25–50; and, Keith Dickson, 'The Jeweled Trees: Alterity in *Gilgamesh*' *Comparative Literature* 59.3 (2007), pp.193–208.

According to scholars of cuneiform, it is not certain that the word 'wool' has been accurately deciphered, but it certainly fits well with a close association that is drawn, throughout the epic, between clothes and the threshold of civil life in the city.

There is no more potent illustration of the close association between clothes and the threshold of civil life than the episode in which Shamhat, a high-class harlot or temple devotee of Uruk, is sent by Gilgamesh to ensnare the wild man Enkidu. King Gilgamesh, potent and unopposed, had grown tyrannical within the enclosure of the city State. Just one of his offences was to exercise the terrible power which, disguised in the politeness of the French language, we call *droit du seigneur*; namely, the formal 'right' of an overlord to have sex with his subjects' brides before the consummation of their marriage.[18] The so-called shepherd of Uruk-the Sheepfold was clearly interfering with his flock in ways quite opposed to his ordained role as its protector. According to the epic, this compelled the king's subjects to appeal to the god Anu, and his response was to commission the goddess Aruru, creator of human beings, to fashion a man, the equal of Gilgamesh in strength, to oppose the tyrannical king.

The man whom Aruru created from a pinch of clay was Enkidu, the archetypal man of nature; a man who delights in the company of wild animals. He is described as one who 'knows not a people, nor even a country' (I.108).[19] He is utterly wild; the epitome of the uncivil and the impolite. Crucially, therefore, he is also quite unadorned by any dress or artificial decoration. We are told that 'his body is matted with hair, / he bears long tresses like those of a woman' and that '[c]oated in hair like the god of the animals, / with the gazelles he grazes on grasses' (I.105–6, 109–10). Here is a man who is uncivilized by the standards of city life but one who has the spirit of a good shepherd. Here is one who can challenge the power of the tyrant who lords it over Uruk-the-Sheepfold. King Gilgamesh knows this, for he has seen Enkidu in his dreams. So when the king is presented with a plan to trap Enkidu, he does not hesitate to put it into action. The plan was laid out to the king by an unnamed 'hunter, a trapper-man' (I.113). The hunter blames Enkidu for filling in his trap pits and freeing animals from his snares and generally for stopping him from 'doing the work of the wild'

---

18   Tablet II, lines 159–62.
19   The reference is to Tablet I, line 108.

(I.160). He has seen Enkidu drinking with his herd at the waterhole, but the wild man is so mighty in strength that the hunter has not dared to approach him. It is the hunter's wise father who invents a scheme to trap Enkidu, and it is this scheme that the hunter presents to the king. These are the terms in which Gilgamesh commanded the hunter to implement the plan:

> Go, hunter, take with you Shamhat the harlot!
> When the herd comes down to the water-hole,
>   she should strip off her raiment to reveal her charms.
> He will see her, and will approach her,
>   his herd will spurn him, though he grew up amongst it. (I.162–6)

Thus commanded, the hunter took Shamhat down to the waterhole to wait for Enkidu, and when 'Shamhat saw him, the child of nature', the hunter instructed her thus:

> This is he, Shamhat! Uncradle your bosom,
>   bare your sex, let him take in your charms!
> Do not recoil, but take in his scent:
>   he will see you, and will approach you.

> Spread your clothing so he may lie on you,
>   do for the man the work of a woman!
> Let his passion caress and embrace you,
>   his herd will spurn him, though he grew up amongst it. (I.180–7)

Shamhat duly 'unfastened the cloth of her loins', 'spread her clothing' and Enkidu 'lay upon her' (I.188, 191). Here, then, is a potent image of the hierarchy on which political power is founded. The king commands a man and he in turn commands a woman who, being a prostitute or a temple devotee, lies both within and without the political realm of the city State. Are there echoes of the same power operating today when a Crown-appointed magistrate, sitting beneath the royal crest in an English courtroom, exerts authority over a veiled woman who, being a devout Muslim, stands both within and without the modern idea of a secular State?[20] Alev Çınar argues in this vein that 'during the founding years' of the 1920s and the 1930s

---

20   See the discussion in Chapter Five at p.143.

when Turkey reinvented itself as a post-Ottoman secular State, 'the secular state used the medium of the female body and women's public visibility as a strategic means' in order to institutionalize its new identity so as to satisfy 'global audiences'.[21] Nevertheless, if there is a 'masculine' agency of power at work, there is good reason to suppose that males are equally subject to it. After all, in the Turkish context it was the male fez and turban rather than the female 'veil' that was targeted by The Hat Law of 1925.[22] In *The Epic of Gilgamesh*, it is Enkidu, the male outsider, who is brought under the regulatory power of the State of dress. The distinctive quality of the female body in the epic is that it is enlisted to perform the role of portal between the civil State and the state of nature. John A. Armstrong has observed that 'peculiar architecture, dress, and manners', as well as 'words', can all operate as 'symbolic border guards' of a particular culture.[23] For Çınar, women in Turkey became 'symbolic border guards' of the new secular State.[24]

The image of the naked Shamhat, spread out upon her clothing, is a potent symbol of the city limit; of the threshold between the civilized and the uncivilized. She is liminal. She makes herself a living portal to the world of men. And she does *make herself* the portal. She might be a trap set by men, but she is also complicit. She exercises her own power within the confines of her role. She seeks to tempt Enkidu to return to Uruk and King Gilgamesh by using every seductive art of sex and speech. (Conveniently, Enkidu had been created fully conversant in the local language.) Once she has succeeded in seducing him sexually, she undertakes the task of civilizing him, and her first act in that endeavour is to clothe him in part of her own garment (II.70*).[25] Then, before taking him to Uruk-the-Sheepfold, she accompanies him to a humble 'shepherd's camp, the site of the sheep-pen' (II.37). There she teaches him the rudiments of social dining and he receives his first experience of (and surely the earliest recorded instance

---

21   Alev Çınar, *Modernity, Islam, and Secularism in Turkey: Bodies, Places, and Time* (Minneapolis: University of Minnesota Press, 2005), pp.59–60.

22   See, generally, Camilla T. Nereid, 'Kemalism on the Catwalk: The Turkish Hat Law of 1925' *Journal of Social History* 44.3 (2011), pp.707–28.

23   John A. Armstrong, *Nations before Nationalism* (Chapel Hill: University of North Carolina, 1982), pp.6–8.

24   Çınar, *Modernity, Islam, and Secularism in Turkey*, p.60.

25   The asterisk indicates that the script was missing from the main source tablet of the Standard Version and has been interpolated from another tablet source (in this case, the Old Babylonian 'Pennsylvania' tablet).

of) what nowadays is termed 'male grooming'. He also receives his first garment:

> The barber groomed his body so hairy,
>   Anointed with oil he turned into a man.
> He put on a garment, became like a warrior . . . (II.108–10*)

One part of Shamhat's persuasive plea especially confirms the strong connection between dress and the *demos*. It is the line: 'Go, Enkidu, to Uruk-the-Sheepfold, / where young men are girt with waistbands!' (I.226–7). Consider how closely the idea of a fold for sheep mirrors the concept of a gird for a young man's waist. Shamhat is telling (the then still naked) Enkidu that there is a place where wild animals have been domesticated and contained within an enclosure and in this place the wildness of young men is 'girt', which is to say that the young men have been domesticated and enclosed in clothes. The etymology of the English words 'girt' and 'gird' is highly apposite, for it directly ties clothing to our idea of domestic settlement. According to Mallory and Adams, the reconstructed PIE lexicon contains 'a series of words for some form of enclosure'. One of those words is **ghórdhos*, derived from **gherdh-* ('to gird'). The root **ghórdhos* became *chórtus* (farmyard) in Greek and *hortus* (enclosed garden) in Latin. The same word later became 'court' in French and English, so we can see that the writers of Shamhat's lines have hit upon a connection between clothing, the architectural domain of regulated domestic settlement and law. William Shakespeare might have seen a corresponding connection between the girt waist and regulated life when, in *Macbeth* (c.1606), he referred to 'the Belt of Rule' (5.2.17–18).[26] To gird and to rule also combine in the office of the *Evzones* (*Εὐζωνες*), the elite soldiers who guard the Presidential Mansion in Athens and who can therefore be considered in ceremonial terms to be the guardians of the polis. (Their name, which has antecedents going back at least as far back as Homer, roughly translates as 'the well-belted ones'.[27]) In all this talk of etymology, I do not overlook the fact that 'gird' is not the actual word used in the original Akkadian language and the fact that the

---

26 Or he might simply have been alluding to the fact that in England in the early seventeenth century, a plain black girdle was a regular feature of judicial costume (John H. Baker, 'A History of English Judges' Robes' *Costume* 12 [1978], pp.27–39, 29).

27 Homer, *Iliad* 1.429; 6.467.

Akkadian language is not part of the PIE family of languages. Nevertheless, the Babylonians and their Indo-European contemporaries lived similar lives of strife and settlement, of hunting and farming, of wilderness and civilization. The cultural connection between the enfolding of sheep and the girding of men within the civil 'wall of wool' would have been as obvious and undeniable to the authors of *The Epic of Gilgamesh* as it has been, until now, obscure and undiscovered by us.

It has been observed that the tale of Shamhat and Enkidu has some resemblance with the story of Adam and Eve. There are indeed points in common, the most obvious being that the tempting agency of the woman lures the man from his state of innocent, native bliss into a state characterized by knowledge or reason. We are told that after 'Enkidu had defiled his body so pure', he was 'weakened, could not run as before, but now he had *reason*, and wide understanding' (I.199, 201–2).[28] There are, on the other hand, important differences between the two accounts, many of which hardly need spelling out. The major difference, so far as law and dress is concerned, is that whereas the story of Adam and Eve looks to a prelapsian era before humans ever fabricated clothes or law, *The Epic of Gilgamesh* demonstrates how dress and law were synonymous in the early city civilizations of postdiluvian Mesopotamia. On the other hand, something that both accounts have in common is that they connect clothing to the moral reason that distinguishes humans from the rest of the animal world. According to the biblical tale of Adam and Eve, the first human infringement of a divine command, the eating of the forbidden fruit of the tree of the knowledge of good and evil, had three immediate and related consequences. The first was that humans acquired knowledge of good and evil; the second was that humans donned dress; the third was that humans were physically excluded from paradise. There are many differences in detail between the biblical tale and *The Epic of Gilgamesh*, but in both accounts, the loss of animal innocence and the acquisition of human reason is accompanied by dress that marks humans out from the rest of zoological nature. In the biblical narrative, the gird of the loin became a memento and vestige of the garden of God:

> The LORD God made garments of skin for Adam and his wife and clothed them. And the LORD God said, 'The man has now become like one of us,

---

28   The word *'reason'* is italicized because the decipher is insecure.

knowing good and evil. He must not be allowed to reach out his hand and take also from the tree of life and eat, and live forever.' So the LORD God banished him from the Garden of Eden to work the ground from which he had been taken. After he drove the man out, he placed on the east side of the Garden of Eden cherubim and a flaming sword flashing back and forth to guard the way to the tree of life. (Gen. 3.21–24)

Whether or not we take the story of Adam and Eve literally, we should take it seriously. Its meaning may be metaphorical, but we have observed that in matters of culture (not least in the matter of the foundations of civil culture) metaphor can be meaningful.[29] The story of Adam and Eve is the product of the collective cultural endeavour of an early people group to understand the nature of humanity and its place in the world. Bearing that in mind, it is of prime significance that, for some reason, they concluded that humans are not the same as other animals and they concluded that dress is a key feature that distinguishes humans from the rest of zoological nature. The early Semitic people asked themselves the question: 'why on earth do we go dressed?' It must have struck them as most peculiar to observe that mankind, uniquely among the animals, feels an imperative to dress by artificial means quite regardless of the weather.[30] The story of Adam and Eve provides their account of the reason why we dress. In the following extract, we join the tale after Eve has been tempted by the serpent (a creature which, given its ability to shed its skin, is a fitting choice for an account of the origins of dress):

When the woman saw that the fruit of the tree was good for food and pleasing to the eye, and also desirable for gaining wisdom, she took some and ate it. She also gave some to her husband, who was with her, and he ate it. Then the eyes of both of them were opened, and they realized they were naked; so they sewed fig leaves together and made coverings for themselves. Then the man and his wife heard the sound of the LORD God as he was walking in the garden in the cool of the day, and they hid from the LORD God among the trees of the garden. But the LORD God

29   See the discussion in the Author's Preface at pp.xv–xvi.

30   As people in hot climates wear clothes despite the heat, so people in colder climes follow fashion despite the chill: 'it is by no means an uncommon occurrence, in an inclement climate, for people to go ill clad in order to appear well dressed' (Thorstein Veblen, *The Theory of the Leisure Class*, Oxford World's Classics [1899] [Oxford: OUP, 2007], p.111).

called to the man, 'Where are you?' He answered, 'I heard you in the garden, and I was afraid because I was naked; so I hid.' And he said, 'Who told you that you were naked? Have you eaten from the tree from which I commanded you not to eat?' (Gen. 3.6–11)

The only reference to shame in the biblical account is a reference to the *absence* of any feeling of shame in the naked state as God created it.[31] It follows that, even if shame was their motive for dressing after the fall, there is no reason to suppose that Adam and Eve regarded their naked human form as the cause of their shame. Such a reading would make no sense according to the internal logic of the Genesis text. The text implies that Adam and Eve have been in the habit of walking naked in paradise, in the company of their God and his creatures. On acquiring knowledge of good and evil, they instantly desired to hide their nakedness, but this cannot be because of any newfound knowledge that the naked body is somehow inherently shameful or 'evil'. On the contrary, they would have known that God is happy for them to live a naked existence. Their newfound knowledge could not have revealed that to be naked is evil, but it might have revealed that to be dressed is somehow superior. Where could they have got that idea from? One answer that presents itself from the biblical account is that their newfound knowledge of good and evil had revealed to them the significance of a difference that they had observed between God and his creatures, namely that God is dressed and his creatures are not. According to this reading, Adam and Eve hid themselves because they had encountered the truth that to dress is to be God-like. They hid themselves from God because they were embarrassed when their attempts to imitate divine dress (by putting on 'fig leaves') fell woefully short of what they had witnessed of the raiment of God. This reading of the Eden story fits with Lawrence Langner's psychoanalytical account of the reasons for the dress imperative. Applying Alfred Adler's theory of the so-called inferiority complex (the theory that 'psyche has as its objective the goal of superiority'),[32] Langner argued that '[m]an from the earliest times has worn clothes to overcome his feeling of inferiority and to achieve a conviction of his superiority to the rest of creation . . . '.[33] Were

---

31   Gen. 2.25.
32   *Über den nervösen Charakter* ('The Neurotic Character') (Wiesbaden: Verlag Bergmann, 1912).
33   Lawrence Langner, *The Importance of Wearing Clothes* (New York: Hastings House Publishers, 1959), p.12.

the writers of Genesis somehow inspired to see a connection between dress and human civil ambition? The translators of the King James version were certainly inspired, for in their rendition the naked Adam is described as having been placed in the Garden of Eden 'to dress it' (Gen. 2.15).

Returning to *The Epic of Gilgamesh*, we can note that the intended effect of Enkidu's induction into the city life of Uruk was to introduce a check or counterweight to the king's tyrannical force. Enkidu had declared in advance that he would 'change the way things are ordered' (I.222), and his resolve to do so was confirmed with righteous anger when he heard that King Gilgamesh intended yet again to exercise *droit du seigneur* at a forthcoming wedding. The threat of impending abuse was reported to Enkidu in the familiar metaphorical language of nuptial dress: 'for Gilgamesh, the king of Uruk, the centre of political power, / the veil will be parted . . .' (II.156–7*). Enkidu was true to his destiny and true to his word. His first action following his entry into Uruk was to step forward in the street to block the path of Gilgamesh. Then 'Enkidu with his foot blocked the door of the wedding house, / not allowing Gilgamesh to enter' (II.111–12). Enkidu, straddling the threshold to prevent the unveiling of the virgin, effectively performs the perfect symbolic counterpart to Shamhat's threshold activity. She had stripped away her city clothes to entice Enkidu in from the wild; now the man of the wilderness, newly invested in the law and order of the city, keeps the king out.

The notion that the invested authority of a citizen might form a barrier even to the invested authority of the king must strike us as a remarkably modern feature of such an ancient tale. The threshold of the *domus* is crucial to the modern English notion of a subject's legal liberty from interference by the monarch, which we see expressed in the saying 'an Englishman's home is his castle'. The legal origin of this saying is *Semayne's Case* (1604),[34] which was decided early in the reign of James I of England. In one of his many judicial efforts to curtail the royal prerogative, Sir Edward Coke, chief justice of the King's Bench, held in that case that the owner of a private home has the right to defend his house even against search and entry by the king's sheriffs, for 'the house of every one is to him as his Castle'.[35] The homeowner has the right 'to shut the door of his own house'.[36]

---

34 (1604) 5 Coke Rep 91a.
35 Ibid., 91b.
36 Ibid., 93a.

The threshold to civic architecture frequently seeks to articulate the individual's connection to the social collective and the individual's separation from it. In so doing, it can be said to mimic the threshold function of the private *domus*. Legal precincts speak particularly powerfully of the liminal quality of being both within and without the civil domain. 'Liminal' can be understood here in the anthropological sense in which Victor Turner employed it to describe the threshold place in a rite of passage which places the initiate neither fully outside the initiated state but not yet fully within it. David Evans employs Turner's concept of liminality to situate London's Inns of Court[37] 'within the medieval context of symbol and ritual'.[38] In a passage 'On the Threshold of the Law', Evans describes the liminal experience of entering and exploring the labyrinthine network of the Inns:

> The visitor is perpetually 'on edge' . . . for throughout each interior, an endless succession of bifurcating thresholds and passages produces a vertiginous sensation of being at once inside and out. (4)

Evans argues that 'the architecture of the Inns of Court stages the deferral of bodily interiority through which the Law simultaneously derives its infinite remove and its authority' (1). In other words, the precincts of the Inns of Court perform the law's ideal of being at once always open and perpetually inaccessible. Evans suggests that the effect is to entice the visitor to quest for the inner sanctum of law's truth while simultaneously keeping its secret concealed. This anticipation and deferral creates a 'remove' that enhances the law's authority: 'The Law is the "not yet" of an encounter that builds its reality out of the infinite anticipation of the revelation that will disclose its hidden truth' (25). The end of all this is finally to conceal the 'radiant secret' of the law (25). Thus far I would agree with Evans, but I disagree when he concludes that the secret of the law is 'nothingness' (25). As I see it, the secret of the law is utterly material. The law creates the enticing illusion of an inner sanctum not to disguise the fact that its interior is empty, which it may be, but to distract the inquirer from the truth that what matters is the

---

37   The halls and associated tenements in which the barristers' branch of the legal profession of England and Wales has passed on its traditions since at least as far back as the fourteenth century.

38   David Evans, 'Theatre of Deferral: The Image of the Law and the Architecture of the Inns of Court' *Law & Critique* 10.1 (1999), pp.1–25. Numbers in parentheses denote page numbers.

materiality of the threshold itself. The door is the law's domain. The face is the law's domain. Dress is the law's domain.

Washington, DC, is surely the most architecturally eloquent city on earth. The rhetoric of its many constructions has persuaded a disparate people that they are a unified nation. From the Capitol Building at its head to the monuments of the founding fathers – Jefferson and Washington – at its feet, the architecture of Washington, DC, dressed in flags and symbolic ornament, incorporates the tangible form of a united body politic without which there would be only an intangible idea of a State. In the monumental myth of Washington, DC, no architectural feature is more persuasive and articulate than the main doors to the US Supreme Court. The creator of the doors understood their significance: 'Out of all of our monumental projects, spread over two lifetimes, the Supreme Court doors are the only work that we ever signed – that's how important they were.'[39] The photograph of the bronze doors (Figure 2.1) cannot convey their impressive scale. Together they measure 17 feet high by 9 ½ feet wide and weigh around 13 tons. They are decorated with bas-relief panels depicting celebrated landmarks in the history of the rule of law, and by the same token celebrated landmarks in the history of dress. The panels range from the trial scene that was said to have been represented in the embellishment of The Shield of Achilles,[40] in which two lawyers are depicted, each draped in a Greek *himation*,[41] through a series of togate Romans and medieval and early modern Englishmen until the final panel in which Chief Justice Marshall and Justice Story of the US Supreme Court, dressed in fashionable cravats tailcoats and breeches, are shown conversing the momentous case of *Marbury* v. *Madison* (1803).[42] The photograph reproduced as Figure 2.2 shows in detail the second panel from the top of the right-hand door. It depicts Lord Chief Justice Coke barring King James I from the Court of the King's Bench, recalling such judgments as that in *Semayne's Case*, mentioned earlier, and *The Case of Proclamations*,[43] in which Coke affirmed that the king was subject to the law

---

39   John Donnelly Jnr (sculptor) quoted in David Mason, 'The Supreme Court's Bronze Doors' *American Bar Assn Jnl* 63 (1977), p.1395.

40   Homer, *Iliad* 18.490–508. See Raymond Westbrook, 'The Trial Scene in the Iliad' *Harvard Studies in Classical Philology* 94 (1992), pp.53–76.

41   'A properly arranged himation reflected good breeding and proper order' (Mireille M. Lee, 'Clothing' in Gagarin and Fantham, *The Oxford Encyclopedia of Ancient Greece & Rome*, Vol. 2, pp.228–32, 230.

42   5 US 137 (1803). This case established the independence of the US judiciary from the legislative and executive branches of government.

43   (1610) EWHC KB J22.

Figure 2.1 Entrance doors to the United States Supreme Court (exterior). Designed by Cass Gilbert and John Donnelly Snr. Sculpted by John Donnelly Jnr.

Source: Image © Gary Watt 2011.

Figure 2.2 Entrance doors to the United States Supreme Court (exterior, detail: second panel top right, Lord Chief Justice Coke and King James I). Designed by Cass Gilbert and John Donnelly Snr. Sculpted by John Donnelly Jnr.

Source: Image © Gary Watt 2011.

and not master over it. Coke standing at the threshold of the court, barring the king's access, also evokes Enkidu standing at the domestic threshold and barring access to King Gilgamesh. Enkidu, dressed in civil form, is the incarnation of the ordered layer of law. The same office is performed by Coke, dressed in his judicial robes and invested with legal authority.

It is appropriate that the doors to the US Supreme Court should depict the law barring access to a monarch, for the decoration on the doors is only visible when the doors of the court are closed. What is less appropriate is that even when the doors are open, they are no longer open to visitors. Not even the parties to cases being heard in the Supreme Court can enter by the main doors, and neither can their attorneys. Presumably only the Justices themselves, and other securely vetted employees of the US Supreme Court, can now enter the court through the main doors. Since 4 May 2010, visitors may leave by the main door but they are required to enter through a new side entrance. The Supreme Court Justices all appreciated the seriousness of the security concerns that prompted this change, but two were firmly of the view that security concerns should not override the semiotic importance of the public having access through the symbolically significant main doors. Justice Breyer, with the concurrence of Justice Ginsburg, issued a memorandum objecting to the closure. He observed that to his knowledge 'no other Supreme Court in the world . . . has closed its main entrance to the public' and argued that '[t]o many members of the public, this Court's main entrance and front steps are not only a means to, but also a metaphor for, access to the Court itself'.[44] One commentator adds that the closure of the doors represents a threat to Americans' 'basic architectural literacy'.[45]

To close the front doors to a courthouse during operational hours represents a political failure; a failure of the ideal of a persuasively performed political State. Franz Kafka critiqued this species of failure in his short story 'Vor dem Gesetz' ('Before the Law').[46] It tells of 'a man from the country' who is denied access to the law. The following brief extract will give an impression of what is at stake. The reader will note that within the few lines in which

44 'Statement Concerning the Supreme Court's Front Entrance', 3 May 2010 (*Journal of the Supreme Court of the United States* [2009], pp.831–2).

45 Philip Kennicott, 'Closing Main Doors to the Supreme Court Sends Troubling Message', *Washington Post*, 4 May 2010.

46 *Almanach dem Neuer Dichtung* (Leipzig: Kurt Wolff Verlag, 1916). The story is retold in Franz Kafka, *Der Prozess* ('The Trial') (Berlin: Verlag Die Schmiede, 1925).

the visitor from the country describes the doorkeeper, Kafka dwells on some significant features of the doorkeeper's dress:

> [T]he law is supposed to be accessible to everyone and at all times, he thinks, but as he now looks more closely at the door-keeper in his coat of fur, at his great pointed nose and his long and straggly black Tartar beard, he decides it would be better to wait until he gets permission to enter. The door-keeper gives him a stool and lets him sit to one side of the door. There he sits for days and years.[47]

The man from the country eventually dies waiting. Richard Carstone, the tragic young man of Dickens's *Bleak House* is also gradually worn to death waiting for his cause to come to a final resolution in court. In an advanced stage of his demise, he was discovered in his room '. . . half dressed – in plain clothes . . . not in uniform – and his hair was unbrushed' (45).[48] Carstone died in limbo. Not only did he die before the final hearing of his cause (the assets at issue were all consumed in legal costs before the cause could be heard), but he died when still a law student. The description 'half dressed' efficiently depicts the fact that he was not yet a fully fledged lawyer. In Kafka's story, in contrast, the doorkeeper is completely dressed, being covered even to the extent of a beard and fur coat. Perhaps Kafka chose the fur coat to symbolize the power and status of judges and others who administer the law. Perhaps he was merely informing us that here is a man who is dressed to bear all weathers. The man from the country is duly warned that he will be worn down long before the doorkeeper's coat wears thin. The doorkeeper's dress performs a promise of access and openness: the beard frames the mouth for speech and the coat, curtain-like, conceals the hope of human appearance and humane action. In short, the dress performs as the door performs (and as the Inns of Court perform in Evans's analysis): by summoning a spectator, by fostering the anticipation of access and by determinedly delaying admission. The lesson of the story may be that there is no truth and justice behind the door of the law and that one had better adjust one's expectations to appreciate what truth and justice there might be in the door itself. The superficial procedures and

47 Franz Kafka, *The Trial*, Penguin Classics (trans. Idris Parry, 1994) (London: Penguin, 2000), p.166.
48 Quotations are taken from Charles Dickens, *Bleak House* (serialized 1852–3) (Harmondsworth: Penguin English Classics, 1971). The figure in parenthesis following the quotation refers to the relevant chapter of the novel.

externalities of law furnish a form of truth and justice if we are prepared to see it as such. If we are not prepared to see it as such, we might be in for a long wait before we see something better.

Peter Goodrich tells another tale of a doorkeeper of the law who kept his spectators enthralled with anticipation. Lord Robert Goff, now retired, is one of the most distinguished judges to have sat, in recent memory, in the highest court in the jurisdiction of England and Wales. Some years ago, he turned up 30 minutes late to deliver a talk to students. There is nothing especially noteworthy in that, except for what turned out to be the cause of the delay. Goodrich reports that when he enquired of a colleague why his lordship had turned up late, his colleague gave the following explanation:

> [T]hat after partaking of some tea in the common room and just five minutes before the lecture was to begin, Lord Goff announced that he needed to change his trousers. There was nothing visibly wrong with his trousers but his request was acceded to and the noble Lord and learned brother was directed to the bathroom where he apparently and at length changed. The new trousers were as grey and non-descript as the previous ones. What was important was the rhetoric of delaying appearance, of keeping the audience waiting. It marked a special space, a build up, an aura of importance, a deference that was viscerally incorporated in the students' silent attentiveness, their willingness to wait in reverence of the eminence to come.[49]

Professor Goodrich interprets the episode in a way that makes plain the shared liminal location of dress and law. He suggests that Lord Goff (whom he likens to a 'Gownman' in the same order as a 'Chief Druid') 'brought his ritual status with him in the form a trouser-changing routine'.[50]

In ancient city States, the threshold was often not merely the entrance to the law court, but the very site of judicial judgment. In the Old Testament, Job associates the invested nature of legal authority with the architectural location of the gate:

> When I went to the gate of the city and took my seat in the public square … I rescued the poor who cried for help, and the fatherless who had none

---

49   Peter Goodrich, 'Druids and Common Lawyers: Notes on the Pythagoras Complex and Legal Education' *Law and Humanities* 1.1 (2007), pp.1–30, 29.

50   Ibid., p.30.

to assist him . . . I put on righteousness as my clothing; justice was my robe and my turban.[51]

References to judgment at the gate are widespread in ancient literature. For example, in Deuteronomy it is said that parents will take a rebellious son 'to the elders at the gate of his town' (21.19); a law report from ancient Babylon describes how a judge sent a land dispute to be determined at 'the gate of Marduk', because that was where the disputed land transfer had been witnessed.[52] The 'trial' of Jesus of Nazareth before Pontius Pilate concluded at the judge's seat outside of Pilate's palace, at the place known as the 'Stone Pavement'.[53] In the gospel account, as in *The Book of Job*, the liminal location of the judgment seat is closely associated with dress as a locus of law. It seems that Pilate and Jesus both wore seamless garments at the 'trial'. Jesus was made to wear a robe of royal purple, and this was presumably placed over an undergarment. The gospel narrative states that at his crucifixion, when Jesus' overgarment was removed and divided between the Roman soldiers, he was left wearing an undergarment that was 'seamless, woven in one piece from top to bottom'.[54] This description is intended to identify Jesus with the Jewish Temple in Jerusalem, where the inner sanctum – 'the holy of holies' – separated God's presence from the world by means of a curtain or veil. As Jesus' undergarment was woven from top to bottom (from heaven to earth), so the curtain spontaneously split from top to bottom at the moment of his death.[55] This signified the removal of the fabricated cloth of formal law that had separated humans from the divine presence since the fall.

Pilate was dressed in a toga. Jesus was born in the reign of Caesar Augustus, the first Emperor of Rome, and Augustus insisted that all Romans should wear the toga in public meetings. Virgil's Jupiter describes the Romans as 'the masters of the material world and the people of the toga'.[56] It is said that Augustus quoted this on an occasion when he was outraged to see Romans improperly attired in a public assembly, whereupon he forbade any Roman

---

51   Job 29.7,12,14. See also 1 Sam. 1.9; Jer. 38.7.

52   Henry W. F. Saggs, *The Babylonians* (1962) (London: The Folio Society, 2002), p.178. Compare Gen. 23.17–18.

53   Jn 19.13.

54   Jn 19.23.

55   Mt. 27.51.

56   '*Romanos, rerum dominos gentemque togatam*' (*Aeneid* 1.286).

to enter the forum without their toga.[57] The newly invested Caesar Augustus was represented in statuary 'as the togate citizen, often with his toga pulled reverently over his head (*capite velato*)'.[58] So much was the toga the defining mark of Roman civilization, that the toga was removed from any citizen banished from Rome.[59] It is true that the highest-ranking Romans were keen to shed the heavy, hot toga as soon as they were able when out of the public eye at home or at holiday,[60] but it is certain that Pilate would have worn one when sitting in judgment at the threshold to his palace.

The toga was awkward to arrange and burdensome to wear, but in many respects it was functionally perfect. Suppose you are a tribe in the ancient world that wishes to spread your idea of civilization abroad. How will you communicate the message of your political life to nations to whom your speech is alien and whose speech appears to you to be mere babbling? You will want something that communicates with what Shakespeare calls a 'speechless dialect'.[61] It must speak silently but eloquently of the settled life of the sheepfold, it must tell of legal and architectural order and it must demonstrate your wealth in clear and conspicuous terms. The Roman toga is perfectly suited to the task. Within the considerable weight and precisely ordered arrangement of the white woollen folds of the Roman toga, one can plainly see the security of the sheepfold and the architectural and legal order of the political structures that grew out of the idea of the primitive polis. In the weight and whiteness of the toga, even more so in the purple-edged or full-purple toga, one can also see the wealth and power that flows from established political stability. The fact that the toga virtually disables the left arm from manual labour tells the world that Roman citizens enjoy a superior style of life. No wonder that ambitious barbarians were pleased to adopt the toga as a mark of civilization, even after the fall of Rome. Around the year 510, the Gothic king Theoderic appealed to residents in the Gallic provinces to adopt Roman attire:

Now that you are restored to your ancient liberty through God's favour, clothe yourselves in the customs of the toga (moribus *togatis*), divest

<hr>

57 C. Suetonius Tranquillus, *Divus Augustus* (Alexander Thomson [ed.] *Suetonius: The Lives of the Twelve Caesars; An English Translation* [Philadelphia: Gebbie & Co, 1889], chapter 40).

58 Jonathan Edmondson, 'Public Dress and Social Control in Late Republican and Early Imperial Rome', in Jonathan Edmondson and Alison Keith (eds), *Roman Dress and the Fabrics of Roman Culture* (Toronto: University of Toronto Press, 2008), p.23.

59 Pliny the Younger, *Epistulae* 4.11.3.

60 Tertullian, *De pallio* 5.1–2.

61 *Measure for Measure* 1.3.66.

yourselves of barbarity, cast aside savagery of the mind, since it is not fitting for you to live in accordance with alien customs when these times of ours are so fair and equitable.[62]

The toga was required costume in law courts and its rhetorical dimension could prove useful. Cicero employed it to good effect when he wore the pure-white toga (*toga candida*) for his famous oration against Lucius Sergius Catilina ('Catiline').[63] Related to its rhetorical dimension, the toga also had theatrical or performative potential. Jonathan Edmondson argues that *tragoedia* or stagecraft was enhanced by 'the elaborate nature of Roman public dress, which created a sense of civic uniformity across the citizen body, while at the same time marking difference and rank'.[64] The magistracy, for instance, were marked out by a purple stripe along the border of their toga, and, even higher up, the censors wore entirely purple togas.[65] The toga, wherever it was and whatever form it took, was a gateway to Rome; a portable portal to the eternal polis.

Strange as it may seem, the dress that formed the door to Rome is in one sense still open, for the Byzantine branch of the Roman Empire retained a vestige of the toga in the uniform of their magistrates and other officials. The Byzantine *loros* (or '*lorum*'), that was derived from the decorated *toga picta* worn by Roman consuls, was a long embroidered scarf which, like the toga, was worn draped and wrapped in an orderly fashion. The *loros* survived, in turn, in vestigial form as the *armelausa* which was the mantle worn by judges throughout the Middle Ages and into the early modern period. The mantle is still retained in modern form as the judicial gown in many jurisdictions (the jurisdiction of England and Wales included) down to the present day.[66] The legal historian J. H. Baker notes that until sometime between 1615 and 1625, the mantle was fastened over the right shoulder and fell over the left arm, so that it had to be folded back to make the left arm useful.[67] The left arm was therefore occupied with supporting the mantle in much the same way that it had formerly been occupied with supporting the folds of the toga. Crucially, the *armelausa*, as vestige of the toga, still leads to the greatest edifice that

---

62   Cassiodorus, *Variae* 3.17.1, quoted in Edmondson, 'Public Dress and Social Control', p.39.
63   64 BC.
64   Edmondson, 'Public Dress and Social Control', p.38.
65   Ibid., p.29.
66   William Norman Hargreaves-Mawdsley, *A History of Legal Dress in Europe Until the End of the Eighteenth Century* (Oxford: Clarendon Press, 1963), p.49.
67   Baker, 'A History of English Judges' Robes', p.28.

remains of Rome, for it is judges who wear the *armelausa* and it is judges who preside over laws that still owe a great deal to the laws of Rome. Some modern jurisdictions remain, in essence, Roman Law jurisdictions; but even in the jurisdiction of England and Wales and in other Common Law jurisdictions which pay no great tribute to Roman Law, there remains some vestige of the Roman scheme.[68] The survival of Roman Law is attributable to the consolidation of Roman Law into the *Corpus Juris Civilis* under the Byzantine Emperor Justinian I; so we can say that the Byzantine branch of the Roman Empire not only transformed the toga into the *loros* and thereby assured the survival of the sartorial door to Rome, but it also ensured that the door would continue to lead to Rome's greatest edifice of civil thought: its law.

If it can be shown that dress is culturally equivalent to architecture and that architecture is culturally equivalent to law, we will have gone a long way towards demonstrating that dress is culturally equivalent to law. What I mean by cultural equivalence is that a culture finds meaning in dress by relating it to law through metaphorical language (and vice versa, that it finds meaning in law by relating it to dress), and that such metaphorical meanings reveal close functional, semiotic and aesthetic similarity between law and dress. It is straightforward enough to demonstrate the cultural equivalence of architecture and law. Both are technical systems built by rule to contain, exclude and accommodate. In the modern world, jurists claim that their modes of thought and practice are 'scientific', science being the modern paradigm of accuracy and truth. In ancient times, the architect was the paragon of the civil ideal, and lawyers would have been pleased to emphasize the correspondence between their skills and those of the *arkhi-tekton* (the 'ruling' or 'master' technician).

A moment's reflection will suggest numerous points in common between the functions of dress and architecture: both frequently operate to cover, protect, beautify, accommodate, glorify, signify and secure. Foucault has famously described the architectural capacity of the built environment to discipline and punish,[69] but it is surely right to observe that 'many of his terms suggest that this can be extended to the analysis of dress'.[70] Most

---

68   Herbert Felix Jolowicz, *Roman Foundations of Modern Law* (Oxford: Clarendon Press, 1957).

69   Michel Foucault, *Discipline and Punish: The Birth of the Prison* (London: Penguin, 1977).

70   Alexandra Warwick and Dani Cavallaro, *Fashioning the Frame: Boundaries, Dress and the Body* (Oxford and New York: Berg, 1998), p.78.

important in fundamental and definitional terms is the fact that both disciplines are concerned to 'order'. Where there seem to be functional differences between them, these often turn out to be differences in degree only. Storage, for example, is rarely a primary aim of dress but it is frequently a primary aim of architecture. The shelter function is clearly something that dress and architecture have in common (the English words 'hall' and 'cell' are derived from the PIE root *kel-*, which means to 'to hide' or 'to enclose'), and it is sometimes hard to decide under which heading a thing should fall. The umbrella, for example, is simultaneously dress-like and shelter-like. One might as well ask if a snail wears its shell or is housed in it.[71]

Beyond functional similarities between dress and architecture, there are aesthetic similarities. When it comes to accommodating the human body, neither architecture nor dress is exclusively concerned with mere functionality. Considerations of scale and style apply. Architecture may be functionally ergonomic, but if its proportion is wrong it will fail in aesthetic terms. It is not enough that a building should be technically fit for human habitation; it should also be aesthetically fitting to a humane sense. The architecture of Hitler's Nazi Germany fails because the scale is wrong, and the strictness of the design is wrong.[72] The rectilinear architecture of Nazi Germany, like the politics of the regime, was too *recht*. Rigorously straight lines are inherently unaccommodating to the curves of the human form. There is more to good order than lines drawn by rule. Consider Anthony Trollope's contemplations on the architecture of a Gothic church in his novel *The Warden*:

> The stone work also is beautiful; the mullions of the windows and the thick tracery of the Gothic workmanship is as rich as fancy can desire; and though in gazing on such a structure one knows by rule that the old priests who built it, built it wrong, one cannot bring oneself to wish that they should have made it other than it is. (12)[73]

---

71   John Carl Flügel, *Psychology of Clothes* (1930) (London: The Hogarth Press, 1950), p.83.

72   The error of excessive scale is especially evident in Hitler's plans for a new Berlin: a *Welthauptstadt Germania* ('World Capital Germany') as drawn up by Hitler's architect Albert Speer (see Albert Speer, *Inside the Third Reich* [New York: Macmillan, 1970]).

73   Anthony Trollope, *The Warden* (London: Longman, Brown, Green and Longmans, 1855). The figure in parenthesis following the quotation refers to the relevant chapter of the novel. All quotations are taken from the Penguin Popular Classics edition (London: Penguin, 1994).

The sense that precise rectilinear order might not be perfectly pleasing applies as well to the human face and the dressed human form as to architecture. Trollope describes the warden's eldest-daughter Eleanor almost as if she were the human equivalent to that Gothic church: she is not 'perfect in every line, true to the rules of symmetry', but she is 'very beautiful when seen aright' and 'you could hardly pass an evening with her and not lose your heart' (11). We admire symmetry, but not when it is too strict. The aesthetic appeal of 'error' in dress is a poetic conceit of long standing. Consider the following lines that appear in the poem 'Delight in Disorder' by Robert Herrick (1591–1674):

> A Sweet disorder in the dress
> Kindles in clothes a wantonness:
> . . .
> A careless shoestring, in whose tie
> I see a wild civility:
> Do more bewitch me than when art
> Is too precise in every part.

An equivalent disposition in matters of dress has been observed by the author of *Watching the English*, who at one point writes that 'we English are at our sartorial best when we have strict, formal rules and traditions to follow – when we are either literally or effectively "in uniform"';[74] before adding that '[w]e are at our best when we are "in uniform" but rebelling just slightly against it'.[75] This practice of bending rules to fit the human form is not unique to England, but it must have been exceedingly useful to the Anglo-Saxons (who may be considered the originators of English language and English law) as they sought to accommodate wave after wave of alien laws brought into the realm by the Roman Church, the Danes and the Normans. The practice of bending rules without breaking them, features in law and culture by the name of 'equity'.[76]

Architecture and dress share the function and art of articulation in various ways. They articulate in the sense that they join or connect: dress joins the individual to the collective, and articulate architecture – such as doors,

<hr>

74 Kate Fox, *Watching the English* (London: Hodder & Staughton, 2004), p.269.
75 Ibid., p.294.
76 Gary Watt, *Equity Stirring: The Story of Justice beyond Law* (Oxford: Hart, 2009).

bridges and arches – join parts together to make a whole. They also articulate in the sense that they separate, for to connect things is to acknowledge that they are different to each other. When we talk of 'articulate' speech, we are generally referring to the quality of speech that is characterized by the art of connecting words while keeping them distinct. Articulate features of urban architecture have the same quality of separating parts even as they join the parts together. William L. MacDonald makes the following observation on the syntax of urban architecture in the Roman Empire:

> arches and way stations established articulative urban frames, marking off segments of passage, of one length here, another there. As a result the whole could be grasped cumulatively . . . the net result was a cognitive system of largely functional units dividing urban texts into chapters and paragraphs.[77]

The threshold of the private home is a significant linguistic component of the urban story. It can be considered the point of articulation; the point that joins the individual to the social collective and which at the same time separates the individual from the political State. Even today, we tend to dress somewhat differently when we are inside our homes to when we are outside. It is acceptable to leave one's house in dressing gown and slippers, but only as far as the garden gate. To enter the public street dressed that way is considered an infringement of the customary dress code, unless the context (e.g. the emergency context of a fire or such like) excuses unusual dress.[78]

Architectural grammar and syntax can be read not only in the articulation of the urban plan, but it can also be read within individual architectural elements. Architectural ornamentation can be likened to the embroidery or embellishment of clothes. In Roman architecture, following the Greek, even the ornamentation of individual pillars followed rules resembling the

---

77 William L. MacDonald, *The Architecture of the Roman Empire II: An Urban Appraisal* (New Haven and London: Yale University Press, 1986), p.108.

78 On context-based exceptions to dress codes, see, for example, Erving Goffman, 'Attitudes and Rationalizations Regarding Body Exposure', in Mary E. Roach and Joanne B. Eicher (eds), *Dress, Adornment, and the Social Order* (New York and London: John Wiley & Sons, 1965), pp.50–2. Goffman says that a lawyer will be forgiven for wearing a sweater instead of suit if he (or she) is working overtime on a Saturday, because 'mere presence in the office at an off hour is sign enough of regard for the work world' (p.52).

laws of language construction. These rules constituted distinct architectural 'orders':

> The vocabulary or decorative details of each order are arranged according to an architectural grammar and syntax that makes each one recognizable, yet allows for flexibility of the orders in scale and proportion.[79]

Figure 2.3 shows a diagrammatic epitome of the five orders of classic architecture: Tuscan, Doric, Ionic, Corinthian and Composite. Figure 2.4 shows William Hogarth's satirical rendition of periwigs in terms of five architectural orders of his own invention, each one corresponding to one of the classical orders.[80] Hogarth's orders are: Episcopal, Old Peerian (or Alder Manic), Lexonic, Queerinthian (or Queue de Renard) and the Composite (or Half Natural). Lexonic refers to the judicial wig, of which more will be said in Chapter Four. Suffice to say at this juncture that in addition to the sense of order they convey, judicial dress and judicial architecture also set the stage for the theatrical performance of law.[81] It has been suggested that the judicial periwig 'acts as a sort of frame for the oratory issuing from the mouth of the lawyer'.[82] Hogarth's satire on the periwig hits upon the historical fact that architectural orders and styles have been directly reflected in dress throughout human history. The Greek *chiton* came in Doric and Ionic styles that were 'clearly designed to resemble their architectural counterparts',[83] and styles of architecture and dress continued to connect into the Middle Ages, most clearly in the similarity between the elongated, pointed style of Gothic architecture and such features as men's elongated, pointed shoes and women's elongated, pointed hats (the conical 'hennin'). A close connection between architecture and dress can also be seen in the eighteenth- and nineteenth-century chimney-like ('stovepipe') top hat and in the streamlined style of the 1920s. A final point to make on the cultural

---

79   Architecture 'Forms and Terms', in Gagarin and Fantham, *The Oxford Encyclopedia of Ancient Greece & Rome*, Vol. 1, pp.216–20, 216.

80   William Hogarth, *The Five Orders of Periwigs as They Were Worn at the Late Coronation Measured Architectonically* (1761) (etching).

81   For an extensive discussion of law's performative aspect, see Chapter Four.

82   Thomas Woodcock, *Legal Habits: A Brief Sartorial History of Wig, Robe and Gown* (London: Ede and Ravenscroft, 2003), p.25.

83   Marilyn J. Horn and Lois M. Gurel, *The Second Skin: An Interdisciplinary Study of Clothing*, 3rd edn (Boston: Houghton Mifflin & Co, 1981), p.75.

Figure 2.3 'Five orders of Architecture' from Ephraim Chambers (ed.) *Cyclopaedia*, volume 1 (1728).

Source: Image in the Public Domain.

equivalence of architecture and dress is that '[d]esigners and fashion editors frequently talk about the "construction" of clothes' and that 'underwear before the 1960s was referred to as "foundation" garments'.[84]

If underwear is the foundation of clothing, then nudity is the bedrock of dress. People who live in societies where the dress code requires clothing are

---

84   Warwick and Cavallaro, *Fashioning the Frame*, p.79.

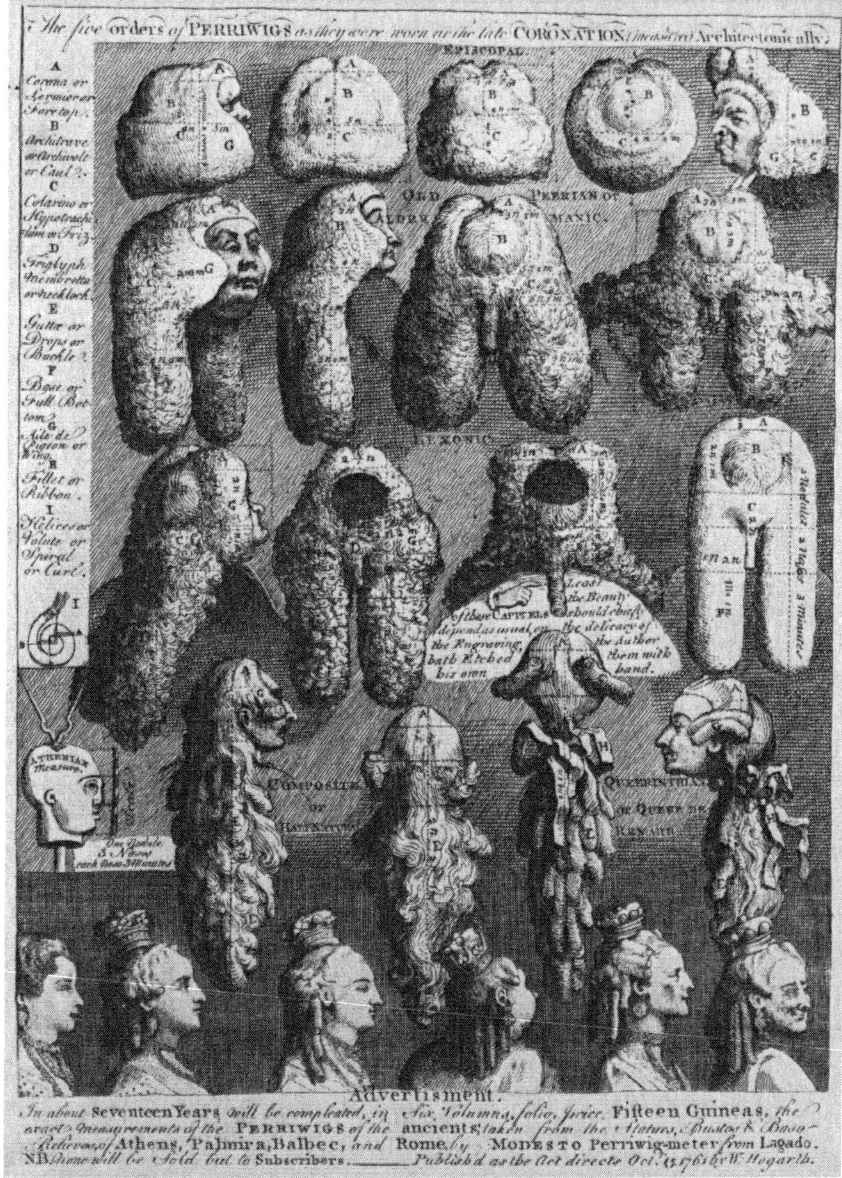

Figure 2.4 William Hogarth, 'The Five Orders of Periwigs' (includes James Stuart; William Warburton; Samuel Squire; George Bubb Dodington, Baron Melcombe; Charlotte Sophia of Mecklenburg-Strelitz; Elizabeth Percy [née Seymour], Duchess of Northumberland).

Source: © National Portrait Gallery, London.

captured by cladding almost as soon as they are born. They are naked for just a moment at the fleeting threshold of birth: one minute swaddled in their mother's womb, the next minute held in the folds of her arms and the next minute swaddled in the first folds of cloth. How much of our instinct to dress is a desire to replicate the mother's corporal embrace? In Chapter Five, we will consider a range of issues arising from the way in which legal authorities respond to unauthorized nudity within the public spaces of polite society, but here I want to attend to two arguments – the argument for the 'neutral' and the argument for the 'natural' – that are sometimes raised in favour of adult public nudity in cultures where the dress code requires covering by cloth.

An example of the argument for nudity on the ground of neutrality is one that is sometimes put forward by women who claim that they should be free to go topless in public places wherever men are permitted to go topless. US commentators note that this claim usually fails in the courts.[85] (In the United States, it has been observed across a range of legal contexts that 'when it comes to public nudity, plaintiffs tend to lose';[86] this can be contrasted with the position in Germany, where it is accepted that the individual has more latitude to exhibit a naked persona in public places.[87]) At the root of women's claim to go topless where men go topless, there is an assumption that the law is unequal because it treats identical cases – the case of the male and the case of the female – differently. The essence of the argument is that the distinction typically observable between the naked torso of an adult man and that of an adult woman should not be a relevant distinction in law. One might be sympathetic with that argument on certain grounds – including the ground of equal opportunity for self-expression – but the argument is unconvincing when it is advanced on the basis of strict neutrality. If there is any context in which gender is not in any meaningful sense a 'neutral' factor, it is in the public perception of the naked adult form. The argument might be made that a law which requires women to cover their upper torsos is a law

85   See Kimberly J. Winbush, 'Regulation of Exposure of Female, But Not Male, Breasts' *A.L.R.* 67.5 (1999), pp.453–57, 431. Winbush cites *People* v. *Santorelli* 80 NY 2d 875; 600 NE 2d 232 (1992) as one of the rare cases in which the argument succeeded.

86   Gowrie Ramachandran, 'Freedom of Dress: State and Private Regulation of Clothing, Hairstyle, Jewelry, Makeup, Tattoos, and Piercing' *Maryland Law Review* 66 (2006), pp.11–93, 72. See, generally, Pat Marie Maher and Ann C. Slocum, 'Freedom in Dress: Legal Sanctions' *Clothing and Textiles Research Journal* 5.4 (1987), pp.14–22.

87   James Q. Whitman, 'The Two Western Cultures of Privacy: Dignity Versus Liberty' *Yale L Jnl* 113 (2004), pp.1151–221.

made by men for men and that there is a feminist argument for challenging it on that basis alone, but is that argument really convincing? One suspects, on the contrary, that this is a context in which gender distinction in the law will be supported as much by women as by men.

Public nudity is sometimes promoted on the ground that it is natural. Stephen Gough, the so-called naked rambler, claims that he is doing what comes naturally,[88] and that the artificial and unnatural thing to do is to cover our naked form with fabrications. Of course in one sense it is perfectly true to say that the naked state really is a state 'au naturel'. We are born naked and in that literal sense it is our native state to wear no clothes at all. We also know that adults who are native to certain cultures prefer to dress in ways that do not involve covering with cloth. It cannot be denied that nudity is literally native and that to be unclothed can be culturally natural. From this it follows that clothing can certainly be considered unnatural. But what of that? The real question is not whether it is natural to clothe but whether it is natural to dress, and to that question we get a very clear answer. So far as humans are civilized social animals, it appears from all experience that it is in our very nature to dress. We may debate the source of this apparently innate feature of human civil society, but there is no doubt that the habit of dress is a perfectly natural one. It is my argument that the habit of dress is natural in the way that the habit of law is natural. This does not mean that dress and law are not artificial constructs made by human hand and mind, but it does mean that dress and law are natural in the sense that it is in our nature to fabricate such things. J. C. Flügel argues that '[c]lothes . . . though seemingly mere extraneous appendages, have entered into the very core of our existence as social beings'.[89] I would not limit that observation to clothes: dress, whatever form it takes, occupies the 'core of our existence as social beings'. The centrality of dress to our social self-perception is such that in a dress-dominated society it is practically impossible to go undressed in public. This is precisely because the undressed human form in a domain of dress is not considered on its own terms, but in terms of an absence of dress. It is considered to be in a state of *un*-dress. Indeed, it is as impossible to go dress-free in a domain of dress as it is to pass a law to bring the rule of law to an end. So long as a state of lawlessness is defined in

88   For discussion of Stephen Gough's appearance in court see Chapter Five at pp.127–31.
89   Flügel, *Psychology of Clothes*, p.16.

terms of law, we never truly escape the rule of law. So long as a dress-free state is defined in terms of dress, we never truly escape the domain of dress. On this view, Stephen Gough, the naked rambler, is not truly naked. He is, on the contrary, extremely well covered. When he is not under supervision in the solitary confinement of his prison cell, he attracts the intense gaze of the public eye. Hans Christian Andersen's morality tale of *The Emperor's New Clothes* has this strange thread of truth in it: that a clothes-free person in a clothed domain is the best dressed, and most looked upon, person in town.

If 'naturism' aspires to do 'that which comes naturally to humans', we should inquire as to the notion of 'nature' to which naturism aspires. Without prejudging the merits of naturism, it cannot be assumed that everything that 'comes naturally' to humans is always a good thing. Indeed one reason why our idea of social civilization depends upon law is because we are inclined to be nasty and brutish when we do only that which comes naturally to our selfish instincts. Prejudice ('naked prejudice' as it is sometimes termed) is an entirely natural human trait. If prejudice were not natural in a basic psychological sense, we could hardly function. When one sits on a chair it is because one prejudges that it is there and that it will support one's weight. We are all to a great extent prejudiced to perceive the world in a way that confirms our preconceptions of the world. This is what psychologists call 'confirmation bias'.[90] It is psychologically natural to presume that people who are 'like me' are more likely to like me and to perceive the 'other' as being more likely to present a threat. Such prejudice is natural and this is precisely why, as social creatures, we naturally need the artifice of law to counter it. There may be reasons that will sufficiently justify adult nudity in public places, but the claim that 'it is natural' is not one of them. Indeed, one of the strongest justifications for adult nudity in public places – nudity 'in the name of art'[91] – is quite opposite to the claim that nudity should be permitted 'in the name of nature'.

An assault upon the requirement 'to clothe' does not reach to the root of the requirement 'to dress'. If 'to dress' is, as I have argued, 'to order', it

---

90   Jonathan St B. T. Evans, *Bias in Human Reasoning: Causes and Consequences* (Hove: L. Erlbaum Associates, 1989).

91   Individuals have installed themselves naked on the 'fourth plinth' in London's Trafalgar square as part of sculptor Antony Gormley's project *One & Other* (6 July–14 October 2009). Consider, also, the large-scale nude installations by photographer Spencer Tunick.

will follow that law as a universal fact of human civil life is not concerned with covering merely. When the law requires women to cover their breasts when they appear in public, the law is more concerned to maintain the appearance of 'order' than it is to promote the appearance of cloth. The law would not only intervene to restrain someone from diving into a public swimming pool naked, but it would also intervene to restrain someone from diving into the pool wearing a full business suit. Sometimes the law requires individuals to dis-cover themselves for the sake of orderly appearance. We will examine the example of the Islamic 'veil' in depth in Chapter Four, but even a seemingly innocuous instance can be informative. For example, the case of the policemen in the State of Massachusetts who were required to shave off their moustaches even though some of the men had worn them for decades.[92] This followed the decision of the US Supreme Court in *Kelley v. Johnson*,[93] which upheld the uniform dress code of police officers on the ground that 'similarity in appearance of police officers is desirable'.[94] When we put the case of the topless women immediately alongside the case of the moustachioed police officers, it is apparent that the law's concern is not to require covering up per se but to require orderly public dress. Police officers are contractually committed to accept a degree of uniformity, of course, but what about the woman who is required to cover her breasts before she leaves home? What is the source of her obligation to put on clothes? The law is generally reluctant to impose a duty to perform a positive act in the absence of a particular pre-existing duty. England is especially laissez-faire in this regard. Suppose a topless woman is sitting on a bench in a public park as a small child (a stranger to her) starts to drown in a shallow pond before her eyes. The law will not compel her to rescue the child, but it will compel her to cover up her exposed flesh.

Whether the code of dress requires covering or uncovering by clothes seems to depend entirely upon the prevailing cultural mores in the particular context. In Finland, for example, the sauna was traditionally the threshold zone in which Finnish mothers gave birth and where the sick were tended, thus hygiene determines that all users should be naked. (Nudity is also in keeping with the association between the sauna and the threshold of birth – after all,

---

92   'Mustaches Are Issue for Police', *The New York Times*, 1 July 1992.
93   425 US 238 (1976).
94   Ibid., p.248.

none of us ever came clothed into the world.)[95] Clothing is no more acceptable in a Finnish sauna than nudity is acceptable on a Finnish street. One must remove clothing before one enters the sauna and one must don clothing before one re-enters the wider public domain. The sauna may therefore be considered an exception to the general dress code that requires covering by clothes, or the general dress code may be considered an exception to the clothes-free code of the sauna. If the sauna is a sort of 'state within a State', it provides an interesting point of comparison with schools, where general dress freedoms (such as the freedom to wear the Islamic 'veil') may be set aside in order to promote norms that are deemed to be enshrined in school uniform.[96] The theatrical stage is another zone of exception.[97] Indeed, even in the public street, theatrical dress or 'fancy dress' is less confrontational to the civil authorities than more serious, but ostensibly similar modes of dress. A ghost outfit worn on Halloween or for a party, for example, will be considered an innocuous exception even in States that outlaw public coverings worn for religious or political purposes. The theatrical stage proper is, like the sauna or the school, a genuine zone of exception in which the usual laws of dress may be wholly suspended or repealed. Naked and sexual performance is permitted on the stage, and within the confines of the theatre, which would certainly be deemed criminal outside.[98]

The skin has been described as the 'symbolic stage upon which the drama of socialization is enacted'.[99] Foucault also employed the metaphor of theatrical performance in this context, as Judith Butler explains:

> Although Foucault writes that the body is not stable and cannot serve as a common identity among individuals cross-culturally or transhistorically,

---

95   This may be compared to the possibility that the rite of baptism, which symbolizes spiritual 'new birth', may have been undertaken naked in some sections of the early Christian church (Gregory Dix, *The Treatise on the Apostolic Tradition of St. Hippolytus of Rome, Bishop and Martyr*, 3rd rev. edn [Abingdon: Routledge, 1992], p.33).

96   *R (on the application of Begum)* v. *Denbigh High School Governors* [2006] UKHL 15; [2007] 1 AC 100 (House of Lords). Lieve Gies, 'What Not to Wear: Islamic Dress and School Uniforms' *Feminist Legal Studies* 14 (2006), pp.377–89.

97   See Edward Ross Dickinson, '"Must We Dance Naked?": Art, Beauty, and Law in Munich and Paris, 1911–1913' *Journal of the History of Sexuality* 20.1 (2011), pp.95–131.

98   An extreme example is *Un peu de tendresse bordel de merde!* (Dave St-Pierre dance company, 2010), which more than fulfilled its promise to breach the 'fourth wall' between performers and audience.

99   Terence S. Turner, 'The Social Skin', in Catherine B. Burroughs and Jeffrey Ehrenreich (eds), *Reading the Social Body* (Iowa City: University of Iowa Press, 1993), pp.15–39. See, generally, Claudia Benthien, *Skin: On the Cultural Border between Self and World* (trans. Thomas Dunlap) (New York: Columbia University Press, 2002).

he nevertheless points to the constancy of cultural inscription as a 'single drama,' suggesting that this drama of historical 'inscription' enjoys the very universality denied to the body per se.[100]

Butler indicates that Foucault sees something in the artificial arrangement of skin that is constant throughout human history. If that is right, then Foucault sees something in the ordering of skin that is akin to the pan-historical constancy that I see in dress generally. One element that is constant in dress, whether it employs the medium of skin or the medium of cloth, is the constant of 'performance'. Both media supply a stretched-out stage for the formal enactment of social regulation. Particularly potent examples of cloth-less dress are the tattoo and other forms of dermal scarification. They are more fleshy and fundamental than text and textile, and since they are sub-textile they are subtle in the most literal and beguiling sense.

Tattoos and other forms of dermal scarification have traditionally marked the civil world from the animal world.[101] The anthropologist Claude Lévi-Strauss observed that '[t]he purpose of Maori tattooing is not only to imprint a drawing onto the flesh but also to stamp onto the mind all the traditions and philosophy of the group'.[102] Maoris practice facial tattooing. The same practice is popular among the Ramnami people of central India, who tattoo their skin with the name of the deity Ram (Rama) in Sanskrit – sometimes over almost the entire surface of their bodies. Originally a sign of religious devotion, it became a sign of the sect's defiance of the Hindu-caste system under which, as so-called untouchables, they were required to dress and adorn themselves in a manner that would mark them out from members of supposedly superior castes.[103] It has been observed that tattoos and body painting have been 'variously used to mark outlaw status and nobility, insiders and outsiders'.[104] The cultural history of marking criminality is truly ancient, for according to the biblical narrative, when Cain killed his brother Abel, God 'set a mark upon Cain, lest any finding him should kill

100   Judith Butler, 'Foucault and the Paradox of Bodily Inscriptions', in Donn Welton (ed.), *The Body* (Oxford: Blackwell Publishers, 1999), pp.307–13, 309 (first published in *The Journal of Philosophy* 86 [1986], pp.601–7).

101   Susan Mullin Vogel, *Aesthetics of African Art: The Carlo Monzino Collection* (Exhibition Catalogue) (New York: The Center for African Art, 1986), p.25.

102   Claude Lévi-Strauss, *Structural Anthropology* (New York: Basic Books, 1963), p.257.

103   Ramdas Lamb, *Rapt in the Name: The Ramnamis, Ramnam, and Untouchable Religion in Central India* (State University of New York Series in Hindu Studies) (Albany: SUNY Press, 2002).

104   Enid Schildkrout, 'Inscribing the Body' *Annu Rev Anthropol* 33 (2004), pp.319–44, 325.

him'.[105] The sense that dermal decoration marks out civil life from animal life suggests new significance to the fact that Cain, the marked-man, is said to have founded the first human city on earth.[106]

The story of the mark of Cain relates a clear and present reality. We no longer brand criminals, as once we did, but we uniform them, number them, tag them, photograph them and ink their prints. Giorgio Agamben urges us to resist the means, including fingerprints and retina scans, by which modern States attempt to mark non-criminals as if they were criminals; a process that he refers to as 'biopolitical tattooing':

> What is at stake here is none other than the new and 'normal' biopolitical relation between citizens and the State. This relation no longer has to do with free and active participation in the public sphere, but instead concerns the routine inscription and registration of the most private and most incommunicable element of subjectivity – the biopolitical life of the body.[107]

The idea of the tattoo as an institutional ideological stamp or imprint (tattoo as brand) is combined with the notion of tattoo as marker of social status (tattoo as boundary) in Franz Kafka's 1914 short story *In Der Strafkolonie* ('In the Penal Colony').[108] This chilling tale relates the final days of a penal colony that houses a machine which dispenses a form of institutionalized justice by executing prisoners and simultaneously inscribing the text of its 'judgment' on the prisoners' skin. Jeanne Gaakeer describes it thus:

> Starting as a kind of tattooing, the process soon turns into torture. When the condemned person finally deciphers the sentence, six hours after the infliction of pain has begun, it takes another six hours to bring about death as the needles keep piercing the body more deeply. In short, the machine makes an imprint of the crime of which the condemned person is guilty, and thus executes the sentence.[109]

---

105 Gen. 4.15.
106 Gen. 4.17.
107 Giorgio Agamben, 'No to Biopolitical Tattooing' (trans. Stuart J. Murray) *Communication and Critical/Cultural Studies* 5.2 (2008), pp.201–2, 202.
108 Franz Kafka, *In Der Strafkolonie* (1914) (Berlin: Klaus Wagenbach, 1985).
109 Jeanne Gaakeer, 'The Legal Hermeneutics of Suffering' *Law and Humanities* 3.2 (2009), pp.123–49, 139.

The Austro-Hungarian architect Adolf Loos associated the making of tattoos with criminality and 'degenerate' mentality. It was not the *wearing* of tattoos that Loos considered to be degenerate, but the primitive urge to make the mark (which Loos compared to making markings on walls).[110] How telling, then, that the Nazis chose tattooing as a method of marking out concentration camp prisoners. Applying Loos's reasoning, Nazi infliction of tattoos was a sign, not of any fault in their victims, but of their own degeneracy. It is clearly inhuman to tattoo another person against their will as the Nazis did, but it is quite another thing to give or receive a voluntary mark.[111] A voluntary tattoo might actually be considered a paradigm of dress and a paradigm of law.[112] It achieves what laws aspire to achieve: order that is stable and enduring, but sufficiently flexible to accommodate a degree of change and growth. It should be recalled that Magna Carta is a tailored panel of parchment, of skin. As we read in *Sartor Resartus*:

> [A]ll Forms whereby Spirit manifests itself to sense, whether outwardly or in the imagination, are Clothes; and thus not only the parchment Magna Charta, which a Tailor was nigh cutting into measures, but the Pomp and Authority of Law, the sacredness of Majesty, and all inferior Worships . . . are properly a Vesture and Raiment.[113]

Sometimes the layer of law is only skin-deep. When one looks closely at an original of the Magna Carta, one finds that it is a form of dress as thin as the social mask that Maori tribes folk wear, for over time the black iron-gall ink has impregnated the vellum and become one with the skin. The founding document of our law is a tattoo.

110   Adolf Loos, 'Ornament und Verbrechen' ('Ornament and Crime') (*Trotzdem*, 1908) published in *Die Schriften von Adolf Loos* (Innsbruck: Brenner Verlag, 1931), pp.79–80.

111   On the use of tattoo as a medium for writing a will, see Catherine O. Frank, 'Of Testaments and Tattoos: The Wills Act of 1837 and Rider Haggard's *Mr Meeson's Will* (1888)' *Law & Literature* 3 (2006), pp.323–41.

112   The Bible indicates that the Divine judge is tattooed (Rev. 19.11–16).

113   Carlyle, *Sartor Resartus*, Book III, chapter 9.

CHAPTER THREE

Shakespeare on Proof and Fabricated Truth

*[B]lessed he who has a skin and tissues, so it be a living one, and the
heart-pulse everywhere discernable through it.*[1]

The imaginary English editor of Carlyle's *Sartor Resartus* observes that the imaginary philosopher Teufelsdröckh 'though a Sanscullotist, is no Adamite'.[2] Commenting on this, Michael Carter explains that Teufelsdröckh (and, by implication, Carlyle) 'will have nothing to do with the notion that if we were to strip off our outer casings truth, equality and justice would blossom', for he knows 'that social being is "clothed-being"'.[3] It is true that Carlyle wrote that man 'is by nature a *Naked Animal*; and only in certain circumstances, by purpose and device, masks himself in Clothes', but that observation was made in the context of comparing human zoological nature to the biological nature of plant and animal life.[4] His point was only that the human is somewhat under-covered in its zoological nature compared to the almost complete covering that one sees on birds and most land-dwelling mammals. *Sartor Resartus*, Carter further elaborates, 'was never a renunciation of clothes, or even a criticism of elaborate costume. It was a manifesto for authenticity'.[5]

In this chapter, we will examine early modern suspicion of superficialities and the corresponding early modern appreciation that the truths on which civil life relies may be fabricated things. The very phrase 'naked truth' was a poetic fiction coined in the early modern period by the Scottish poet Alexander Montgomerie,[6] a favourite of King James VI of Scotland (James I of England). This chapter will reveal that 'truth', for purposes of legal proof, is as much a fabricated or 'coined' fiction as the contemporary poetic concept of 'naked truth'.

---

1   Thomas Carlyle, *Past and Present* (London: Chapman & Hall, 1843), Book II, chapter 17.

2   Thomas Carlyle, *Sartor Resartus: The Life and Opinions of Herr Teufelsdröckh* (1833–4) (Boston: James Munroe and Co, 1836), Book I, chapter 9.

3   Michael Carter, *Fashion Classics from Carlyle to Barthes* (Oxford and New York: Berg, 2003), p.5.

4   Carlyle, *Sartor Resartus*, Book I, chapter 1.

5   Carter, *Fashion Classics*, p.11.

6   'The Cherrie and the Slae' (c.1585) (Edinburgh: Robert Waldegrave, 1597), stanza 82. (Stanza 81 commences with a call to test a truth by confrontation 'face for face'.)

Lorna Hutson has located *The Invention of Suspicion*[7] in the early modern period, and she finds significant clues to a culture of suspicion in the creative, including theatrical, culture of England at that time. The focus of this chapter is specifically upon suspicion of dress in early modern England and the relation that this had to the trial of truth in society at large and in courts of law in particular. Significant indicators of that cultural connection are to be found within contemporary polemic (e.g. Phillip Stubbs complained in his *Anatomy of Abuses in England* that the 'confuse mingle mangle of apparell' had produced 'general disorder')[8] and within literary and dramatic works, not least in the works of William Shakespeare (the son of a Warwickshire glove-maker and sometime lodger with a London wig-maker).[9] Of course, suspicion, indeed cynicism, regarding proof and truth in courts of law was no new phenomenon. In Plato's *Phaedrus*, the character of Socrates makes an observation that must have rung as true in Shakespeare's day as it did in ancient Greece, as it does today:

> [H]e who is to be a competent rhetorician need have nothing at all to do, they say, with truth in considering things which are just or good . . . For in the courts, they say, nobody cares for truth about these matters, but for that which is convincing; and that is probability, so that he who is to be an artist in speech must fix his attention upon probability.[10]

In the early modern period, general suspicion of an individual's capacity to perform a false public persona was widespread, for this was the age in which the modern individual was beginning to emerge from the cocoon of collective social identity that had prevailed in the societies, guilds and feudal categories of the Middle Ages. Suspicion of evident forms was acute in the English law court, especially in relation to contractual and other documentary formalities in a world of increased monetary lending and mercantile trade, but it was nowhere more acute than in relation to individuals' physical appearance in an England gripped by suspicion of covert Roman Catholicism (including concealed Jesuit spies) and even of witches in disguise. The rising popularity

---

7   Lorna Hutson, *The Invention of Suspicion: Law and Mimesis in Shakespeare and Renaissance Drama* (Oxford: Oxford University Press, 2007).

8   Phillip Stubbs, *Anatomy of Abuses in England* (London: Richard Jones, 1583), sig. C2ᵛ.

9   Charles Nicholl, *The Lodger: Shakespeare on Silver Street* (London: Allen Lane, 2007).

10   *Plato in Twelve Volumes* (trans. Harold N. Fowler), Vol. 9 (Cambridge, MA: Harvard University Press, 1925), pp.272d–e.

of the 'masque' form of entertainment at the English court throughout the early modern period can be seen as an attempt by the ruling class to reassert respect for superficialities in the face of their diminishing reliability.[11]

At the end of the sixteenth century, sumptuary laws were still on the statute books and dress was in theory supposed to be a trusty indicator of social role and social standing, but in practice the sumptuary laws were hardly enforced and dress was considered to be an increasingly unreliable indicator of social role, social rank and individual identity. There was great suspicion of dressing out-of-status, and that concern was particularly strong in relation to martial dress. In Shakespeare's *Henry V* when the herald from the King of France declared 'You know me by my habit' (3.6.87), he was declaring what was certainly true in the days of the historical Henry V but which had become much less certain in 1599 when Shakespeare first staged his play. Dress continued to operate in early modern England 'as a form of material memory' that 'incorporated the wearer into a system of obligations',[12] but respect for dress prescriptions were in decline. As the force of collective dress codes was on the wane, so the freedom and responsibly to fashion oneself appropriately was on the rise. Jurists understood this. William Dugdale wrote of the contemporary lawyer that 'even as his Apparell doth show him to be, even so shall he be esteemed'.[13] This same responsibility is expressed in the advice Polonius gave his son Laertes in Shakespeare's *Hamlet*:

> Costly thy habit as thy purse can buy,
> But not expressed in fancy; rich, not gaudy:
> For the apparel oft proclaims the man,
>
> . . .
>
> This above all: to thine own self be true,
> And it must follow, as the night the day,
> Thou canst not then be false to any man. (1.3.73–5, 81–3)

11   Jennifer Chibnall, '"To That Secure Fix'd State": The Function of the Caroline Masque Form', in David Lindley (ed.), *The Court Masque* (Manchester: MUP, 1984), pp.78–93, 80–1; Robert I. Lublin, '"Whosoever Loves Not Picture, Is Injurious to Truth": Costumes and the Stuart Masque', in Cynthia Kuhn and Cindy Carlson (eds), *Styling Texts: Dress and Fashion in Literature* (Youngstown, NY: Cambria, 2007), chapter 4.

12   Peter Stallybrass and Ann Rosalind Jones, *Renaissance Clothing and the Materials of Memory* (Cambridge: Cambridge University Press, 2000), p.22.

13   William Dugdale, *Origines Juridicales* (London: F and T Warren, 1666), fo. 197.

The irony is that the theatre was a prime forum for the performance of falsehood. Indeed, the growing popularity of theatre served to heighten general mistrust of dress as an indicator of social status, not least because actors sometimes wore garments handed down from their noble patrons.[14] (Although it has been observed that 'when characters in Shakespeare's plays change their clothes, and hence their status, they never of their own (represented) volition disguise up the social scale'.[15]) Meanwhile, courtiers were accused of dressing like actors.[16] In the martial context, a significant contributor to the culture of mistrust was the fact that, although early Tudor militia regulations had communicated the debt of service 'inherent in the king's coat' and had defined the ways in which it 'covered men's legal status',[17] the modern idea of military uniform did not yet exist.[18] It was therefore expedient for vainglorious individuals to employ dress to make an outward but empty show of valour. It is with such doubts in mind that in Shakespeare's *Henry V* the Duke of Orleans and the Constable of France take opposing sides in a mock trial of the Dauphin's valour. Orleans argues that the Dauphin's valorous virtue is obvious, to which the Constable contradicts that 'never anybody saw it but his lackey. 'Tis a hooded valour' (3.7.80–1). On the eve of The Battle of Agincourt, Henry, disguised at this point as a gentleman soldier, prays that God will 'steel' his soldiers' hearts (4.1.245). Earlier he had directly summoned his soldiers to '[d]isguise fair nature with hard-favoured rage' (3.1.8), just as their fathers had proved themselves in war and thereby been made 'war-proof' (3.1.18). Such language indicates the widespread contemporary suspicion that fair and feint nature was all too often concealed in martial disguise, not only at war, where one might find a 'counterfeit cowardly knave' (5.1.51), but more especially in the counterfeit valorous dress adopted in peaceful civil life. Certain false or misleading indicators of martial prowess, such as the doublet (originally the comfortable

14   Peter Stallybrass, 'Worn Worlds: Clothes and Identity on the Renaissance Stage', in Margreta de
      Grazia, Maureen Quilligan and Peter Stallybrass (eds), *Subject and Object in Renaissance Culture*
      (Cambridge: CUP, 1996), pp.289–320.

15   Susan Baker, 'Personating Persons: Rethinking Shakespearean Disguises' *Shakespeare Quarterly*
      43.3 (1992), pp.303–16, 313.

16   Thomas Nashe railed against 'England, the players' stage of gorgeous attire, the ape of all nations'
      superfluities'. (*Christ's Teares Over Jerusalem* [1593] [London: Longman, 1815], p.135.)

17   Vimala C. Pasupathi, 'Coats and Conduct: The Materials of Military Obligation in Shakespeare's
      Henry Plays' *Modern Philology* 109.3 (2012), pp.326–51, 366.

18   In the Middle Ages, sumptuary laws had been passed in an attempt to prevent wealthy lords from
      kitting out private armies of retainers in their livery: Jane Ashelford, *The Art of Dress: Clothes and
      Society, 1500–1914* (London: National Trust, 1999), p.289.

second or 'double' layer worn under a breastplate) and slashed cloth were even items of general fashion at this time, and not just for men. The problem of false representation of martial valour was exacerbated by the fact that real soldiers, if we can read a contemporary complaint into Shakespeare's line, had savage manners and dressed in 'diffused attire' (5.2.61).

One of the recurring themes of Shakespeare's plays is that even the ceremonial vestments of kings are no sure proof of true kingship. The premise of Shakespeare's *Henry V* is that the King of France rules under a false title; that his title is founded on mere 'shows of truth' (1.2.74). At the start of the play, King Henry invites his counsellor, the Archbishop of Canterbury, to outline Henry's true title to France, and in doing so the king warns the archbishop to speak truthfully – not to 'fashion', 'colour' or 'suit' falsely (1.2.15–19). Having been reassured as to his own true title to France, Henry sends the Duke of Exeter to France, where he demands that the French king should 'divest' himself and 'lay apart . . . / all wide-stretched honours that pertain / By custom and the ordinance of times / Unto the crown of France' (2.4.82, 86–8). The metaphor represents the royal title of the French king as a stretched-out layer of 'costumary' title with which he has been falsely invested. The dress dimension of Shakespeare's notion of kingship is confirmed later in the play when King Henry, reflecting on the nature of a king, observes that 'his ceremonies / laid by, in his nakedness he appears but a man.' (4.1.96) and wonders to himself if a king's ceremony is anything other than 'place, degree and form / Creating awe and fear in other men?' (4.1.200–1). All of which recalls the moment when he became king of England and donned the 'new and gorgeous garment majesty' (2 *Henry IV* 5.2.45).[19] In Shakespeare's *King Lear* we see how naked a king may become when he divests himself of his invested authority.[20]

What does it mean to 'prove' a title? What qualifies as 'proof'? The word 'proof' is nowadays used to indicate material that withstands physical trial (we talk of 'bulletproof' and 'waterproof' clothing) and to indicate material evidence that withstands legal trial. When Shakespeare was writing, proof as a quality of clothing and adjudicatory proof as a quality of legal evidence

19   We might say that 'kingship itself is a disguise, a role, an action that a man might play': David Scott
      Kastan, '"The King Hath Many Marching in His Coats": Or, What Did You Do in the War, Daddy?', in
      Ivo Kamps (ed.), *Shakespeare Left and Right* (New York: Routledge, 1991), pp.241–58, 252. Compare
      the passing of the royal robes to the biblical King David, Israel (1 Sam. 18.4).
20   In the 2007 Royal Shakespeare Company production, directed by Trevor Nunn, Sir Ian McKellen in
      the title role made the point by baring himself completely below the waist.

were associated by a shared suspicion of appearances and a shared desire to employ processes of probation (processes of 'probing') to discover hidden things. The witch trials that were pervasive in the Old World and the New World throughout this period are terrible testimony to the force of this concern, for they were focused to a large extent upon the skin of alleged witches. One preferred mode of proof was to 'prick' or 'to probe' the suspect's skin at the site of so-called devil's marks.[21] What makes this relevant to us today is that an awareness of Shakespeare's (and other early modern) insights into proof can serve to cultivate a critical appreciation of the fabricated nature of modern legal notions of truth.

In *Othello*, we find what is surely the most famous of Shakespeare's references to proof. It occurs when Othello challenges Iago to provide incontrovertible evidence of Desdemona's marital infidelity: 'Be sure of it: give me the ocular proof . . . / Make me to see't, or at the least so prove it / That the probation bear no hinge nor loop / To hang a doubt on, or woe upon thy life!' (3.3.398, 403–5). Othello demands proof through direct physical witness of Desdemona's betrayal (so-called ocular proof). This is the sort of proof that we have when someone is caught 'in the act' or, which is the next-best thing, caught 'red-handed'. When someone is caught red-handed, the staining of the skin with blood is deemed to obviate the need to probe any deeper to find the truth of the offence. This idea of the marked hand as (literally) 'manifest' proof goes back to antiquity; Cicero, for example, refers to *facinus manifesto compertum* ('clear and manifest crime') in his *Defence of Aulus Cluentius Habitus*.[22] As it happens, Othello will settle for a lesser standard of material evidence of Desdemona's infidelity, provided it admits of no relevant doubt (what he calls 'probation' that will 'bear no hinge or loop'). When we understand what is meant when Othello refers to 'probation' without 'hinge' or 'loop', we will have fashioned a key to unlocking the significance of the idea of proof, not only in the works of Shakespeare but also in the world of law.

In the notes to his 2001 Arden edition of *Othello*, E. A. J. Honigmann relies on the Oxford English Dictionary entries for 'hinge' and 'hang' to

---

21   Heikki Pihlajamäki, '"Swimming the Witch, Pricking for the Devil's Mark": Ordeals in the Early Modern Witchcraft Trials' *The Journal of Legal History* 21.2 (2000), pp.35–58. See, further, Orna Alyagon Darr, *Marks of an Absolute Witch: Evidentiary Dilemmas in Early Modern England* (Farnham: Ashgate, 2011). Darr describes other skin-focused practises, including 'scratching'.

22   *Pro A. Cluentio Habito* XIV.41. Michael Grant (trans.), *Cicero: Murder Trials*, rev. edn (London: Penguin, 1990), pp.121, 145.

support the view that Othello is referring to something that swings or pivots, so that Othello is demanding proof so secure 'that doubts will not move it'.[23] As an explanation, this is insufficiently precise. In the 1958 Arden edition of the play, M. R. Ridley had observed that Othello's metaphor of 'hinge' and 'loop' is very unusual in Shakespeare's works, and that 'we have therefore to start from scratch' in discerning its meaning. Ridley continues: 'it is not easy to see what the force of the figure is', observing that it is not like Shakespeare 'to combine in one picture incongruous specific concrete details', and, significantly:

> This may all seem to be making a fuss about nothing, since the 'general sense' is clear; but with an artist of Shakespeare's vivid pictorial imagination we should never, I think, be easily satisfied with 'general sense' and a consequently woolly apprehension when he himself is being concretely specific.[24]

It is submitted that the hitherto mysterious signification of Shakespeare's supposedly mixed metaphor of 'probation', 'hinge' and 'loop' is to be found in the technical terminology of military dress. 'Probation' is an allusion to the process by which medieval and early modern armourers tested or 'proved' their finished work for weaknesses, a process which required the armour to be, quite literally, 'probed' by a range of weaponry. The 'hinge' and 'loop' in Othello's quote refer to the weak points in a suit of armour – these are, as Othello puts it, the main sites of 'doubt'. No suit of armour could function without the loops or buckles by which it was strapped together, and in certain places sections of armour were joined by metal hinges. As Charles Ffoulkes writes:

> It is almost superfluous to mention the straps which join the various portions of the suit. These are always placed, where possible, in positions where they are protected from injury; as, for example, on the jambs they are on the inside of the leg, next to the horse when the wearer is mounted, and the *hinge* of the jamb being of metal is on the outside.[25] (emphasis added)

23   William Shakespeare, *Othello* (E. A. J. Honigmann ed.) (London: Arden Shakespeare, 2001), p.232.
24   William Shakespeare, *Othello* (M. R. Ridley ed.) (London: Arden Shakespeare, 1965), p.115.
25   Charles Ffoulkes, *The Armourer and His Craft* (London: Methuen, 1912), pp.54–5.

Thus Othello's image of 'probation', 'hinge' and 'loop' is not an inconsistent mix of metaphors, but a single extended metaphor, and one that he, as a military general, would naturally employ. The metaphor also fits perfectly well with Othello's express concern to establish adjudicatory 'proof'. Armour that passed the process of probation (the process of being proved) was said to qualify as 'proof'. This sequential process is paralleled in an earlier part of Othello's narrative, where he says: 'I'll see before I doubt; when I doubt, prove; /And on the proof, there is no more but this: / Away at once with love or jealousy' (3.3.213–15).

In the medieval and early modern periods an armourer's proof found distinctively physical expression in the very surface of his work. The armourer would shoot arrows and crossbow bolts to establish the thickness of his armour and the resulting 'proof marks' would be left on display (and sometimes decorated) deliberately to demonstrate the impenetrable quality

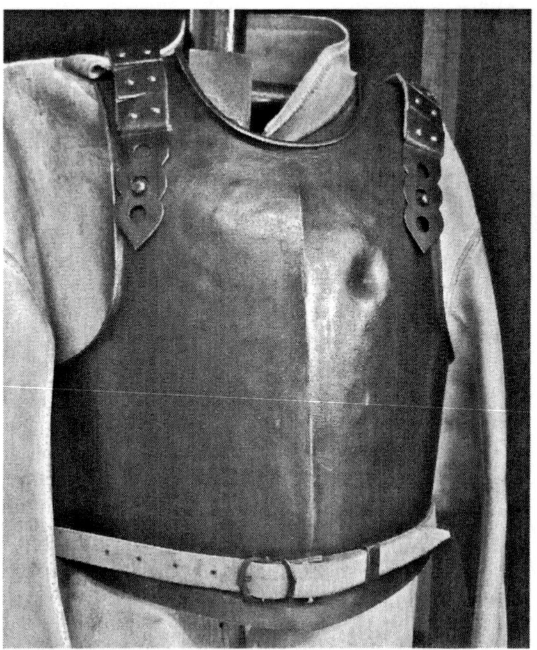

Figure 3.1 Bullet 'proof mark' on an English Civil War era breastplate (courtesy of The Stratford Armories, Warwickshire).

Source: Image © Gary Watt 2012.

of the metal.[26] (Figure 3.1 shows a seventeenth-century breastplate complete with proof mark and hinges).

As early as the end of the fifteenth century, firearms were in frequent use and several pieces of armour from this period 'show a proof mark: a bullet "bruise" in some inconspicuous place, by which the armourer had proved that the plate could withstand the shot of handguns'.[27] The armourer's practice of probation and proof continued to be current and widespread in Shakespeare's lifetime.[28] Proof was frequently made by bullet or crossbow bolt, but it could also be made by the stroke of a sword. Ffoulkes observes that 'as late as the seventeenth century we have evidence that armour was proved by the "*estramaçon*" or sword blow',[29] noting that armour was graded as 'full proof' (*à toute épreuve*) or 'half proof' (*à demi épreuve*) according to its resistance to different types of weapon. Such gradation of proof is highly reminiscent of those theories of legal proof (which had prevailed in the Civil Law of mainland continental Europe since the early medieval period), that distinguished 'full proof' (*plena probatio*) from 'half proof' (*semiplena probatio*).[30] Thus the language for describing the quality of legal proof established by degrees of ocular and other evidence developed in a culture in which remarkably similar language was taken to indicate the quality of material proof as evidenced by the marks which armourers inflicted upon the surface of their work. A similarly close cultural relationship existed between legal and material proof in England, which should not surprise us when we consider that trial by battle had been a normal method of disposing of legal disputes in England after the Norman Conquest, and that it survived as an occasional novelty (but latterly without actual combat) until it was finally abolished in 1819.[31]

We can be confident that it is a military and metallic metaphor of proof that Othello is applying to the evidence of Desdemona's infidelity when he refers to probation without a 'hinge' or 'loop' of doubt. Elsewhere in *Othello* we find frequent clues to the fact that Othello (and, by extension,

26   Ibid., p.55.

27   Stephen Slater, *The Illustrated Book of Heraldry* (London: Hermes House, 2006), p.21.

28   Harold Arthur Dillon, 'a Letter of Sir Henry Lee, 1590, on the Trial of Iron for Armour' *Archaeologia* 51 (1888), pp.167–72.

29   Ffoulkes, *The Armourer and His Craft*, p.62.

30   See James Franklin, *The Science of Conjecture: Evidence and Probability before Pascal* (Baltimore: The Johns Hopkins University Press, 2001), pp.15–23.

31   Stat 59 Geo III c46. See James Bradley Thayer, *A Preliminary Treatise on Evidence* (Boston: Little, Brown, & Co, 1898), pp.7–46.

Shakespeare) has in mind an idea of proof that measures the quality of external evidence by its thickness, as if it were clothing, armour or some other thing that covers the unclothed state that is optimistically imagined to be the 'naked truth'. When Roderigo makes a pass at Cassio with his sword, the undercoat to Cassio's armour protects him from injury. Presumably Cassio had been struck between the joints of his armour. If so, he seems, like Othello, to conceive the joint as a site of doubt. Thus he emphasizes Roderigo's inability to know if he (Cassio) is protected beneath his metal outside: 'That thrust had been mine enemy indeed, / But that my coat is better than thou know'st: / I will make proof of thine' (5.1.24–6). Early in the play, when Othello's own probity is called into doubt, the weakness of the evidence against him is directly compared to the thinness of clothing: 'To vouch this is no proof, / Without more wider and more overt test / Than these thin habits and poor likelihoods / Of modern seeming do prefer against him' (1.3.118–21). It is fitting, then, that when Iago presents Othello with the final damning piece of 'evidence' to establish Desdemona's supposed infidelity, it takes the form of a thin piece of cloth. Desdemona's strawberry-spotted handkerchief (Othello's first gift to her) is the thin material which, added to the rest, will, as if it were armour, at last attain the thickness of sufficient 'proof'. As Iago puts it: 'this may help to thicken other proofs / That do demonstrate thinly' (3.3.473–4). Significantly, and tragically, we know that this fabricated 'proof' did not provide an authentic account of Desdemona's conduct, even though it was taken to be a sufficient show of truth.[32]

As we noted earlier, when Shakespeare was writing and staging his plays, fashionable dress had a distinctly military feel. The fact that the doublet was worn by Queen Elizabeth at once confirmed and confused its military pretensions. The culture of suspicion or doubt concerning external martial appearances coincided with a concern to discover the quality of a person's inner metal. Central to this concern was a renaissance of Plato's metaphorical categorization of citizens in his mythical Republic according to different types of metal.[33] A version of Plato's idea was reprised by Barnaby Rich (the same who supplied the immediate narrative source for

---

32   On forging, fabrication and the weaving of lies in *Othello*, see, further, Catherine Bates, 'Weaving and Writing in Othello' *Shakespeare Survey* 46 (1993), pp.51–60.
33   Plato, *The Republic* III.4 (trans. D. Lee), 2nd edn (Harmondsworth: Penguin, 1974).

Shakespeare's *Twelfth Night*) in his 1578 work, *Allarme to England*.[34] In another publication of 1578, Walter Darell's treatise *Concerning Manners and Behaviours*, we find the earliest reference in the English language to inner 'metal' or 'mettle' as a quality of character that is resistant to a probe (and which would therefore qualify as 'proof' of character). Darell's complaint is that he sees too many gloriously adorned courtiers who 'like tender mylkesops that can beare no brunt: or that, / beside a glorious outside, haue not mettall inough in / them to abide a flea byting'.[35] Shakespeare's late drama, *Cymbeline* (1610), treats a number of the motifs that concern us here, including false proof of female infidelity, cross-dressing and disguise. In its final act we find a speech of Posthumus Leonatus which precisely echoes *Walter Darell's* concern to expose the deceit inherent in the fashion for glorious garb:

> Let me make men know
> More valour in me than my habits show.
> Gods, put the strength o'th'Leonati in me!
> To shame the guise o'th'world, I will begin
> The fashion, less without and more within. (5.1.29–33)

Sir John Falstaff is a Shakespearean archetype of the fashion for false outward show of martial valour. In *The First Part of Henry IV*, when Falstaff claims he is 'no coward' (2.2.48), Prince Henry's short response is most meaningful when we appreciate that outward appearance and inner character are connected by material considerations of probation and metallurgy. Henry simply says: 'We'll leave that to the proof' (2.2.49). Later in the play, Falstaff employs the language of false form ('counterfeit') to describe the action of faking his death on the battlefield in order to save his life: 'to counterfeit dying, when a man thereby liveth, is to be no counterfeit, but the true and perfect image of life indeed. The better part of valour is discretion.' (5.3.116–17). Another Shakespearean exemplar of the type is the character of Sir Andrew Aguecheek in *Twelfth Night*. Sir Toby Belch advises Sir Andrew, ahead of his encounter with Cesario (the disguised Viola), to set

---

34   Barnaby Rich, *Allarme to England foreshewing what perilles are procured, where the people liue without regarde of martiall lawe* (London: Henrie Middleton, 1578).

35   Walter Darell, 'Concerning Manners and Behaviours', in *A Short Discourse of the Life of Servingmen* (London: Ralphe Newberrie, 1578), p.56.

up an outward show of martial prowess as a false proof of the inner metal which in truth he lacks:

> [S]o soon as ever thou see'st him, draw, and as thou draw'st swear horrible, for it comes to pass oft that a terrible oath, with a swaggering accent sharply twanged off, gives manhood more approbation than ever proof itself would have earned him. (3.4.132–5)

Yet another example is Parolles, a follower of Bertram in *All's Well That Ends Well*. In one scene, Bertram defends Parolles as a soldier of 'very valiant approof', but Lafeu does not trust the outward appearance of the man: 'there can be no kernel in this light nut. The soul of this man is his clothes. Trust him not in matter of heavy consequence' (2.5.33–4). The name 'Parolles' would have amused the lawyers and landed gentry in Shakespeare's audience, for they will have been aware that title to land could be proved by formal deed or by non-documentary (parole) evidence.[36] The typical non-documentary evidence was word of mouth supported by public performance of transfer known as livery of seisin.[37] The joke is that the form and deeds of Parolles, the liveried follower of Bertram, present contrary evidence for the state of his character. It is significant, therefore, that at the end of the play Parolles is called by the king to act as a witness in the trial of Bertram's character.

For all the orthodox associations that are made between men and martial metal, it is the women in Shakespeare's plays who supply some of the most interesting studies in the probation of appearances and the proof of inner matter. This is in part because of the layering inherent in the fact that the women in Shakespeare's plays were originally young male actors dressed in female garb. It is also, in related part, because Queen Elizabeth portrayed herself as a palimpsest of military man concealing woman's flesh concealing a man's heart. The 'Virgin Queen' invited public probation to the point of her inner metal, most famously at Tilbury Docks when she addressed the troops assembled to repel the Spanish Armada of 1588: 'I know I have the body of a weak and feeble woman, but I have the heart and stomach of a king, and

---

36 It was generally said that a person is not permitted to 'create an uncertain estate in land by parol' (quoted in Sir Edward Coke, *The First Part of the Institutes of the Laws of England* [1628], III.299).

37 Samuel E. Thorne, 'Livery of Seisin', in *Essays in English Legal History* (London: The Hambledon Press, 1985), pp.31–50.

a king of England too.'[38] In *Twelfth Night*, when Viola asks, in reference to Sir Andrew Aguecheek, 'what manner of man is he?', Fabian's (mocking) reply cuts straight to the point of form and substance; of clothing and proof: 'Nothing of that wonderful promise, to read him by his form, as you are like to find him in the proof of his valour.' (3.4.199–200). In her reply, Viola admits that she is not martially inclined but is one who would 'rather go with sir priest than sir knight'; adding, crucially, 'I care not who knows so much of my mettle' (3.4.203–4).

Shakespeare explores in numerous places women's potential to demonstrate proof of inner metal. In *Hamlet*, it is demonstrated negatively where the Prince complains that his mother should have a heart that is penetrable and human rather than of impenetrable proof metal: 'let me wring your heart, for so I shall, / If it be made of penetrable stuff, / If damnèd custom have not brazed it so / That it is proof and bulwark against sense' (3.4.40–3). In *Julius Caesar*, it is demonstrated positively where Brutus's wife, Portia, employs the yielding frailty of her flesh to demonstrate the fortitude of her character; piercing the surface of her skin to prove herself and to leave a proof mark in the form of a scar:

> Tell me your counsels, I will not disclose 'em.
> I have made strong proof of my constancy,
> Giving myself a voluntary wound
> Here in the thigh: can I bear that with patience
> And not my husband's secrets? (2.1.310–14)

Even today, men and women seek to prove their mettle by their mode of dress. The painful and permanent marking of tattoo is an especially potent form of wound or mark by which to prove individual character and social allegiance. Prisoners and gang members are frequently marked out this way. Prison officers are also marked out by distinctive dress. Like the members of many other uniformed services, prison officers must pass through a probationary period as part of their ritual initiation into the uniformed corps. Probation is an intriguing liminal state in which the probationer has been set

---

38 'Queen Elizabeth's Armada Speech to the Troops at Tilbury' (9 August 1588), in Leah S. Marcus, Janel Mueller and Mary Beth Rose (eds), *Elizabeth I: Collected Works* (Chicago: University of Chicago Press, 2000), p.326. See Carla Spivack, 'The Woman Will Be Out: A New Look at the Law in *Hamlet*' *Yale J L & Human* 20 (2008), pp.31–60, 46.

apart from the general polis but has not yet been fully admitted to the role of its protector. The probationary process can be observed in most uniformed professions, perhaps most notably in the military, where servicemen and women are often admitted to their corps by the appropriation of coloured headdresses – red berets, green berets and so forth. When police cadets in New York City pass their probation, they change from probationary grey uniforms to the standard blue.[39] Similar probationary processes existed in the ancient world; indeed the word 'probation' alludes to the requirement that a man be shown to be of good quality (*probatus*) before admission as a legionary in the Roman Army. We still 'decorate' soldiers who prove their martial metal in time of war, by awarding them a piece of metal (a medal) to be worn on their uniformed chest where once upon a time they would have borne an armoured breastplate.

As Shakespeare's *Othello* establishes the connection between proof of an accusation and proof of armour, so Shakespeare's *Twelfth Night, or What You Will* connects these concerns to early modern preoccupation with documentary proof and procedural proof in courts of law. It has been said of Shakespeare's *Twelfth Night* that the 'plot is a pretext' and the 'theme of the play is disguise'.[40] Disguise is introduced as an important theme at the very outset of the play. In the second scene, when the freshly shipwrecked Viola conceals herself in the clothing and outward form of her brother Sebastian, whom she fears has died in the wreck, she invites the ship's captain to assist in her concealment and she employs the language of disguise to express her confidence in the captain's character: 'I will believe thou hast a mind that *suits* / With this thy fair and *outward* character . . . / *Conceal me* what I am, and be my aid / For such *disguise* as haply shall become / The *form* of my intent' (1.3.52–3, 55–7) (emphases added). The theme of disguise makes a brief appearance even as early as the short opening scene of the play, where we are told that the lady Olivia will not entertain the suit of Orsino, Duke of Illyria, but instead, in mourning for her recently deceased brother, 'like a cloistress . . . will veilèd walk' (1.1.29). Later in the play, the lady Olivia also declines to entertain the suit of her steward Malvolio, who is tricked into proving his affection for his mistress by appearing before her in cross-gartered yellow stockings. The lady Olivia, is, in turn, spurned by the disguised Viola (masquerading as the

---

39   See, generally, Nathan Joseph and Nicholas Alex, 'The Uniform: A Sociological Perspective' *American Journal of Sociology* 77.4 (1972), pp.719–30.
40   Jan Kott, *Shakespeare Our Contemporary* (London: Methuen, 1965), p.207.

gentleman Cesario). When Olivia falls for Viola's seeming masculinity, Viola muses: 'Fortune forbid my outside have not charm'd her! . . . / Disguise, I see, thou art a wickedness, / Wherein the pregnant enemy does much' (2.2.13, 22–3). The central theme of the play is disguise, but the theme of disguise can also be read as a theme of proof. Consider the scene in which Viola, disguised in her brother Sebastian's outward form, is mistaken for him by Sebastian's rescuer, Antonio. Viola naturally translates the language of dress and disguise into the language of proof:

> Prove true, imagination, O, prove true,
> That I, dear brother, be now ta'en for you!
>   . . . even such and so
> In favour was my brother, and he went
> Still in this fashion, colour, ornament,
> For him I imitate. O, if it prove,
> Tempests are kind and salt waves fresh in love. (3.4.296–7, 301–5)

When Sebastian is finally reunited with his twin Viola (she disguised as the man Cesario), he probes the apparition of himself with a salvo of questions: 'Do I stand there? . . . what kin are you to me? / What countryman? What name? What parentage?' (5.1.211, 215–16). In early modern England, this quick-fire form of interrogation was a standard method for proving ('probing' or 'testing') facts in the context of legal and ecclesiastical inquisition. In the religious context, the orthodoxy of an adherent's faith was proved through catechism, and in the Court of Chancery, which was originally an ecclesiastical court, the concern of the court was to interrogate the conscience of the party, to which end it employed a method of serial questioning which seems to have been inspired by the methodology of religious catechism.[41] W. J. Jones notes that the Court of Chancery asked such questions as: 'do you not know or have you not credibly heard or are you not fully persuaded in your conscience that it was the true intent, will and meaning of the said Nicholas Bristowe, deceased, that . . . ?'.[42] Elsewhere in *Twelfth Night*, Shakespeare makes express reference to proof by catechism and to proof by constant

---

41   Oliver W. Holmes, 'Early English Equity' *Law Quarterly Review* 1 (1885), pp.162–74, 162 n.1. Citing
       Rot Parl 84; 3 Hen V pt 2 46, No23.
42   William J. Jones, *The Elizabethan Court of Chancery* (Oxford: Clarendon Press, 1967), p.238;
       cited in Dennis R. Klinck, *Conscience, Equity and the Court of Chancery in Early Modern England*
       (Farnham: Ashgate, 2010), p.84.

question. On both occasions the process of proof appears, as we would now expect, in the context of a related concern to probe through the external coverings of dress.

The first instance appears in the witty interchange between Olivia and her licensed fool, Feste, in which, through diverse probations, he attempts to persuade his mistress to cast off her mourning veil. It begins with Feste's aside in which, making an apostrophe to 'Wit', he asserts that '[t]hose wits, that think they have thee, do very oft prove fools' (1.5.25–6). The relevant passage deserves to be quoted at length for the way in which it shows how Feste employs processes of testing or probation (including syllogism and catechism) to demonstrate the unreliability of external appearances presented in the form of clothes. The text of the passage is a tapestry in which themes of probation and proof are interwoven with textile references to the fool's official garb (the motley), to sartorial processes of patching and mending and to the maxim *cucullus non facit monachum* ('a hood does not a monk make'). The stimulus for the scene is Olivia's request that her servants should take away the 'fool':

> FESTE   . . . bid the dishonest man mend himself. If he mend, he is no longer dishonest; if he cannot, let the botcher mend him. Anything that's mended is but patched: virtue that transgresses is but patched with sin, and sin that amends is but patched with virtue. If that this simple syllogism will serve, so. If it will not, what remedy? As there is no true cuckold but calamity, so beauty's a flower. The lady bade take away the fool: therefore, I say again, take her away.
>
> OLIVIA   Sir, I bade them take away you.
>
> FESTE   Misprision in the highest degree! Lady, *cucullus non facit monachum*: that's as much to say as I wear not motley in my brain. Good madonna, give me leave to prove you a fool.
>
> OLIVIA   Can you do it?
>
> FESTE   Dexteriously, good madonna.
>
> OLIVIA   Make your proof.
>
> FESTE   I must catechize you for it, madonna. Good my mouse of virtue, answer me.
>
> OLIVIA   Well, sir, for want of other idleness, I'll bide your proof.
>
> FESTE   Good madonna, why mourn'st thou?

OLIVIA   Good fool, for my brother's death.
FESTE   I think his soul is in hell, madonna.
OLIVIA   I know his soul is in heaven, fool.
FESTE   The more fool, madonna, to mourn for your brother's
         soul being in heaven. Take away the fool, gentlemen.
OLIVIA   What think you of this fool, Malvolio? Doth he not mend?
         (1.5.33–55)

The themes of this passage anticipate the scene later in the play in which Malvolio, who has been 'misprisioned' (arrested) and wrongfully imprisoned on a charge of madness, is visited by Feste disguised as a priest. On that occasion, Malvolio submits to probation by interrogation, saying 'I am no more mad than you are. Make the trial of it in any constant question' (4.2.34–5). What we see in the scene between the lady Olivia and the fool Feste is the fool's attempt to prick a hole in the formality of his lady's mourning as represented in the form of her veil. He does so by means of logical (syllogistic) probation and by catechism-like interrogation. Today we might describe his efforts by means of another sartorial metaphor used in legal contexts: 'picking holes' in an argument.

Of the classical rhetorical proofs that will still persuade a court today, one of the most significant is the commonplace proof. Judges will accept without trial or probation that 'apples fall down', that 'rain makes wet' and that 'night follows day'. They are said to take 'judicial notice' of such things. They hold, as the drafters of the *United States Declaration of Independence* once held, that certain truths are 'self-evident'. Shakespeare places an example of commonplace proof in the mouth of the provincial judge, Justice Shallow, in *The Second Part of Henry IV*: 'Certain, 'tis certain, very sure, very sure: death is certain to all, all shall die . . .' (3.2.26–7). Another example appears in *Twelfth Night* where, demonstrating yet another aspect of the play's central concern with proof, Viola observes ''tis a vulgar proof / That very oft we pity enemies' (3.1.104–5).

There is, though, a wide range of facts that the law will not accept as proof unless they are established by a certain documentary form or by a process of trial. The law will not always accept the factual evidence – the evident outer appearance of proof – but will sometimes demand that a claim be clothed or armoured in a certain pre-approved form or will demand that unfamiliar facts be proven, like unfamiliar armour, by process of trial. Take the fact of an oral promise. If I orally promise to make a gift to you, the promise is not enforceable against me in the absence of an actual transfer of the subject matter of the gift.[43] The same is true of a voluntary promise to enter a bargain. If the other party makes no promise to give or do something in exchange, my promise is considered to be a 'bare' promise. Writing in 1530, Christopher St German put it this way:

> *What is a nude contract, or naked promise, and whether any action may lie thereon*
>
> Student: . . . a nude contract is, when a man maketh a bargain, or a sale of his goods or lands without any recompence appointed for it: as if I say to another, I sell thee all my land, or else my goods, and nothing is assigned that the other shall give or pay for it . . . no action lieth in those cases, though they be not performed . . . for it is secret in his own conscience whether he intended for to be bound or nay. And of the intent inward in the heart, man's law cannot judge, and that is one of the causes why the law of God is necessary, that is to say, to judge inward things.[44]

The discovery of inner truth under outward signs is, of course, a perennial theme, and the human need of divine assistance in that process of discovery figured especially prominently in the theology of Thomas Aquinas (1225–74). As Lorna Hutson has observed, the passage from St German, just quoted, expresses a 'Thomist commonplace'.[45]

St German rationalizes the problem posed by a bare promise (*nudum pactum*) as a problem of proof. The reason the law will not enforce the promise is because the law has no means to probe inner conscience. What the law requires, therefore, is that intent should be clothed by some outward form that will withstand the law's probation and thereby qualify as sufficient proof. Even today in English law, a unilateral voluntary promise (i.e. a promise not made in exchange for a benefit promised by the other party) is not binding on the promisor, whereas the same promise made in the documentary form of a deed is regarded as a binding covenant.[46] It

---

43   It is said that there is no equity to perfect an imperfect gift (*Milroy* v. *Lord* [1862] 4 De G F & J 264).

44   Christopher St German, *Doctor and Student* (1530) (Theodore F. T. Plucknett and J. L. Barton eds) (London: Selden Society, 1974), pp.228–31.

45   Hutson, *The Invention of Suspicion*, p.55.

46   Patrick S. Atiyah, *Introduction to the Law of Contract* (Oxford: Clarendon Press, 1961), pp.22–3.

is significant that legal suspicion of mere words and legal insistence upon proper documentary form reached a peak (though by no means its only peak) at precisely the time that Shakespeare was writing and first staging *Twelfth Night*. The first known performance of *Twelfth Night* occurred on 2 February 1602 in the Hall of the Middle Temple (one of the 'Inns of Court'), and the important litigation in *Slade's Case*, which had been running since 1596, finally concluded in November 1602.[47] The essential question in *Slade's Case* was whether an action for debt had to be pursued by an exceedingly formal writ of debt in the Court of Common Pleas, or whether a claim in debt might be expedited by the less formal action of *indebitatus assumpsit* in the court of King's Bench under which the plaintiff would put it to a jury that the debtor's oral promise to pay amounted to a binding assumption of liability. The case concerned basic questions about the enforceability of contracts, and it therefore became famous beyond the walls of the lawyers' world.[48] The uncertainty caused by the case as it progressed through various courts had an impact on commercial practice. The legal historian David Ibbetson notes that '[t]he records of the King's Bench for 1600 show a significant shift away from the use of *assumpsit* in place of debt'.[49] Eventually the judges decided that debt could be pursued on *assumpsit* as an alternative to the old form of action in debt, and thereby opened the way to a modern flexible law of contract. The following extract from the report of the final judgment emphasizes that one of the major sticking points in *Slade's Case* was the question of proof:

> And as to the Objection which hath been made, that it shall be mischievous to the Defendant . . . forasmuch as he might pay it in secret: To that it was answered, That it shall be accounted his folly that he took not sufficient witnesses to prove the paiment he made.[50]

Twelfth Night was written during the period in which (as Professor Ibbetson notes) there was a 'significant shift away from *assumpsit*', so we should expect to find that if the play alludes to *Slade's Case*, it will do so by casting

47   *Slade's Case* (1602) 4 Co Rep 91 (Court of Exchequer Chamber).
48   William J. Jones, *Politics and the Bench: The Judges and the Origins of the English Civil War* (London: Allen and Unwin, 1971), pp.49–50.
49   David Ibbetson, 'Sixteenth Century Contract Law: *Slade's Case* in Context' *Oxford Journal of Legal Studies* 4.3 (1984), pp.295–317, 303.
50   *Slade's Case* (1602) 4 Co Rep 91 at 92b, 95a.

doubt upon words unsupported by formal documentation. We do indeed find such doubts expressed in the play, notably when Feste laments that 'words are grown so false, I am loath to prove reason with them' (3.1.17–18). For the lawyers in Middle Temple Hall who constituted the first known audience for the play, there could hardly have been an issue of greater topical interest than that of doubtful words. The documentary evidence for the first performance on 2 February 1602 is an entry in the diary of John Manningham, a student barrister at the Middle Temple. It is notable that Manningham fixes upon the significance of a counterfeit document:

> A good practice in it to make the steward believe his lady-widow was in love with him, by counterfeiting a letter as from his lady, in general terms telling him what she liked best in him and prescribing his gesture in smiling, his apparel, etc. and then, when he came to practice, making him believe they took him for mad.

As we have seen, there was a side to the debate in *Slade's Case* that was resistant to the avoidance of the old documentary formalities and that emphasized the unreliability of mere spoken words. Here the student lawyer picks up on the fact that Shakespeare was playing on the equally unreliable nature of documentary evidence. In the scene where Malvolio scrutinizes the counterfeit letter and satisfies himself as to its meaning and import, he concluded that his interpretation of the document was 'evident to any formal capacity', before admitting, a little later, that his interpretation does not stand up to 'probation' (2.5.90, 98). How deep must have been the resonance of these lines with Shakespeare's audience of lawyers, who, when they weren't feasting and watching plays, would have been mooting the points of *Slade's Case*. The dress aspects of the play would also have appealed to them. Student barristers were infamous for their obsession with fashionable dress. *An Act for the Reformacyon of Excesse in Apparayle* (1533),[51] which was the last statute to lay down sumptuary laws in the reign of Henry VIII, had been relatively indulgent to students of the Inns of Court or Chancery. It allowed them to wear doublets and partlets of satin, damask and camlet or jackets of camlet, if received as gifts. They were not permitted to wear crimson, purple, scarlet or blue, but they could wear marten and

---

51   Statute 24 Hen VIII c13.

black rabbit fur.[52] Apparently the Inns of Court indulged the students within the licence of the law, provided that their apparel indicated 'no lightness or wantonness in the wearer'.[53] That licence must have been stretched to snapping point by the time of the vainglorious fashions of the 1580s, for in the period 1580 to 1600, the various Inns of Court introduced strict orders concerning the wearing of gowns.[54] No doubt the rules were followed as a matter of form, but they did nothing to suppress the students' passion for fashion. Sir Thomas Overbury complained that student barristers were more concerned with their luxurious clothes than with their legal cases.[55]

In civil (non-criminal) cases, including cases of contract law, the required standard of proof is proof established 'on the balance of probabilities', which is sometimes called proof that is 'more likely than not' or proof based on a likelihood of at least 51 per cent. In criminal matters, the defendant is presumed innocent until proven guilty and the defendant should be acquitted unless the jury is 'sure that the defendant is guilty'.[56] The traditional formulation of being 'sure' is that the jury is satisfied of the defendant's guilt 'beyond reasonable doubt' (variously expressed as 'beyond a reasonable doubt', 'beyond any reasonable doubt' and 'beyond all reasonable doubt'). Recall Othello's willingness to waive his demand for positive 'ocular proof' in favour of a lesser degree of proof that will, in a negative sense, 'at least' be proof against doubt. Consider how close that formulation is to the legal standard of 'proof beyond reasonable doubt'. Neither formulation is concerned to establish fundamental truth. Each formulation is concerned only to remove evident doubt.

There is a lively academic debate concerning the nature of the early modern origins of the concept of 'proof beyond reasonable doubt'.[57] To that debate we can now add a new and material layer. Barbara Shapiro has

52   Maria Hayward, *Rich Apparel: Clothing and Law in Henry VIII's England* (Farnham: Ashgate, 2009), p.38.

53   John H. Baker, 'History of the Gowns Worn at the English Bar' *Costume* 9 (1975), pp.15–21, 16.

54   These sumptuary regulations might represent an effort 'to represent in visual terms the polity of the Protestant State' (Paul Raffield, *Images and Cultures of Law in Early Modern England: Justice and Political Power, 1558–1660* [Cambridge: CUP, 2004], p.161).

55   Sir Thomas Overbury, *His Wife* (1614) (London: Robert Allot, 1628), sigs K4ʳ–K5ʳ; quoted in Emma Rhatigan, '"The Sinful History of Mine Own Youth": John Donne Preaches at Lincoln's Inn', in Jayne Elisabeth Archer, Elizabeth Goldring and Sarah Knight (eds), *The Intellectual and Cultural World of the Early Modern Inns of Court* (Manchester: MUP, 2011), pp.90–106, 91.

56   *R* v. *Majid* [2009] EWCA Crim 2563.

57   See, for example, Barbara J. Shapiro, 'The beyond Reasonable Doubt Doctrine: "Moral Comfort" or Standard of Proof?' *Law and Humanities* 2.2 (2008), pp.149–73; James Q. Whitman, 'Response to Shapiro' *Law and Humanities* 2.2 (2008), pp.175–89.

convincingly argued that the process of proof beyond reasonable doubt aimed to establish practical satisfaction or moral comfort as inquirers found it increasingly hard to discover the absolute truth of facts within the complexities of the early modern world.[58] We can now see how closely this parallels early modern notions of proving armour. Armour was never required to be absolutely impenetrable. It would be nonsensical to suppose that armour could be made to resist all the weapons of the age in all contexts of conflict, and in fact armour died out precisely because attempts to make it proof against increasingly sophisticated weapons eventually required such a thickness of metal that soldiers were no longer able to bear it. Armour was never required to be positively invulnerable to any possible assault; it was merely required to offer sufficient practical protection and comfort against reasonably likely attack. Proof of armour was not proof as an absolute truth; it was merely proof to the point of practical satisfaction. The same was true, and is true, of legal proof. To sum up, we can say that the concept of satisfactory legal proof in early modern England was formulated in the context of a wider cultural appreciation of proof as a material quality of clothing and of armour in particular. With this in mind, the conclusion we reach is this: that legal proof beyond reasonable doubt is proof with holes in it, but with holes too small to allow the inquirer to probe to a deeper reality and too small, therefore, to admit injury. When such reliable outward proof is established, the law is then content to presume that it has probed to the point of a person's inner mettle and to the point of truth. An eighteenth-century preacher once said in a sermon addressed to judges that righteousness is necessary, but outward judgment is 'perhaps more useful'. He described private righteousness as a silver-embroidered vest and public judgment as a gold-fringed robe.[59] It is said that the law requires, not only that justice must be done but also that it should be seen to be done. One wonders, though, whether the law might not be content for justice to be seen to be done according to its processes regardless of whether it is actually done in fact.

58   Barbara J. Shapiro: *A Culture of Fact: England, 1550–1720* (Ithaca, NY: Cornell University Press, 2000); *Probability and Certainty in Seventeenth-Century England: A Study of the Relationships between Natural Science, Religion, History, Law, and Literature* (Princeton, NJ: Princeton University Press, 1983); *'Beyond Reasonable Doubt' and 'Probable Cause': Historical Perspectives on the Anglo-American Law of Evidence* (Berkeley: University of California Press, 1991).

59   Bunker Gay, *The Accomplished Judge; or, a Complete Dress for Magistrates* (a sermon preached at Keene, at the first opening of the Inferior Court, in the county of Cheshire, 8 October 1771) (Portsmouth, New-Hampshire: D. Fowle, 1773), p.16.

When Pontius Pilate asked, 'what is truth?' in the course of the most significant show trial in history,[60] he no doubt appreciated that the purpose of legal trial is not to discover truth but rather to cover the case in such a way that public onlookers will be satisfied. An argument of the present book is that legal processes of trial, right up until the present day, are still concerned to cover cases with a satisfactory semblance of truth. To express the point in terms of clothing, we can say that legal processes of trial do not seek to discover or uncover layers of lies that might be obscuring naked truth, but rather that they endeavour to cover each case in a way that will deflect doubt. Something similar has been observed by ethnographers investigating local conceptions of what counts as being socially unclean. They have found that 'purity is not simply about following rules but also about the strategic capacity to project a virtuous public image. In other words, one must *appear* to follow the rules'.[61] The dominant metaphor for truth – the *discovery* metaphor – is misleading. The truths that most concern us for the purposes of civil life are not discovered from hidden depths, but fabricated before our eyes. Agamben sees this dynamic at work in the legal context: 'The ultimate aim of law is the production of a *res judicata*, in which the sentence becomes the substitute for the true and the just.'[62] Scott was right when he said that we 'weave' when we 'practice to deceive',[63] but it is also the case that we establish forms of truth through processes of fashioning and fabrication.

To some extent I am agreeing with Warwick and Cavallaro where they observe that 'fashion's penchant for obfuscating the very distinction between deception and truthfulness' renders 'the boundary between "telling lies" and "telling truth" . . . precarious and uncertain'[64] and where they argue that truth may reside *in* 'superficial phenomena'.[65] However, where Warwick and Cavallaro posit the latter possibility to the exclusion of the existence of absolute truth, I would argue that it is entirely compatible with the possibility of absolute truth. Indeed, fabricated truth may be regarded as a

60   Jn 18.38.
61   Adeline Masquelier, 'Introduction', in Adeline Masquelier (ed.), *Dirt, Undress and Difference: Critical Perspectives on the Body's Surface* (Bloomington and Indianapolis: Indiana University Press, 2005), pp.1–33, 11.
62   Giorgio Agamben, *Remnants of Auschwitz* (1999) (trans. Daniel Heller-Roazen) (New York: Zone Books, 2002), p.18.
63   Sir Walter Scott, *Marmion* (1808) 6.17.532–3.
64   Alexandra Warwick and Dani Cavallaro, *Fashioning the Frame: Boundaries, Dress and the Body* (Oxford and New York: Berg, 1998), p.xviii.
65   Ibid., p.133.

counterfeit of, or pragmatic approximation to, absolute truth. Satisfactory proof established by evidence for the practical purposes of civil life is one thing; absolute truth may be quite another thing. Even scientific method, properly-so-called, does not aim to discover underlying truth. It is merely concerned to prove (i.e. to 'probe' or test) working hypotheses.[66] A scientific theory is never 'true'. It can, at best, have the status of being 'not disproved'. Likewise, when a judge makes a finding of fact on disputed evidence in a legal case, the effect is to create a fact where previously there had been merely conflicting theories. The judge in this sense makes a reality in legal terms that is satisfactory for legal purposes. Science operates in the same way. It identifies scientific 'facts' in terms that are satisfactory for scientific purposes. Indeed, the 'fic' in 'scientific' is a clue to the fact that scientific proofs comprise knowledge (*scientia*) that is fashioned (*facere*). Facts may be manufactured things.

When Warwick and Cavallaro assert that 'dress, by encouraging us to make and remake ourselves over and again, renders the very idea of essence quite absurd',[67] they are making a statement which, in its absolutism, is essentialist in itself. In any case, the fact that there is variety in the nature of particular forms of dress does nothing to indicate that there is no essence to dress. It may be that for certain practical purposes we do not need to identify an essential truth, but this does not mean that there isn't one. No matter how we dress, the essential fact is that we do dress. Warwick and Cavallaro make a similar mistake when, having observed that the language of dress may assist us to question such metaphysical categories as true and false, they go on to claim that it also has the potential to subvert all such 'binary mythologies'.[68] Actually, talking dress confirms such truths as the truth that we all, for some reason, go dressed in public. Talking dress therefore confirms the binary distinction between dress and non-dress. If any myth is threatened by the timeless cultural category of dress, and such cognate categories as law, it is the postmodern conceit that there are no such categories anymore. Warwick and Cavallaro eventually seem

---

66   For Francis Bacon, 'penetration' was a preferred metaphor for the 'discovery' of knowledge about nature (see, for example, Francis Bacon, *Novum Organum* [London: John Bill, 1620], Aphorism XVIII). The metaphor has proved controversial with some feminists because Bacon personifies nature as a female.

67   Warwick and Cavallaro, *Fashioning the Frame*, p.116.

68   Ibid., p.xxiii.

to admit as much, when they confess that '[a]s a moulding agency, dress may seal the body's subjection to invincible collective mythologies'.[69] They also acknowledge, likewise, that the social subject's 'vestimentary envelope will inexorably carry traces of its primordial fantasies of self-realization and pre-linguistic expression, which challenge the requirements of the adult domain of laws and institutions'.[70] Warwick and Cavallaro are right to suggest that dress allows for 'playful experimentation' with categorical boundaries, but it is an error to think that this playfulness is a threat to the essential existence of those boundaries. On the contrary, playing with a boundary is a mode of making it; just as lawyers' practice of playing with laws contributes to their creation.

There is a painting hanging in the main criminal courtroom of the Palais de Justice in the town of Montpellier in the South of France which seems to me sum up the fact that lawyers conceive of truth as a fabricated thing. Arrayed within a series of paintings in classical style depicting various virtues of legal process, it depicts the naked female figure of *Veritas*;[71] except this figure of truth is concealing much of her nakedness by means of a book held in one hand and a drape of cloth held in the other (Figure 3.2). Her right breast is exposed, as is the entire contour of her right side – foot, leg, hip and torso – but she is essentially 'decent', as the law requires. The Montpellier image of *Veritas* can be read as an acknowledgement of law's cultural affinity with the layer of cloth and a confession that the true nature of legal trial is not to discover naked truth, but to produce a certain satisfactory proof in the form of textile and text. The covering, not the content, is the heart of the matter in the worlds of dress and law alike. In short, law prefers fabricated truth to the naked variety.

Occasionally the law has gone out of its way to cover up the naked female figure of Justice. The huge statues standing in the Great Hall of the Robert F. Kennedy Department of Justice Building in Washington, DC – the female figure *Spirit of Justice* (which has one breast exposed) and the bare-chested male figure *Majesty of Law*[72] – were for a time concealed behind curtains,

69   Ibid., p.5.
70   Ibid., p.41.
71   The painting, dating to around 1878, is by the Montpellier-born artist Ernest Michel. I am grateful to Professor Nathalie Vienne-Guerrin (Université Montpellier III) and to Ms Dominique Santonja of *La Cour d'Appel de Montpellier* for assistance in identifying the artist.
72   1933–6, C. Paul Jennewein (sculptor).

Figure 3.2 Ernest Michel, 'Veritas' (c.1878).

Source: Image © Ms Dominique Santonja of La Cour d'Appel de Montpellier.

allegedly on the orders of the former Attorney General John D. Ashcroft.[73] One wonders what he would make of the statue *Verity* by Damien Hirst, which was unveiled on the pier of the English seaside town of Illfracombe on 17 October 2012. Standing more than 20 metres tall and weighing more than 25 tonnes, the naked pregnant female figure is an allegory for truth and justice. She holds the Sword of Justice erect in her left hand and with her other hand she holds the skewed Scales of Justice behind her back. She stands on a plinth of books, so there is some contact with text, but there is no textile in sight. Far from being covered up, even her skin is peeled away along the entire front of her right-hand side above the knee. Her skull, the tissue of her breast, her muscle fibres and her unborn child are all displayed in detail. This is how truth might appear if stripped of the curtain of censorship and the artifice of law. The fact is, though, that the arts of law are not as free as other arts. We cannot throw off the artificial fabrication of truth, and nor

73   Dan Eggen, 'Sculpted Bodies and a Strip Act at Justice Dept', *Washington Post*, 25 June 2005.

should we wish to. Fabrications are the nearest thing we have to satisfactory truth for the purposes of law, order and civil life. Still, it will be no bad thing if we dare to doubt the evidence of our eyes and to probe continually the proofs that are placed before them. As Professor Teufelsdröckh informed us: 'The beginning of all Wisdom is to look fixedly on Clothes, or even with armed eyesight, till they become transparent.'[74]

74   Carlyle, *Sartor Resartus*, Book I, chapter 10. On transparency and judgment, see Thomas Docherty, *Confessions: The Philosophy of Transparency (Wish List)* (London: Bloomsbury Academic, 2012).

CHAPTER FOUR

The Face the Law Makes

Has not your Red hanging-individual a horsehair wig, squirrel-skins, and a plush-gown; whereby all mortals know that he is a JUDGE? – Society, which the more I think of it astonishes me the more, is founded upon Cloth.[1]

Law makes the form of a face in the world, and the face of law is one of the faces by which we recognize the world as we know it. Many matters combine together to make the face of the law. Words and deeds, certainly; words *as* deeds also. Then, no less important, there are the forms of architecture and dress that make up the stage and costume of the law's performance.

The word 'face' derives from the Latin *facies* ('form'). If, as seems likely, the word 'face' has an even deeper relation to the Latin verb *facere* ('to make' or 'to do'), then 'face' would share that root with 'fashion'. A 'face' is a made thing, and it is a thing to behold. The Greek word for face, *prosopon* (πρόσωπον), denotes that which is towards (*pro-*) the eye (*ops*), and the visive sense is equally obvious in the French and German words for 'face': *visage* and *Angesicht*.

The law, having made a face for itself, makes its subjects in its own image. Individual human beings cease to be fully human in the eyes of the law and become, instead, abstract constructions. This is why the legal subject is said to have 'legal personality'. The word personality derives directly from the Latin *persona*, which was the Roman word for the classical actor's mask. (The Greeks called the actor's mask by the name of 'face': *prosopon*.) The law's practice of concealing and deprecating human reality under a simplistic mask of legal personality was clearly demonstrated in the old Common Law doctrine of *femme couverte*. By that doctrine 'the very being or legal existence' of a married woman was 'suspended during the marriage', or at least 'incorporated and consolidated into that of the

---

1   Thomas Carlyle, *Sartor Resartus: The Life and Opinions of Herr Teufelsdröckh* (1833–4) (Boston: James Munroe and Co, 1836), Book I, chapter 9.

husband'. Husband and wife were considered 'one person' in law.[2] The law fabricates a face for us that will be capable of having regard to the artificial face that the law has made for itself. The law fashions itself and it fashions us in its own image for the purpose of mutual regard. Foucault explained that the law is always watching us.[3] It is also the case that we are always watching it. Law is a regarded thing. Law commands our gaze. As the well-known maxim puts it: 'ignorance of law is no defence.' If humans are persons (masks, fabricated faces) vis-à-vis the law, how much more mask-like are wholly artificial creatures of the law such as corporations. It is only with reluctance that a court will occasionally lift the so-called veil of a corporation's legal personality to reveal the human puppet-masters who operate the underlying business organization.[4]

In Chapter Five, we will consider the nature of the law's response today when the 'abutting fronts' of the individual and the State conflict; especially in the context of public face-covering and public nudity. In this chapter, we will be concerned mainly with the significance of the law's own modes of dress, including the judge's robe, the lawyer's gown and the police uniform. We will see that legal costume, as a factor in the formation of the face of law, can be regarded as an aspect of the lawyers' performative (i.e. form-making) arts. Script, stage, props and costume all play a part in the performance of legal authority. While maintaining an outlook that is global and concerned with perennial features of law and dress, we will focus closely upon the fashionable worlds of mid-nineteenth-century London and Paris. The tale of these two cities in the period 1825 to 1875 is a tale of how the modern world, including its legal aspect, established itself through dress. It was during this period that the wig was retained by lawyers despite the fact that everybody else (with the exception of coachmen in the British Royal Household) had given it up. Anyone who clung on to the wig was considered downright old-fashioned. President James Monroe, who held office from 1817 to 1825 (and who was a lawyer by profession), is reputedly the last US president to have worn the powdered wig along with old-style knee breeches and tricorne hat. His dress was considered so out of fashion that it earned him

---

2   William Blackstone, 'Of Husband and Wife', in *Commentaries on the Laws of England* (in four volumes), 1st edn (Oxford: Clarendon Press, 1765–9), I.xv

3   Michel Foucault, *Discipline and Punish: The Birth of the Prison* (London: Penguin, 1977).

4   *Salomon v. A Salomon & Co Ltd* [1897] AC 22; *VTB Capital Plc v. Nutritek International Corp & Ors* [2012] EWCA Civ 808.

the sobriquet 'The Last Cocked Hat'.[5] It was around the same period that the modern police uniform was invented. When Sir Robert Peel established London's Metropolitan Police Force on 29 September 1829, the uniform included a blue swallowtail coat, a stovepipe top hat and white gloves.

The tale of fashion in the mid-nineteenth century is a tall tale and a broad tale, as befits the ambition of the age. Male fashion reached new heights in the mid-nineteenth century when the trendsetting Prince Albert, consort to Queen Victoria, adopted the top hat around 1850. Within a decade or so, a lawyer by the name of Abraham Lincoln had extended his already impressive 6 feet and 4 inches by some 8 inches of 'stovepipe' ('chimney-pot') hat, and he went on to become President of the United States. It was around the same period that the female fashionable silhouette expanded to an extremely broad ambit by means of the steel-hooped 'crinoline'. The American W. S. Thomson purchased the rights to Amet and Milliet's 1856 patent and put the steel crinoline into mass production. It then went on to reach its broadest extent in the 1860s before gradually dying away.[6] The lightweight steel and tape structure of the crinoline allowed skirts to extend to great width without the drawback of oppressive weight that had accompanied earlier attempts to achieve bulk with multiple layers of cloth, sometimes supported on skeletons of whalebone or wood. Indeed, the steel crinoline could make a woman as broad as she was high,[7] much to the delight of caricaturists working for the journals of Paris and London in the 1850s. Dress in this period was a significant stimulant to the creative arts and cultural commentary. The focus of this chapter is accordingly upon the ways in which such contemporary figures as Daumier and Baudelaire in Paris and Dickens and Carlyle in London help us to appreciate the numerous interfaces between the public performance of dress and law.

While the hats of men, such as the engineer Isambard Kingdom Brunel, seemed to mimic the industrial chimney stack;[8] women, puffed out with huge skirts which wholly obscured their feet, bore more of a resemblance

---

5   Anne Hollingsworth Wharton, *Social Life in the Early Republic* (1902) (New York: Benjamin Blom, 1969), p.135.

6   See Lucy-Clare Windle, 'Over What Crinoline Should These Charming Jupons Be Worn? Thomson's Survival Strategy during the Decline of Crinoline' *Costume* 41 (2007), pp.66–82. (I am grateful to the author for providing me with further historical detail on the crinoline.)

7   Alfred L. Kroeber, 'On the Principle of Order in Civilization as Exemplified by Changes of Fashion' *American Anthropologist* 21.3 (1919), pp.235–63, 248.

8   On hat height as a male status symbol, see James Laver, *Modesty in Dress* (Boston: Houghton Mifflin, 1969), pp.121–3.

to hens nesting on eggs. Each gender was therefore performing, through theatrical forms of dress, a role which at that time was considered an ideal. The man was ambitious for public renown and social advancement. The married woman, for whom the ideal was to be mistress over a well-ordered house, was ambitious to locate herself at the hub of a private domain of domestic care and control.[9]

The lessons we learn from Europe may be compared to experiences elsewhere in the world. Such a task of comparison cannot be undertaken in a comprehensive way here, but even brief consideration of the position in China, for example, reveals that the notion of the fabricated social 'face' is at least as important in mainstream Chinese culture as it is in the European mainstream. Indeed, so great is the cultural appreciation of the dressed or performed public face in China that 'the nude' – one of the pillars of European art – is not a feature of Chinese art. In China, the clothed body is regarded as a more true representation of the person.[10] Oscar Wilde would have approved, for he once expressed the opinion that a mask 'tells us more than a face'.[11]

There is something in the dynamics of dress that tends to produce hierarchy, regularity, uniformity and conformity. Perhaps that 'something' is the aspect of dress that identifies it with law and order. There are notable examples of hierarchy, regularity, uniformity and conformity in dress jurisdictions throughout the world. China, to stay with the example of that country, provides instances that have become stock examples in dress scholarship. The practice of binding women's feet, which continued into the last quarter of the nineteenth century, demonstrated social hierarchy by conforming the feet of women in higher-status (or aspirational) families to a shape that rendered the women unfit to labour for a living.[12] The *Zhongshan* (or 'Mao') suit, which was ubiquitous in China in the twentieth century, exemplified the power of dress to confirm social uniformity. The same features (hierarchy, regularity, uniformity and conformity) are equally visible in the fashions of Paris and London in the middle of the nineteenth

9   See, generally, Lynda Nead, *Myths of Sexuality: Representation of Women in Victorian Britain* (Oxford: Basil Blackwell, 1988); Elizabeth Langland, *Nobody's Angels: Middle-Class Women and Domestic Ideology in Victorian Culture* (Ithaca: Cornell University Press, 1995).

10   John Hay, 'The Body Invisible in Chinese Art?', in Angela Zito and Tani E. Barlow (eds), *Body, Subject, and Power in China* (Chicago: University of Chicago Press, 1994), pp.42–77.

11   Oscar Wilde, 'Pen, Pencil and Poison: A Study in Green' *Fortnightly Review* (January 1889), pp.41–54.

12   C. Fred Blake, 'Foot-Binding in Neo-Confucian China and the Appropriation of Female Labor' *Signs* 19.3 (1994), pp.676–712.

century, for example in rib-crushing corsets for women and near uniformity of colour and cut in formal dress for men.

Part of the face that the law has made in the world is the formal dress of the legal profession. Official legal dress in the jurisdiction of England and Wales has recently undergone a number of changes. One of the most noticeable changes has been the elimination of the 'full-bottomed' (shoulder-length) wig from the ceremonial dress of the highest court in the land, the Supreme Court of the United Kingdom. The only clothing retained as a ceremonial head covering at the 'swearing in' of the first judges of that court was the academic-style doctor's hat which the solitary female Justice (Baroness Hale of Richmond) chose to adopt[13] (Figure 4.1). Accordingly, ceremonial judicial dress in the inner sanctum of UK law now resembles church dress: the women wear hats and the men do not. Nevertheless, the architects who designed the interior of the new Supreme Court building have endeavoured to demonstrate that it is not an inaccessible holy-of-holies, sitting as it were at the top of a ziggurat of legal hierarchy. Interior walls of transparent glass are designed to foster a sense of open and accessible justice. (A sense that was only temporarily obscured when press and other media were not permitted to be physically present for the ceremonial swearing in of the new Justices.[14])

The wigs have gone, and so has the full-length enclosed judicial robe (in contrast, the judicial robe worn by Justices of the Supreme Court of the United States is still of the enclosed variety), but there is one notable survival in the ceremonial dress of the Justices of the UK Supreme Court: the gown is still there. The style of the gown, with its long, gold-embroidered side panels (with arm slits) hanging free below the arms like the ends of a stole or scarf, evokes the Byzantine *loros* and reminds us that the judicial mantle is traceable, in one form or other, back to the Roman toga.[15] To judge from the official photograph of their lordships on the day of their swearing in, the style of gentleman's suit worn under the gown by the male Justices of the Supreme Court is almost perfectly uniform, as is the style of gentleman's shoe (see Figure 4.1). There is, however, some revealing variety in detail.

13   On the significance of 'face' in photographic judicial portraiture, see Leslie J. Moran, 'Judging Pictures: A Case Study of Judicial Portraits of the Chief Justices, Supreme Court of New South Wales' *Intl Jnl Law in Context* 5.3 (2009), pp.295–314, 303.

14   'Public Ban at Supreme Court Opening', *The Guardian*, 1 October 2009. Linda Mulcahy is suspicious of glass as a metaphor for judicial openness (*Legal Architecture: Justice, Due Process and the Place of Law* [Abingdon: Routledge, 2010], p.153).

15   See the discussion in Chapter Two at pp.35–6.

Figure 4.1 Justices of the Supreme Court of the United Kingdom (detail, Rear: Baroness Hale, Lord Walker, Lord Brown. Front: Lord Hope, Lord Phillips).

Source: © Crown Copyright.

It is noticeable, for instance, that only one of their lordships is wearing the barrister's customary garb of sharply pinstriped suit comprising trouser, jacket and waistcoat. One other is wearing a black coat jacket and waistcoat with sharply striped trousers of the morning-suit variety. Others appear to be wearing plain dark suits (or suits with subtle pinstripes) and matching or black waistcoats. The waistcoat, like the gown, is something of a survivor. Although it was adopted from Persian fashion, the English form of waistcoat may be considered a successor to the doublet it replaced; proving that some fashions become extinct as the dinosaurs became extinct: by adapting and hiding in plain sight.[16]

From what can be discerned from the formal photograph of the first Justices of the Supreme Court of the United Kingdom on the day that they were sworn in to office, the one judge who is unmistakably wearing the barrister's traditional uniform of sharp pinstriped three-piece suit (in this case white stripes on a charcoal-grey cloth) is Lord Phillips of Worth Matravers, the first president of the court. That the one judge wearing that traditional lawyer's garb should be the president of the court is perhaps predictable enough, were it not for the fact that Lord Phillips pioneered the recent reforms of official legal dress in the United Kingdom. His lordship's retention of the most stereotypical and traditional form of lawyer's suit eloquently expresses the truth that the English reforming spirit is rarely a radical one.

And why should it be radical? History shows numerous examples of societies in which radical regime change has been accompanied by the outright removal of old forms of legal dress, only for those traditional forms to be reintroduced in related form after some years' absence. So far as the advocate's gown is concerned, the most impressive revival may be its reintroduction to the Czech Republic after an absence of 60 years.[17] As for the judicial gown, Hargreaves-Mawdsley observes that '[w]here, as in Austria, France, North Germany, and Scandinavia, the long costume was abandoned as a result of the policy of revolutionary or "enlightened" governments, it was later reassumed'.[18] France provides a good example of this phenomenon.

---

16   Evolutionary biologists inform us that our best-dressed creatures, the birds, are really dinosaurs in disguise. See, for example, Gregory S. Paul, *Dinosaurs of the Air: The Evolution and Loss of Flight in Dinosaurs and Birds* (Baltimore: The Johns Hopkins University Press, 2002).

17   Legal Profession Act 1996 (Statute No 85) s.17a (added by Act No 219/2009), in force, 1 June 2011.

18   William Norman Hargreaves-Mawdsley, *A History of Legal Dress in Europe Until the End of the Eighteenth Century* (Oxford: Clarendon Press, 1963), p.3.

Judicial dress, with its aristocratic overtones, was scrapped in the immediate aftermath of the 1789 revolution, but instinct for some sort of uniform could not be resisted for long. In 1800, Napoléon Bonaparte introduced as uniform dress for all courts 'a short flap-collared *manteau à petit collet*, black and of silk, a long lawn cravat, and a three-cornered black hat'.[19] The red judicial robe was abandoned in the early years of post-revolutionary America, but it has made a modest comeback in the State of Maryland.[20] More recently, in Australia, where the judicial practice of robe wearing was abandoned in family proceedings, it has since been resumed, and at least one English judge has called for it to be reintroduced into family proceedings in English courts.[21] In English courts, judicial gowns can nowadays be completely discarded in civil (non-criminal) cases where the relevant Head of Division, the Senior Presiding Judge or the President of the Court of Protection 'agrees for good reason' that they should not be worn.[22] Will the gown ever be discarded utterly? That is doubtful. The evidence of history suggests that, in law, 'old habits die hard'.

There is a tradition of regarding the dignity of an official role as something that is invested in the official dress associated with the role rather than in the person who wears it. In the case of a judge, the robe acts symbolically as a barrier to the divine judgment that is threatened on the judge if he or she were to pass judgment in their private capacity. (The Bible stipulates that 'in the same way as you judge others, you will be judged'.)[23] James Q, Whitman in his book *The Origins of Reasonable Doubt* notes that medieval ecclesiastic lawyers took the view that a judge's error in judgment, if sinful, 'built him a mansion in Hell'.[24] In theory, the private individual of the judge was shielded from damnation by the fact that the performance of public judgment resided not in his private person, but in his robe of office. One drawback of this attitude was that it enabled the judge to exercise judgment

19   Ibid., p.45.
20   Rudolf B. Lamy, *A Study of Scarlet: Red Robes and the Maryland Court of Appeals* (Annapolis: Maryland State Law Library, 2006).
21   Mr Justice Paul Coleridge, 'Lets Hear It for the Child; Restoring the Authority of the Family Court, Blue Skies and Sacred Cows', 21st Annual Conference of the Association of Lawyers for Children (Southampton: 26 November 2010).
22   Practice Direction (Court Dress) (No 5) [2008] 1 WLR 1700. (One 'good reason' for not wearing a gown is the risk of intimidating minors.)
23   Mt. 7.2.
24   See James Q. Whitman, *The Origins of Reasonable Doubt: Theological Roots of the Criminal Trial* (Yale Law Library Series in Legal History) (New Haven: Yale UP, 2008), p.3.

on others that was hypocritical as regards his own person. In the strangely lucid distraction of his mind, Shakespeare's King Lear rails against such hypocrisy as it is represented in 'the great image of authority':

Thou rascal beadle, hold thy bloody hand!
Why dost thou lash that whore? Strip thy own back:
Thou hotly lusts to use her in that kind
For which thou whip'st her. The usurer hangs the cozener.
Through tattered clothes great vices do appear:
Robes and furred gowns hide all. Place sins with gold,
And the strong lance of justice hurtless breaks:
Arm it in rags, a pigmy's straw does pierce it. (*King Lear*, 4.5.160–7)[25]

If one drawback is that the official robe might conceal base motives, another is that it might hide the humane qualities of the individual judge. In Dickens's *Bleak House*, the Lord High Chancellor is portrayed as an obfuscating demon within his official domain of the High Court of Chancery, but as something much more human when conversing with the novel's young protagonists (Richard, Esther and Ada) in the privacy of his chambers. It is telling that in the latter scene, the Lord Chancellor is described as 'plainly dressed in black and sitting in an arm-chair' while his 'robe, trimmed with beautiful gold lace, was thrown upon another chair' (3).[26] The robe is the symbol of his office, that is clear enough, but what haunts this scene is the possibility that the Lord Chancellor might not be fully human until he has cast aside his legal habits. Trollope levels precisely this accusation against a stern Church of England cleric in his novel *The Warden* (1855), of whom he writes that it is only when he has removed the symbols of his office (his shovel hat and 'shining black habiliments') and replaced them with 'a tasselled nightcap, and . . . his accustomed *robe de nuit*, that Dr Grantly talks, and looks, and thinks like an ordinary man'.[27] Returning to *Bleak House*, we find a lawyer there who seems quite incapable of shedding his legal professional skin. His very name 'Tulkinghorn' indicates that he is

---

25   Modern editors frequently change the 1623 (first folio) 'place sins with gold' to 'plate sins with gold'.
26   Quotations are taken from Charles Dickens, *Bleak House* (serialized by installments 1852–3) (Harmondsworth: Penguin English Classics, 1971). The figure in parenthesis following the quotation refers to the relevant chapter of the novel.
27   Anthony Trollope, *The Warden* (London: Longman, Brown, Green and Longmans, 1855), chapter 2.

a mere 'talking-horn', a superficial mouthpiece like one of those dramatic masks of the ancient world. Q. D. Leavis wrote that the 'only extraordinary thing' about Tulkinghorn 'is the contrast between his public self and his private self'.[28] She was alluding to the fact that Tulkinghorn appears in public to be the perfect legal professional, whereas in private he pursues and harasses desperate individuals with a cold and ruthless determination. However, it seems to me that the 'contrast' between Tulkinghorn's public and private life is not as great as Leavis supposes, but, rather, that Tulkinghorn's problem is that he has internalized the worst aspects of his professional persona. Dickens certainly invites us to wonder if the mask has become the man:

> Mr. Tulkinghorn appears. He comes towards them at his usual methodical pace, which is never quickened, never slackened. He wears his usual expressionless mask – *if it be a mask* – and carries family secrets in every limb of his body and every crease of his dress. (12) (emphasis added)

And again:

> One peculiarity of his black clothes and of his black stockings, be they silk or worsted, is that they never shine. Mute, close, irresponsive to any glancing light, his dress is like himself. (2)

Like himself indeed, and also by virtue of 'knee-breeches tied with ribbons, and gaiters or stockings' (2) rather reminiscent of Malvolio, the ill-willed retainer in Shakespeare's *Twelfth Night* whom we encountered in Chapter Three. Another lawyer of *Bleak House*, Mr Vholes, is a family man with an apparently unremarkable private life, but he is more than once described as black-gloved and buttoned up to the chin (37), and he seems to suffer violently when he peels away his professional garb:

> Mr. Vholes, quiet and unmoved, as a man of so much respectability ought to be, takes off his close black gloves as if he were skinning his hands, lifts off his tight hat as if he were scalping himself, and sits down at his desk. (39)

---

28   Frank R. Leavis and Queenie D. Leavis, *Dickens the Novelist* (London: Chatto & Windus, 1970), p.160.

Dickens liked to describe lawyers metonymically in terms of their dress. An early example appearing in *The Pickwick Papers* is the description of Mr Justice Stareleigh as 'all face and waistcoat'.[29] (We can now appreciate that the word 'face' is as much a reference to dress as the word 'waistcoat'.) In *Bleak House*, Dickens referred to the whole mass of lawyers metonymically through the medium of dress. According to John Jarndyce, owner of Bleak House, the legal system, perhaps especially the system of The Court of Chancery, was a 'Wiglomeration'. In his despair, he identifies two key features of law as a social fact: that it is uncertain where the idea of a legal system comes from, but that it inevitably exists: 'How mankind ever came to be afflicted with Wiglomeration . . . I don't know; so it is' (8). We might say the same thing about the social habit of dress.

Lord Neuberger of Abbotsbury, the current president of the UK Supreme Court, employed two face-related metaphors in a speech he gave extrajudicially when he was still Master of the Rolls. He warned his judicial colleagues that they should not let the 'judicial mask slip' in public because of the risk of 'devaluing the coinage' of judicial respectability.[30] However, the corresponding danger, if judges keep the face of the law too firmly fixed, is that they will be unable to remove the mask in private. The perennial challenge to individuals who are invested into the legal profession is to wrestle with the clothes that they are bound to wear. Strange as it might sound, a lawyer should never seek to feel at ease in their professional skin. No scholar has done more than James Boyd White to challenge lawyers to question their professional habits of thought. He asks this deeply disquieting question: 'Is being a lawyer something you can put on and take off like a suit of clothes, or does it somehow change you beyond repair?'[31] It is no doubt necessary that an individual lawyer should be able to represent the law and their client without partiality to the lawyer's own private opinions, and no doubt the lawyer's professional dress serves usefully to disguise the individual within the role, but lawyers should find their professional dress constantly irritating. This is not to say that they should attempt to throw it off, but rather that they

29   Charles Dickens, *The Posthumous Papers of the Pickwick Club etc* (serialized by installments 1836–7) (London: Chapman and Hall, 1837), chapter 34.
30   Lord Neuberger of Abbotsbury MR, 'Where Angels Fear to Tread' Holdsworth Club 2012 Presidential Address 2 March 2012 para [53]. Compare John T. Noonan, *Persons and Masks of the Law: Cardozo, Holmes, Jefferson and Wythe as Makers of the Masks* (Berkeley and Los Angeles: University of California Press, 2002).
31   James Boyd White, *The Legal Imagination* (Boston: Little, Brown and Co, 1973), p.9.

should always remain conscious of the ethical dilemma that is inherent in the role they perform. That role, which will sometimes require the lawyer to advise the apparently corrupt or to represent the apparently guilty, does not of itself demand a deep conviction to any abstract ideal of truth, but only demands a sincere commitment to such procedural forms of truth as are inherent in the lawyer's professional practice. The danger for the individual lawyer does not lie in the dress per se but in the possibility that the wearer may become insensible to the dilemma that is inherent in wearing it. That danger materializes when lawyers become accustomed to their second skin, for then, as with Tulkinghorn, their dress becomes them.

The lawyer is a marginal figure in society; one who must do some of the dirty work that is deposited at the edge of the polite world. The pinstripe suit is significant in this respect. There has been speculation that the pinstripe might be 'a symbolic reference' to the lawyers' ideal of honesty; the straight line being an indicator of straight dealing.[32] There may be some truth in that when one bears in mind how fundamental the architectural ruled line is to legal thought.[33] One might equally speculate that the fine pinstripe is a rhetorical reference to lawyers' attention to fine detail and their ability to pinpoint what is legally material in a dark mass of evidence. Again, there might be some truth in that reading. A more surprising and certainly a more disturbing reading is the one that associates the pinstripe with the lawyer as marginal figure. The lawyer on this view is one who is marked out from polite society and the pinstripe is a tattoo or taint that acknowledges the lawyer's taboo nature as one who deals with the untouchable frontier of the civil world. In his study *The Devil's Cloth: A History of Stripes and Striped Fabric*,[34] Michel Pastoureau lists prostitutes, prisoners, military personnel and gangsters among the marginal class that are marked out by striped clothes. Even bankers are included. We should add lawyers to that list.

The suit itself, whether pinstriped or not, speaks of conformity to regular and standard lines. According to the etymology of the word, a 'suitor' is a 'follower'.[35] The original 'Suit of Court' was a medieval mandate by which

---

32   Toby Fischer-Mirkin, *Dress Code: Understanding the Hidden Meanings of Women's Clothes* (New York: Clarkson Potter, 1995), p.87.

33   See the discussion in Chapter Two at p.36.

34   *Etoffe du diable: Une Histoire Des Rayures et des Tissus Rayés* (Paris: éditions du Seuil, 1991); (English trans. Jody Gladding) (New York: Columbia University Press, 2001).

35   The PIE root *sek^w- is the ultimate source of 'suit', 'sequence' and 'second' (James Patrick Mallory and Douglas Quentin Adams, *The Oxford Introduction to Proto-Indo-European and the Proto-Indo-European World* [Oxford: OUP, 2006], p.267).

the lord of a manor required his tenants to attend his manorial court. 'To suit' was in that early sense a process of complying or conforming: the lord commanded, and the followers followed the command. 'Suit' came to denote a form of dress on broadly the same basis. A lord's followers would wear his colours or 'livery'. In modern times, the suit has become the livery or uniform of legal practitioners, and in wearing it they send out the message that conformity is their creed. When the New York law firm Cadwalader, Wickersham & Taft decided upon a total change from business suits to casual wear, one writer for the *New York Times* reported that the lawyers had 'shed their skins'.[36]

It may be that the legal profession never can (and perhaps never should) wholly divest itself of distinctive forms of dress. A lawyer, or some official representative of the law, is often to be found standing at the threshold of order and disorder at society's edge and at the threshold of significant transformations in individuals' lives. The lawyers' role is therefore, at least to some extent, a ritual role, and their robes might be expected to reflect this. It has been said that 'ritual dress' – the dress we adopt for 'portentous occasions that also tend to involve ritual speech' – lies somewhere 'between theatrical costume and the uniform'.[37] By that definition, legal dress would certainly qualify as 'ritual dress', and not least because the legal speech that is associated with legal dress has the sort of active or operative quality that we associate with ritual. J. L. Austin referred to world-changing words as 'performative utterances'[38] or, as he later termed them, 'speech acts'.[39] He considered that 'operative words' used by lawyers, such as the *habendum* clause ('to have and to hold') in a deed, belong in this category every bit as much as those same words when they appear in a wedding ceremony. Austin informs us that when a bride and groom say 'I do', this is not a mere description but an active deed. By the same token, when a judge says 'guilty', this is not an opinion or a word that passes as mere breath, but a performance that actually changes the form of the world and transforms lives. Just as the material of a legal 'deed' indicates the power of words to perform as a matter

---

36   Cameron Stracher, 'The Law Firm's New Clothes', *New York Times*, 24 March 2000.
37   Alison Lurie, *The Language of Clothes* (London: Bloomsbury, 1992), p.25.
38   John L. Austin, 'Performative Utterances', in James O. Urmson and Geoffrey J. Warnock (eds), *J L Austin: Philosophical Papers*, 3rd edn (Oxford: Clarendon Press, 1979), pp.233, 235–6.
39   John L. Austin, '*How to Do Things with Words': The William James Lectures delivered at Harvard University in 1955*, James O. Urmson (ed.) (Oxford: Clarendon Press, 1962).

of fact, so the formal dress of a lawyer informs us of the power of law to make and unmake the world that matters to us.

Before we proceed to appreciate the theatrical aspect of legal performance, especially by the lights that were turned on it by imaginative artists in nineteenth-century London and Paris, here would seem to be the opportune place to pause on certain dress elements of the ritual performance of law. I am referring to the headdress, the robe and the colour red. In so far as these elements are concerned to stimulate a primal psychological response, they are trying to stimulate the same primitive reaction that once upon a time would have been sought by magical means. In this regard, the glove is also important:

[W]hether as the symbol of power or the gage of security or of defiance, or, as a token of love or favour, or of peace and good order, the glove has been, from the remotest times, an important factor in the manners and customs of the civilised nations of the earth.[40]

The ritual significance of the glove surely originates in and resides in its 'magical' properties. More than any other item of clothing, with the possible exception of the mask (whose liminal significance in law we have already considered), the glove resembles the human body even when there is no body in it. The glove therefore epitomizes two defining dimensions of primitive magic – the sympathetic (because the glove resembles the hand) and the contagious (because the glove has touched the hand). Aside from these magical properties of the glove, there is also the obvious fact that the judicial glove allows the judge to handle unpleasant matters without risk of ritual contamination. The glove demonstrates precisely that liminal quality of being both within and without the polite world which throughout this study we have come to associate with the culture of both dress and law. We will see, next, that the same liminal quality is demonstrated in the headdress, the robe and the colour red.

The history of the legal headdress, especially the judicial headdress, is truly archaic. The Egyptian goddess of justice, Maat, is depicted wearing the typical Egyptian wig and the upright Ostrich feather of truth in her

---

40 James W. Norton-Kyshe, *The Law and Customs Relating to Gloves* (London: Stevens and Haynes, 1901), p.1.

headband. Today in the mainland of continental Europe, the dominant form of headdress, where there is any, is a hat of some form. (The Germans have a nice saying: *Amt gibt Kappen* ['office comes with a hat'].) Until the wig eventually forced it out, a form of hat was also the standard judicial headdress in England. In the fifteenth century, the 'hat' was a *pileus* (skullcap) worn on top of a white cloth coif, and for good measure a hood was worn with the judicial robe.[41] In due course, the coif and cap were retained in the vestigial form of a patch of white cloth incorporating a smaller patch of black cloth. This was placed on top of the wig (Figure 4.2). Eventually the patch disappeared from the wig entirely, although a depression remained in the crown of the wig where the patch had been.[42]

Remarkably, it was as late as 2 January 2008 that the largest branch of the legal profession in England Wales, the solicitors' branch, began to wear the wig; albeit that the option of wearing the wig is reserved to a small subset of the solicitors' profession who conduct advocacy in the higher courts.[43] One of the first to wear it reported that the wig felt 'itchy',[44] thereby reminding the wearer of the constant ethical discomfort that the lawyer should feel in the customary habits of their profession. The barristers' branch of the legal profession is the traditional wig-wearing branch, and barristers are still required to wear the wig for most civil trials and appeals in the High Court. The main exceptions are the Commercial Court, Admiralty Court and hearings in the Family Division, where barristers are only required to wear business suits. Highly significant in terms of the ritual role of legal dress at the thresholds of civil life is the fact that wigs must be worn in contested divorce and nullity proceedings in the Family Division, and the fact that they must be worn whenever 'the liberty of the subject is at issue (save in the Magistrates Court and during Crown Court bail applications which are held in Chambers)'.[45] The wig is generally required in hearings before the UK Supreme Court and before the Judicial Committee of the Privy Council, but in these forums (in both civil and criminal matters), advocates 'may,

---

41   Hargreaves-Mawdsley, *A History of Legal Dress*, p.50.

42   Ibid., p.65. See, further, James G. McLaren, 'Legal Dress: a Brief History of Wigs in the Legal Profession' *International Journal for the Legal Profession* 6.2 (1999), pp.241–50; Sir Victor Windeyer, 'Of Robes and Gowns and Other Things' *The Australian Law Journal* 48 (1974), pp.394–403.

43   Practice Direction (Court Dress) (No 4) [2008] 1 WLR 357.

44   Neil Rose, 'Solicitor-Advocates Finally Put on Wigs in Court', *Law Society Gazette*, 10 January 2008.

45   *Court Dress: Guidance from the Chairman of the Bar Council*, 31 July 2008.

Figure 4.2 Benjamin Ferrers, 'The Court of Chancery during the reign of George I' (includes Philip Yorke, 1st Earl of Hardwicke, Thomas Parker, 1st Earl of Macclesfield, Sir Thomas Pengelly). (Detail)

Source: © National Portrait Gallery, London.

by agreement, dispense with any or all of the elements of traditional court dress'.[46] As for the judges, they no longer wear wigs except for ceremonial purposes and for criminal matters in the higher courts. Their lordships in the UK Supreme Court do not wear wigs or any other element of court dress when hearing cases, and they have even dropped the wig for ceremonial purposes, as has already been noted.

When Quentin Bell observed that 'dress is above all concerned with status',[47] he might as well have been talking about law. The language of law, which has hardly changed in its essentials since prehistoric times,[48] reveals 'status' – and such related concepts as 'stability' and 'stasis' – to be characteristic of legal culture and thought.[49] The words 'statute', 'constitution' and 'State', for example, all derive from the PIE base *sta-* ('to stand'). James Laver's observations on legal dress confirm that the law's tendency towards stability and stasis, as well as its tendency towards 'ruled' or 'straight-line' form, is reflected in the retention and regulation of the judicial full-bottomed wig. Laver contrasts the judicial habit of wearing full-bottomed periwigs with the abandonment of that fashion by military men, and by the general population, by the end of the eighteenth century:

Judges, however, were in different case. Immobile on the Bench or passing in stately procession on circuit, the troubles of the soldier trying to cope with a full-bottomed wig while charging the enemy cannon left the legal luminary, in both senses of the word, unmoved. So he continued to wear it and gradually, in accordance with what seem to be the laws of costume history, it began to fossilize. The loose, tumbling curls became formal rolls; the whole outline of the structure became more rigid . . . no one could possibly mistake the wig of a modern judge for real hair.[50]

The unnaturally formal figure of the judicial periwig has always been a tempting target for satire. When the periodical *Punch* carried a comic

<hr>

46   The Supreme Court of the United Kingdom, *Press Notice*, 21 November 2011.
47   Quentin Bell, *On Human Finery* (1947) (London: The Hogarth Press, 1976), p.117.
48   See, for example, Calvert Watkins, 'Studies in Indo-European Legal Language, Institutions, and Mythology', in George Cardona, Henry M. Hoenigswald and Alfred Senn (eds), *Indo-European and Indo-Europeans: Papers Presented at the Third Indo-European Conference at the University of Pennsylvania* (Philadelphia: University of Pennsylvania Press, 1970), pp.321–54, 321.
49   Gary Watt, 'Rule of the Root: Proto-Indo-European Domination of Legal Language', in Michael Freeman and Fiona Smith (eds), *Law and Language*, Current Legal Issues, Vol. 15 (Oxford: OUP, 2013), pp.571–89.
50   Laver, *Modesty in Dress*, p.52.

illustration entitled 'Legal Effects', which explored the potential to animate lawyers' wigs with hand-held wires for greater theatrical impact and rhetorical power, it was carrying on a long-standing caricature tradition.[51] In 1761, William Hogarth had rendered the long-bottomed judge's wig according to a strict architectural order that he called the 'Lexonic' (see Figure 2.4 in Chapter Two).[52] Aping the standard scheme drawings of architectural orders such as the Ionic (see Figure 2.3 in Chapter Two), Hogarth shows the judicial periwig overlaid with lines to indicate the rules that determine the relative proportions of its parts. The same strand of satire reappeared more recently in the film *Withnail and I*.[53] In the following exchange, the drug-dealer Danny recounts the experience of a fellow drug dealer, the 'Coalman', who had fallen foul of the law and found himself (dressed in a 'kaftan and bell') up before a High Court Judge:

DANNY: 'So there's this judge sitting there; sitting in a cape like f***ing batman with this really rather far out looking hat . . . '

WITHNAIL: 'A wig!'

DANNY: 'No man, this was more like a long white hat. So he looks at the Coalman and says "what's all this. This is a court man. This ain't fancy dress" and the Coalman looks at him and says "you think you look normal, your honour?"'

So great is the gravitational pull of stasis on legal culture that in the lawyer's wig something as freely growing and freely flowing as hair, even the hair of a horse, was turned into an utterly ordered and rigid form of dress. Of course we should no longer be surprised that judges should regard the wig as a potent symbol of their status and retain it regardless of popular fashion. We should not be surprised because we now know that law is dress and dress is law. The well-ordered artificial wig captivated judicial culture (and was captured by it) because it represents the ultimate triumph of human law and dress over the untamed and meagre fur of human hair in its natural naked

---

51   *Punch* 52 (16 February 1867). The image is reproduced in Jonathan P. Ribner, 'Law and Justice in England and France', in Costas Douzinas and Lynda Nead (eds), *Law and the Image: The Authority of Art and the Aesthetics of Law* (Chicago: University of Chicago Press, 1999), pp.178–99, 193.

52   William Hogarth, *The Five Orders of Periwigs as They Were Worn at the Late Coronation Measured Architectonically* (1761) (etching).

53   Bruce Robinson, 1987.

state. The judicial wig, formalized, fossilized and somewhat resembling an architectural doorframe became emblematic of law's place as guardian of the gateway to polite society.

The robe, like the wig, has been employed to confirm the hierarchical status of the judge. Before we consider jurisdictions in which the robe plays a prominent part, it should be acknowledged that there are some European jurisdictions in which there is no official legal dress to talk of. W. N. Hargreaves-Mawdsley writes that 'in several countries, Poland for example, no true legal costume can be said to have existed'.[54] Finland is a good example of such a jurisdiction. Lawyers and judges in Finland dress in smart, everyday clothes.[55] The Finnish people have traditionally regarded justice as a thing in which they have a stake, and 'faith in the law and in the courts' has always been strong.[56] Historically, local hearings have been attended enthusiastically and were taken as an opportunity to participate in judicial decision-making. This atmosphere was no doubt encouraged by the fact that until the twenty-first century, Finnish advocates were not required to have any formal professional qualification.

Poland, which Hargreaves-Mawdsley cites as a jurisdiction with no official dress, is actually an unsupportive example. Whenever they were free of foreign forces, the Poles sought to adopt quite traditional forms of legal dress. In 1928, for example, the Ministry of Justice issued specific regulations on judicial dress, which were enlarged in 1932.[57] The prescribed dress included a formal robe with traditional aspirations that are obvious from its name '*toga*' and a soft cornered hat called a '*biret*' which is clearly inspired by the medieval *biretta* (precursor to the modern academic mortarboard). Today in Poland, only the judges of the Constitutional Tribunal of the Polish Republic (*Trybunał Konstytucyjny*) are required to wear the *biret*.

Returning to the jurisdiction of England and Wales, it can be observed that for ceremonial purposes, circuit judges continue to hold white gloves and to wear a full-bottomed wig, robe, lace jabot, knee breeches, stockings and buckled shoes, but in court in civil cases they are only required to

54   Hargreaves-Mawdsley, *A History of Legal Dress*, preface.
55   Pia Lett-Vanamo and Timo Honkanen, *Lain Nojalla, Ja Kansan Tuella* ('In the Name of the Law, by the Will of the People') (Helsinki: Edita Prima Oy, 2005).
56   Ibid., p.23.
57   *Rozporządzenie Ministra Sprawiedliwości* 872 (15 November 1932). I am grateful to my student Adam Kalinin (the son of a Polish judge) for furnishing me with details of Polish legal dress.

wear their robe with lilac cuffs, edging and tippet (the tippet is the vestige of the mediaeval casting-hood that now looks like a sash drawn over the left shoulder and diagonally down across the torso). All other judges wear the standard black robe when sitting in open session in court, with coloured tabs at the neck to indicate the rank of the judge: gold for the Court of Appeal, red for the High Court, pink for members of the High Court Masters Group and blue for district judges.[58] It is significant that at the very top of the judicial hierarchy, at the level of the UK Supreme Court and the Judicial Committee of the Privy Council, their lordships are not required to wear any gown in court (although, as we noted earlier, a fine gown detailed in gold is worn for ceremonial purposes). The significance of their lordships' freedom from the dress code lies in the fact that it reveals something that is apparently fundamental about the hierarchical dynamics of official and uniform dress, namely that '[w]here uniforms are required, only those with the highest rank can avoid wearing the attire'.[59] Shakespeare expressed this dynamic in the scene in which Henry V woos Katherine of France:

> O, Kate, nice customs curtsy to great kings. Dear Kate, you and I cannot be confined within the weak list of a country's fashion: we are the makers of manners, Kate. (*Henry V* 5.2.219–21)

The norm of wearing a uniform is for suitors ('those who follow'), not for those whom they follow. The flip side of this dynamic is that where the norm is to dress down, one can expect those at the top of the hierarchy to dress up. Thus when the 'Casual Friday' rule was introduced to offices in England, it is said to have been ignored by 'most of the senior management'.[60] Mark Zuckerberg, the Chief Executive Officer of Facebook, caused consternation when he turned up to a meeting of shareholders wearing a hoodie. He probably didn't care, since his position at the top of the hierarchy freed him from the need to follow the uniform of the business suit. But outside of their particular business hierarchy, even CEOs have their superiors. One year previously, Zuckerberg had worn a jacket and tie when he met President

---

58   Practice Direction (Court Dress) (No 5) [2008] 1 WLR 1700.
59   Fischer-Mirkin, *Dress Code*, p.86.
60   Kate Fox, *Watching the English* (London: Hodder & Staughton, 2004), p.269.

Obama. The President had quipped on that occasion: 'I'm the guy who got Mark to wear a jacket and tie.'[61] That was not entirely true, of course. If Zuckerberg had met Obama the 'guy', we can be pretty sure that he would have met him wearing nothing more formal than his hoodie. It is only because he met Obama, the man invested as president, that Zuckerberg felt compelled to dress up. The law here is that dress respects the hierarchy of invested office. Dress respects dress.

On 4 June 1635, judges in the jurisdiction of England and Wales met to discuss the appropriate form of judicial attire. The '*Discourse*' they published determined the mode of judicial dress that continued to be worn right up until the nineteenth century. The *Discourse* included the statement that he who 'gives the charge and delivers the gaol' ought to be in scarlet robes, hood and mantle throughout the assizes, hence the line in Carlyle's *Sartor Resartus*: 'You see two individuals . . . one dressed in fine Red, the other in coarse threadbare Blue: Red says to Blue, "Be hanged and anatomised".'[62]

It is still the norm for judges to wear red at the threshold point where very serious matters first come to trial. High Court judges wear a scarlet robe with fur facings, a black scarf and black girdle (cincture) and a scarlet tippet over the left shoulder. Below them, the circuit judges wear a red tippet over the left shoulder when hearing criminal cases, except in the Central Criminal Court of 'The Old Bailey' in London, where black is worn. Lower down the judicial hierarchy for criminal matters, recorders (part-time circuit judges) wear black gowns, while at the bottom rung magistrates are merely required to wear 'professional and dignified' dress. When criminal matters go on appeal to the Court of Appeal, the judges there wear a dark court coat and waistcoat with skirt or trousers together with collar bands, a black silk gown and a short wig.

No colour could be more suitable to demonstrate law's liminal jurisdiction at the threshold of civil liberty than red, the colour of blood. Blood marks the moment of birth and when it marks the moment of death it does so signally, even violently. In January 1649, just a few years after the 1635 *Discourse*, the 'judge' (he conducted himself more like a prosecutor) in the trial of

---

61   'Mark Zuckerberg wears hoodie to Facebook investor meetings', *The Daily Telegraph* (online), 10 May 2012.

62   Carlyle, *Sartor Resartus*, Book I, chapter 9.

Charles I closed the case not by words alone, but by the colour of his cloth. C. V. Wedgwood reports:

> It was known to most of those present, and certainly to the prisoner, that the purpose of the Court was to pass sentence. To indicate the solemnity of the occasion Bradshaw was, for the first time, robed in red.[63]

The irony for Charles I was that red had originally been adopted as the standard colour of judicial dress because red was the king's colour, and in the Middle Ages judges were given the material for their robes as royal livery.[64] It was deemed suitable that judges, as servants of the Crown, should be liveried in the royal hue. A further irony in Bradshaw's use of a red robe was that judicial scarlet was required (by the *Discourse* of 1635) to be worn not only when trying criminal cases, but also on saints days (so-called red letter days) and on the birthday of the monarch and whenever a judge had to appear in office in the monarch's presence.[65] Even today, High Court judges wear red robes in all court cases (whether civil or criminal) on 'red letter days', which description now encompasses saints' days, anniversaries of senior members of the Royal Family and Lord Mayor's Day. Perhaps Bradshaw employed the red robe to signify that the court was putting to death, not the private man, but the invested office of the king. However that may be, the semiotic significance of the red robe was rather loaded against Bradshaw. Given that it also signified saints' days, Bradshaw's dress could be interpreted as an admission that he was presiding over the creation of a martyr.

The dressed layer of the law comes in other colours. In England and Wales, the police force is often referred to as the 'thin blue line', and similar metonyms for police have spread throughout the Common Law world, including to the United States.[66] The 'thin blue line' evokes the sense that law is a narrow interface of dress which, as the border of polite (policed) society, lies between civil and uncivil worlds. When Sir Robert Peel introduced the first Metropolitan Police uniform to London, blue was chosen primarily to

63   Cicely V. Wedgwood, *The Trial of Charles I* (London: The Reprint Society, 1964), p.154.
64   John H. Baker, 'A History of English Judges' Robes' *Costume* 12 (1978), pp.27–39, 29.
65   Hargreaves-Mawdsley, *A History of Legal Dress*, pp.61–3.
66   Witness the US police drama *Hill Street Blues* (NBC, 1981–7).

distinguish it from the contemporary red of the British soldier.[67] (In the United States today, it has been shown that citizens' initial response to police uniform in the traditional military colour khaki is negative compared to their response to the more traditional police-uniform colour blue.[68]) Perhaps Peel's choice of blue was an inspired choice to represent, or even to encourage, civil peace. Not only has blue been called a conservative colour,[69] but as the colour of water reflecting a cloudless sky, blue also serves symbolically to quench the fire and to cleanse the bloody stain that we associate with dangerous red.

Another colour, or lack of colour, that has a long association with the law is black. As red is associated with the bench, so black is associated with the bar. The black gown became the rule in the 1580s, when it was introduced in response to excesses in popular fashions during that decade.[70] For example, the rules set down for the Middle Temple in 1584 prohibited white doublet and hose, and in the streets, cloaks were not permitted to be worn, but only gowns 'of a sad colour'.[71] Such rules might have dampened individual displays of sartorial splendour, but they made the collective display of legal professional costume all the more distinctive and dramatic. It confirmed the dressed face of the law in society and confirmed the theatricality of legal performance in court.

Courtroom advocates really are performers on a stage. It is sometimes said that courtroom lawyers are pretending to be actors in a theatre, but the truth is the other way round. Stage actors are pretending to be lawyers. The earliest origins of performative arts and legal advocacy are hardly separable, but we can say that orators in ancient Greece were disputing legal matters in front of public audiences long before the invention of theatre in the Thespian mode.[72] So much did the arts of acting and advocacy resemble each other that the authors of the classical rhetorical manuals were happy for rhetoricians

---

67 Wilbur R. Miller, *Cops and Bobbies: Police Authority in New York and London, 1830–70*, 2nd rev. edn (Columbus, OH: Ohio State University Press, 1998), p.33.

68 Richard R. Johnson, 'Police Uniform Color and Citizen Impression Formation' *Journal of Police and Criminal Psychology* 20.2 (2005), pp.58–66. According to this study, members of the public were more positive about 'light blue/navy blue' uniforms than 'black/black' uniforms. Contrast Ernest Nickels, 'Good Guys Wear Black: Uniform Color and Citizen Impressions of Police' *Policing: Int'l J Police Strat & Mgmt* 31 (2008), pp.77–92, 78.

69 Fischer-Mirkin, *Dress Code*, p.87. Blue has been employed by numerous political parties of a 'conservative' disposition.

70 See Chapter Three at p.71.

71 William Dugdale, *Origines Juridicales* (London: F and T Warren, 1666), fo. 191.

72 See discussion of the Shield of Achilles in Chapter Two at p.27.

to learn from actors, but warned them to avoid being mistaken for actors.[73] Even today, the arts of acting and advocacy can seem practically inseparable. Sir John Mortimer QC observed, for example:

> An English criminal trial is a very theatrical occasion – the barristers and judges wear wigs and gowns, some of the judges are in scarlet and ermine and, on State occasions, carry bunches of flowers (once necessary to protect their noses from prison stench). I often left court to go to a rehearsal of a play I had written and felt I had left the world of fantasy and make-believe at the Old Bailey for the harsh reality of the world of art.[74]

The theme of courtroom theatricality was recently reprised in the BBC television drama *Silks*.[75] The following dialogue takes place in the silks' robing room:

Martha Costello QC:	They call you Lady Macbeth, do you know that?
Caroline Warwick QC:	Don't say that name in here.
Costello:	I thought that was only actors in theatres.
Warwick:	What do you think this is? Who do you think we are?[76]

Dickens, an aficionado of drama (and himself a keen actor and stage performer), considered the association between the theatre and the courtroom to be more tragic than comic:

> [T]o see all that full dress and ceremony and to think of the waste, and want, and beggared misery it represented; to consider that while the sickness of hope deferred was raging in so many hearts this *polite show* went calmly on from day to day, and year to year. (24) (emphasis added)

---

73 See, for example, Quintilian *Institutio Oratoria* (1.11.1–3).

74 John Mortimer, 'Introduction', *The Best of Rumpole* (London: Viking, 1993), p.1. See, generally, Sir Edward Parry, *The Drama of the Law* (London: T Fisher Unwin, 1924).

75 Senior barristers who are promoted to the status of Counsel of the Crown (Queen's or King's Counsel according to the gender of the reigning monarch) are said to 'take silk' on account of the silk-faced gowns they are entitled to wear. Thereafter they are referred to as 'silks'.

76 *Silk* Series 2 Episode 1 (Dir: Peter Hoar, BBC television, 2012). I am grateful to my colleague Dr Jane Bryan for bringing this scene to my attention.

Dickens's visual imagination was perfectly attuned to perceive the theatricality of legal courtroom performance, and in this he had an artistic counterpart in Paris, the other of the two cities that features in this part of our tale of tailoring. Dickens's French counterpart is not a novelist, but an artist who is famed for his lithographic caricatures of Parisian society, and famed above all for his caricature of lawyers. He is Honoré Daumier. If we want to appreciate the performance and fabrication of legal professional coverings and facades, we can do no better than to cultivate an appreciation of Daumier's many lithographs, paintings and drawings of lawyers and the life of the law courts.[77] The critique that Daumier draws by the point of his crayons pierces to the point of the legal soul. The philosopher and art critic Baudelaire, who was the first to bring the public's attention to the genius of Daumier, once observed that Daumier was so familiar with the bourgeoisie from his constant observation that he had 'discovered the mysteries of their bedroom' ('*appris les mystères de son alcôve*').[78] As for the legal branch of the bourgeoisie, Geoffrey-Dechaume said of Daumier that he 'knows lawyers, and above all the lawyer, better than they know themselves'.[79] What qualifies Daumier to address us concerning fashioned facades and fabricated forms of truth is that Daumier's work 'reveals the innermost being of us all'.[80] What demands that we should attend to Daumier is the possibility, expressed by the poet and dramatist Émile Bergerat, that 'nobody has served justice and liberty more than this great honest man'.[81]

Not everyone agrees with these glowing assessments of Daumier. The lawyer Jean le Foyer complains that Daumier simply had, and perpetuated, a populist view of lawyers: 'Daumier glanced into the robing room and saw the magistrates or advocates putting on the gown or robe . . . but Daumier never

---

77   The oeuvre of the French artist Pierre Cavellat is also highly informative. Cavellat was a respected member of the French judiciary who secretly smuggled art materials into court up the sleeve of his judicial robe and depicted court proceedings in lively extemporized sketches executed covertly from the vantage point of the raised judicial dias (see Ruth Herz, *The Art of Justice: The Judge's Perspective* [Oxford: Hart, 2012]).

78   Charles Baudelaire, *Salon caricatural de 1846* (Paris: Charpentier, 1846). The quotation is from Baudelaire *Critique d'art*, Folio Essais (Paris: Gallimard, 1992), p.215 (my translation).

79   Quoted in *Daumier, 1808–1879*, Exhibition Catalogue (Ottawa: National Gallery of Canada, 1999; Paris: Galeries nationales du Grand Palais, 1999–2000; Washington: The Phillips Collection, 2000), p.271.

80   Julien Cain, 'Introduction' to Daumier *Les Gens de Justice* (New York: Tudor Publishing Co., 1959), p.25.

81   Émile Bergerat, 'Revue artistique: Exposition des oevres d'Honoré Daumier' *Journal officiel* (26 April 1878), pp.4453–5.

penetrated beyond that.'[82] Perhaps that is a fair criticism, or perhaps we suspect the lawyer of a degree of defensive bias towards his profession. The opening lines of his book confess an unusually close personal identification with his professional costume: '*Je suis de robe. Magistrat. Et mon fils porte aussi l'épitoge.*'[83] No wonder, then, that he appears to have felt Daumier's critique so keenly. However that may be, one thing Le Foyer does not dispute is that Daumier had remarkable artistic talent. Gordon McKenzie puts him on a par with Dickens, observing that '[i]n both men the art of caricature was expressed at its highest level, and as artists in this field there is little to choose between them'.[84] Caricature can be crude and overloaded, but the caricatures of Dickens and Daumier emphasize only to the extent of making the scene on paper feel as real as the scene in life. Daumier's first biographer, Arsène Alexandre praised Daumier's major lithographic series on the legal profession, *Les Gens de Justice* (1844), in terms which make clear that here, as with the novels of Dickens, we are not presented with caricature of the crude variety, but high art – and theatrical art at that. One of the lithographs in the 1844 series (Figure 4.3) shows a lawyer speaking to a colleague as they put on their robes in advance of a hearing. The joke is that the two lawyers will be arguing an identical case to one they had disputed three weeks earlier, but this time each is arguing against the point that he had supported on the previous occasion. The speaker finds the whole thing very 'drôle'. He says that his colleague will use the speaker's own former submissions against him, and the speaker jokes that he, in turn, will send back his colleagues former replies. 'If we need to', he laughs, 'we can prompt each other'.[85] Arsène Alexandre writes:

> Not since Rebelais has the legal breed been more closely observed, more thoroughly investigated, more mercilessly dissected in all its tricks, its obsessions, its effronteries, its wiliness. The black gowns, the shaven faces, the damp chill of the waiting room, the suffocating atmosphere of the courtrooms, Daumier was positively intoxicated by it all.[86]

82   Jean le Foyer, *Daumier au Palais de Justice* (Paris: La Colombe, 1958), p.9 (my translation).

83   'I am of the robe. Magistrate. And my son also wears the lawyer's gown', p.7 (my translation).

84   Gordon McKenzie, 'Dickens and Daumier' in *Studies in the Comic*, Vol. 8.2 (Berkeley: University of California Press, 1941), pp.273–98, 298.

85   Honoré Daumier, lithographic plate 14 in the series *Les Gens de Justice* (Loys Delteil 1350). First published in *Le Charivari* 13 October 1845 (my words in the text are a paraphrased translation of the original legend).

86   Arsène Alexandre, *Honoré Daumier, l'homme et l'oeuvre* (Paris: H Laurens, 1888), p.269.

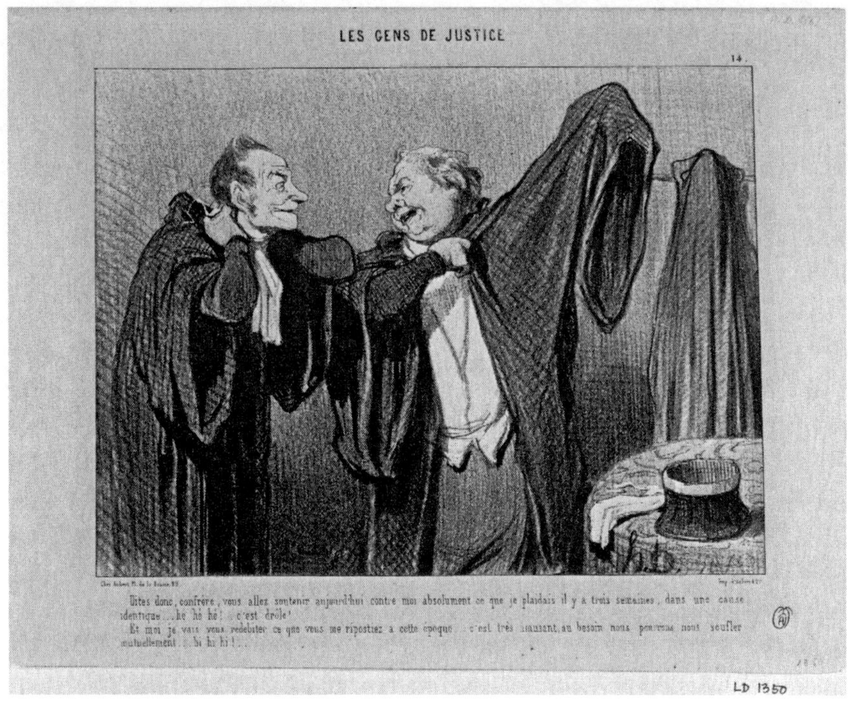

Figure 4.3 Honoré Daumier, lithographic plate 14 in the series *Les Gens de Justice* (Loys Delteil 1350). First published in *Le Charivari* 13 October 1845, accompanied by the legend 'Dites donc, confrère, vous allez soutenir aujourd'hui contre moi absolument ce que je plaidais il y a trois semaines, dans une cause identique . . . hé hé hé! . . . c'est drôle! . . . Et moi je vais vous redebiter ce que vous me ripostiez à cette époque . . . c'est très amusant, au besoin nous pourrons nous soufler mutuellement . . . hi hi hi! . . .'

Source: Reproduced courtesy of the Robert D. Farber University Archives & Special Collections Department, Brandeis University.

The reference to 'black gowns' and 'shaven faces' recalls the 1841 comic pamphlet *Physiologie de l'Homme de Loi* (hereafter *Physiologie*) which identifies these features as characteristics of a lawyer's makeup. That pamphlet combines witty text with rather roughly drawn caricatures on the subject of 'The Man of Law' and was typical of many such 'physiologies' that were popular in France at the time.[87] Julien Cain observes that 'Daumier

---

87   Martina Lauster, *Sketches of the Nineteenth Century: European Journalism and its Physiologies, 1830–50* (Basingstoke: Palgrave Macmillan, 2007).

certainly knew the *Physiologie*',[88] and it is notable that a number of the character sketches in the *Physiologie* bear a striking resemblance to legal characters developed by Daumier in his lithographs; none more so than 'L'Avocat sans causes'.[89] The *Physiologie* engages several of the figurative fundamentals – including the metaphor of theatre and the depiction of dress – which come to dominate Daumier's visual imagination with regard to lawyers (and which, incidentally, are also evident in Dickens's portrayal of the legal profession).

Lawyers' dress dominates the *Physiologie*. The opening chapter identifies the alteration of physical appearance as the key means by which a non-lawyer is ritually transformed into a lawyer. The first stage is to shave off the beard and fancy moustache of the student days: '*Il fait tomber sous le rasoir ses moustaches et sa barbe fantastique*' (7).[90] Hair removed, the lawyer then completes his transformation through the appropriation of professional dress. The effect of the dress on the lawyer is to give him instant unquestioned access to the inner sanctum of the law – the courtroom of the Palais de Justice. Appropriately uniformed, the young lawyer strides into court unimpeded, even on his first day. In contrast, his supporting entourage of family and friends are challenged by the guard at the door to the court (18–19). His family enjoy the spectacle of his first court performance (14), and there is no doubt that the hearing (the French word is 'audience') is perceived in terms of pure theatre. The mother of the junior advocate even prompts him when he stumbles over his lines (21). The *Physiologie* describes the junior lawyer's costume as entirely black, apart from a white cravat (8). The author mischievously suggests that this is symbolic of lawyers' impact on society: for they darken many lives and enlighten few (8). In fact, there was hardly a male professional at the time who didn't wear a predominately black outfit. Baudelaire observed a certain political and poetical beauty, and a form of liminal performance, in that fact:

Is this not the necessary fashion of our time: suffering carried on one's thin black shoulders as a sign of perpetual mourning? Note well that the black coat and redingote have not only political beauty through the expression

---

88   Cain, 'Introduction' to Daumier *Les Gens de Justice*, p.12.

89   *Physiologie,* chapter 3; compare Daumier's lithograph in the series *Les Avocats et les Plaideurs* (*Le Charivari*, 14 November 1851) Loys Delteil, no.2186.

90   *Physiologie.* (Numbers in parenthesis denote pages.) Contrast Shakespeare's 'justice' with 'beard of formal cut' (*As You Like It* 2.7.158).

of universal equality, but also poetic beauty through the expression of the public spirit; – an immense guard of undertakers, political undertakers, amorous undertakers, bourgeois undertakers. We are all performing some funeral.[91]

It should be noted that lawyers' dress in England is genuinely funereal. On the death of Charles II in 1685,[92] the English bar abandoned their legal gown in favour of a black 'stuff' gown of the sort worn by mourners, and this remains the form of gown worn by barristers up to the present day (despite an order of 1697 that required barristers to quit their mourning gowns and return to their former official dress).[93]

According to the *Physiologie*, the other white feature of the lawyer's physical accoutrement (in addition to the cravat) is the large bundle of papers that he carries under the sleeve of his gown (25). The cravat and the white papers, juxtaposed with the lawyers' black costume, produces a dramatic chiaroscuro contrast that Daumier used to great effect in his black-on-white lithographic prints. The profound power of Daumier's 'caricatures' is such that they work disturbingly well without any accompanying legend. A caption can highlight one possible reading of a Daumier image, but in doing so it obscures many more. Look again at the lithograph reproduced at Figure 4.3. It originally appeared with a legend almost certainly written by someone other than Daumier.[94] I have already provided an English paraphrase of the original French legend, but the fact is that the image is just as effective – arguably more so – without the legend. Look again at the image and imagine some of the many ways in which it might be read. Does it not look as if the advocate on the left is tying a bib around his neck as if about to devour something? Is there not something vulture-like in his face, and in the outstretched, wing-like limb of the figure on the right? Do the dark hollows of the sleeves of their gowns not gape like ravenous mouths, or like the hood that traditionally hangs over the head of Death? These lawyers are excited because they are about to feast. They are animated because they are about to perform, and because they have been well paid to perform. In

91   Charles Baudelaire, *Le Salon de 1846*, chapter 8: 'De L'héroïsme de la Vie Moderne'. The quotation is translated from Baudelaire *Critique d'art*, Folio Essais (Paris: Gallimard, 1992), p.154.
92   Hargreaves-Mawdsley, *A History of Legal Dress*, p.86.
93   John H. Baker, 'History of the Gowns Worn at the English Bar' *Costume* 9 (1975), pp.15–21, 18–19.
94   Most likely Charles Philipon, editor of the journal *Le Charivari* in which the image was first published on 13 October 1845 (Loys Delteil, no.1350).

some ways, an even more haunting picture is presented by the impassive pair who are shown descending the main stairway which leads down from the Palais de Justice into the *Cour du Mai* (Figure 4.4). The two lawyers are descending, a few steps apart, each nursing a bundle of documents under his left arm. Each is looking straight ahead in full-frontal profile; their faces are devoid of passion, almost without expression – most un-Daumier-like. Their black robes drop straight, their white official scarves – an elongated equivalent of what English barristers call 'tabs' or 'bands' – hang from their collars rigidly perpendicular, as if stiffly starched. When it was published, the plate was accompanied by the legend 'Grand escalier du Palais de justice. Vue de faces'.[95] This confirms our suspicion that here, in the language of architecture, we are observing a 'front' or 'face' view of the main staircase, and here – in the shape of lawyers – we are confronted with the face of law in the form of two costumed men carved hard and cold as stone.

The perennial stability of ideas of law and order – and of dress – demands that in their essentials such civil ideals should be stable and secure against the shifting whims of whatever might be the democratic fashion for the time being. Accordingly, one reason why uniforms make up a significant aspect of the face of law is because uniforms represent the maximum of dress with the minimum of fashion. Where we see uniforms, for example in the official and ceremonial dress of State institutions, established religions and universities, we tend to find that fashion is absent. Quentin Bell attributes the use of uniform and the absence of fashion in religion and nationalism to the fact that they 'represent ideas which are held to transcend history, to belong either to eternity or to the semi-eternal character of race or country'.[96] Examples of uniforms as national identifier abound, from Nazi Germany to the National Guardsmen of post-revolutionary France.[97] Thomas Carlyle expressed with characteristic efficiency and elegance the centrality of uniform to the fabrication of political society, where he described the 'whole Military and Police Establishment' as 'a huge scarlet-coloured, iron-fastened Apron, wherein society works'.[98]

95   *Le Charivari*, 8 February 1848 (Loys Delteil, no.1372).

96   Bell, *On Human Finery*, p.101.

97   A law of December 1790 provided that 'as the nation is one, there is only one national guard . . . wearing the same uniform': *Legislation Relative à La Garde Nationale de 1789 au 22 Mars 1831* (Paris: Imprimerie P Dupont, 1840), p.12; (trans. Dale L. Clifford), 'Can the Uniform Make the Citizen?: Paris, 1789–1791' *Eighteenth-Century Studies* 34.3 (2001), pp.363–82.

98   Carlyle, *Sartor Resartus*, Book I, chapter 6.

Figure 4.4 Honoré Daumier, lithographic plate 36 in the series *Les Gens de Justice* (Loys Delteil 1372). First published in *Le Charivari* 8 February 1848, accompanied by the legend 'Grand escalier du Palais de justice. Vue de faces'.

Source: Reproduced courtesy of the Robert D. Farber University Archives & Special Collections Department, Brandeis University.

The metaphor of the 'iron-fastened Apron' might remind us of the relation between metal armour and legal proof that I elaborated in the previous chapter, but it is also suggestive of other features of uniforms that are key to their civil role. One is that uniform establishes a bulwark to defend civil authority. Another, related, feature is that uniforms 'articulate'. Uniforms join together and they set apart. This jointed and dis-jointed quality of uniform is deliberately incompatible with the free flow of fashion. It has been said that from a sociological perspective uniforms assist complex organizations to cohere by defining boundaries, assuring conformity and eliminating status-based conflicts.[99] According to the same study, uniform provides 'a certificate of legitimacy' when it is recognizable as 'an indicator of a special status',[100] all of which suggests that uniform is not merely a boundary-creating form of dress but also a boundary-creating form of law. Warwick and Cavallaro argue that '[u]niform is not meant to make everyone look the same, but to produce a hierarchy in which those who need to know can make the necessary distinction'.[101] When the elements that distinguish uniform from non-uniform are apparent only to the initiated, the uniform has a great capacity to guard the ritualized corpus of the uniformed community. Thus it is said that in post-revolutionary France 'edgy National Guardsmen' arrested a citizen 'because the buttons on his uniform were not the Paris model'.[102] No doubt many a wartime spy has been similarly exposed because his or her uniform was not quite right in some crucial detail. More recent evidence of the phenomenon is a fraudster's foiled attempt to infiltrate the proceedings of an English court disguised as a barrister. The judge discovered the impostor after he made a number of legal errors and because he was wearing a barrister's wig with a solicitor's gown. The judge reported that '[a]lthough there may be circumstances in which a solicitor may wear a wig, it struck me immediately as strange. I was surprised to see the confusion of court attire'.[103]

Military uniform is especially potent as an indicator of special status, for it places the soldier outside of (or on the outer side of) the threshold of

---

99   Nathan Joseph and Nicholas Alex, 'The Uniform: A Sociological Perspective' *American Journal of Sociology* 77.4 (1972), pp.719–30.

100   Ibid., p.723.

101   Alexandra Warwick and Dani Cavallaro, *Fashioning the Frame: Boundaries, Dress and the Body* (Oxford and New York: Berg, 1998), p.76

102   Clifford, 'Can the Uniform Make the Citizen?', p.377.

103   Steven Morris, 'Imposter Guilty of Posing as Barrister in Court', *The Guardian*, 5 March 2012.

polite society. To be incorporated back in to civil society, the soldier must discard the uniform and don civilian dress ('civvies'). Military uniform acts as a sort of passport through borders which civilians might not be permitted to traverse alone. A 1950 guide to the duties of an officer of the US Armed Forces states that '[o]n the ordinary post or base, officers of other services will be admitted if wearing uniform, even when accompanied by civilian dependents' (52).[104] The US officials might not have been so trusting of military uniform if they had been aware of the wartime exploits of Sergeant Reading of the British Royal Army Medical Corps. Reading had received bribes to sit silently in the passenger seat of trucks trafficking contraband in Cairo. The mere sight of the uniformed British Officer was enough to guarantee that the trucks could move freely and unchallenged through checkpoints and borders without the additional authority of any spoken or written word.[105]

However relaxed or strict we might be with the rigour of our own dress, we tend to be intolerant of error in official uniform. Military personnel represent the security of the civil State and we expect them to demonstrate secure order in the bodily border that is their own dress. Likewise, uniformed police officers keep order in the civil State and we are disconcerted if they cannot keep order in the state of their own attire. As Quentin Bell puts it:

[I]f but one in the chief constable's constellation of buttons were to be omitted, or if it were to be replaced by some confection of blue glass or silver filigree, one would feel that law and order were overthrown.[106]

The 1950 manual *The Armed Forces Officer* expresses the same rigour with respect to military uniform in the United States:

There is only one correct way to wear the uniform. When any deviations in dress are condoned within the services, the way is open to the destruction of all uniformity and unity. (140)

---

104   *The Armed Forces Officer* Department of the Army Pamphlet No 600–2 (United States Department of Defense, 1950). Page references in parenthesis are to the online version published by the US Marine Corps Association.
105   *Reading v. Attorney General* [1951] AC 507, House of Lords.
106   Bell, *On Human Finery*, p.27.

Uniform can be a highly effective means of disguising or obscuring the individuality of the wearer, but for that very reason the refusal to wear required uniform and the wearing of unauthorized uniform can be especially potent means of expressing individuality.[107] A Jehovah's Witness in the Greek army was sentenced to four-years imprisonment for insubordination for refusing to wear military uniform at a time of general mobilization.[108] On the other side, individuals who wear politically offensive uniforms (for example Ku Klux Klan uniform and neo-Nazi uniform) risk imprisonment in many jurisdictions. Even a legitimate military badge, legitimately worn, may be considered an affront when worn directly in the face of the court. The case of *Regina* v. *Hamilton* was an appeal from a conviction for rape – the basis of the appeal being that interventions made by the judge at first instance had been improper and ought to result in the conviction being quashed.[109] One of those interventions was the judge's demand that the appellant should remove a jacket bearing the badge of the appellant's military regiment. The judge feared that the jury might construe it as evidence of the defendant's good character. The Court of Appeal held that the judge ought not to have obliged the defendant to remove the blazer, but that in any event it would have had no effect on the fairness of the trial. One might add that the mistake made by the trial judge was an entirely understandable one to make in a forum where the appearance of justice (as much as the substance of justice) is at stake.

It is probably a truism to state that all professions are guardians of boundaries, if only the boundary of their own professional spheres, but there is something especially liminal about certain professions. The military, the police, prison guards and border guards all wear uniforms that mark the boundary between civil and uncivilized life, but certain other professions have recourse to modes of dress which, if not strictly speaking 'uniform', nevertheless serve to mark them out from the general body of citizens and to mark them out as guardians of significant thresholds, including ritual thresholds, in the progress of a civil life. Among these professions we can include the priest, the physician and the lawyer. When the cloth of a

---

107   See Jennifer Craik, *Uniforms Exposed: From Conformity to Transgression* (Oxford and New York: Berg, 2005).

108   *Thlimmenos* v. *Greece* (34369/97) (2001) 31 EHRR 15 (ECHR [Grand Chamber]).

109   [1969] Crim LR 486 (Court of Appeal). I am grateful to John Curtis, barrister-at-law, for bringing this case to my attention.

professional costume overtly occupies and overrules the naked contours of individual identity and natural life, this serves as an image of, indeed something to be identified with, the profession's professed power to occupy and overrule a significant threshold of our social lives.

Fashion may be considered the polar opposite to uniform. It is true that members of the 'fashionable set' all wear similar things, so that they demonstrate a degree of uniformity in that sense, but the 'fashionable set' flock together like starlings: forever changing shape as they follow a collective, but largely unpredictable, sense of direction; whereas the uniformed professions flock together like geese: always following a designated leader in orderly ranks shaped like the 'V' of a sergeant's stripes. Views on fashion range from those who consider it to be a tyrannical and capricious force akin to dictatorship to those who consider it to be a liberating and expressive force akin to democracy. Situating himself somewhere within or near the former camp, Quentin Bell argues:

> Fashion for those who live within its empire is a force of tremendous and incalculable power. Fierce and at times ruthless in its operation, it governs our behaviour, informs our sexual appetites, colours our erotic imagination, makes possible but also distorts our conception of history and determines our aesthetic valuations.[110]

He suggests that 'it is not fashion which results from human nature but human nature which is itself subject to fashion'.[111] Bell points out that 'the laws of fashion seem to be accepted without a murmur' and that even 'the leaders of fashion seem to be incapable of raising a finger in their own defence'.[112] He quotes one monarch à la mode, the fashion designer Paul Poiret:

> I must undeceive you with regard to the powers of a king of fashion. We are not capricious despots such as wake up one fine day, decide upon a change in habits, abolish a neckline, or puff out a sleeve. We are neither arbiters nor dictators. Rather we are to be thought of as the blindly obedient servants of woman.[113]

---

110   Bell, *On Human Finery*, p.62.
111   Ibid., p.94.
112   Ibid., p.64.
113   Ibid., p.92. Translated from Paul Poiret, *En habillant l'époque* (Paris: Grasset, 1930), p.266.

In the camp of those who regard fashion as a benevolent democratic force, it is said that 'the age of fashion remains the major factor in the process that has drawn men and women collectively away from obscurantism and fanaticism'.[114]

Dress has always not only accommodated the human body, but it has also, to greater or lesser extent, fashioned the body to conform with social conventions. In Vigarello's terminology, the body has been 'trained' by its clothes.[115] This training or fashioning of the body was highly visible and violent in the early modern period, when '[g]arments, instead of following the outline of what they covered, imposed their own shape to adhere to contemporary conventions'.[116] The fashionable costume of the period 'did not allow for abrupt gestures, and thus abided by the rules for graceful aristocratic movement'; 'costume was designed to impose difficulties on the body'.[117] In witness of this we may consult the many formal portraits of the period which show royalty and courtiers in rigid regalia.[118] Even allowing for a degree of exaggeration in the portraiture, it must be the case that such standard elements as the rigid doublet and ruff of the 1580s exerted severe restraints upon body shape and movement. In that period, we see a form of fashion which quite literally fashioned the body to a certain form. Making the psychological point, Norbert Elias argues that the 'interpersonal external compulsion' of early modern dress was transformed into 'individual internal compulsion'.[119]

In the early modern period, fashionable Spanish women wore lead plates over their breasts to flatten their chests. In the nineteenth century, the same industrial advances that produced the steel crinoline also resulted in steel busks and steel eyelets for corsets and thereby facilitated the practice

114   Gilles Lipovetsky, *L'Empire de l'éphémère: la mode et son destin dans les sociétés modernes* (Paris: Gallimard, 1987); (trans. Catherine Porter), *The Empire of Fashion: Dressing Modern Democracy* (Princeton, NJ: Princeton University Press, 2002), p.12.

115   Georges Vigarello, 'The Upward Training of the Body from the Age of Chivalry to Courtly Civility', in Michel Feher and Ramona Naddaff (eds), *Fragments for a History of the Human Body*, Vol. II (New York: Zone Books, 1989), pp.148–99.

116   Ronnie Mirkin, 'Performing Selfhood: The Costumed Body as a Site of Mediation between Life, Art, and the Theatre in the English Renaissance', in Joanne Entwistle and Elizabeth Wilson (eds), *Body Dressing* (Oxford, New York: Berg, 2001), pp.143, 156; citing Vigarello, 'Upward Training of the Body', p.155.

117   Mirkin, 'Performing Selfhood', p.156

118   See Jane Ashelford, *A Visual History of Costume: The Sixteenth Century* (London: Batsford Ltd, 1993); *The Art of Dress: Clothes and Society, 1500–1914* (London: National Trust, 1999).

119   Norbert Elias, *Über den Prozess der Zivilisation* (1939); (trans. Edmund Jephcott) *The Civilizing Process* (Oxford: Blackwell, 1978), p.257. Cited Mirkin, 'Performing Selfhood', p.158.

of 'tight lacing'. Whereas the crinoline increased the comfort of the wearer, conformity to a tight-laced corset had the potential to kill.[120] Children were spared the fetishistic extremes of tight lacing, but they were routinely put into 'stays'. The Victorian artist, George F. Watts, who was a passionate campaigner against the unnatural restrictions of contemporary female dress, lamented the case of a little girl of 12 who 'being for the first time jammed into the abomination' of her corset and complaining that she could not breathe, received the curt answer from her mother's French maid: 'Il faut souffrir pour être belle'.[121] In this way, he observed, 'the deformity of the poor child's body and mind' commenced.[122] The so-called *Redresseur* corset was specifically marketed to be worn by adolescent girls whose mothers had omitted to follow the fashion of putting their daughters in a corset ('stays') at a younger age. Leigh Summers observes that the *Redresseur* was 'punitive and regulatory',[123] but notes that these qualities were defended by at least one male commentator at the time, who considered the *Redresseur* a 'safe and most efficient contrivance' designed to be 'a corrective and improver to the figure'.[124] A sufficiently oppressive cut and weight of cloth can also serve to impose sartorial servility. Quentin Bell observes:

> When Veblen wrote *The Theory of the Leisure Class* the world seemed to be divided, almost as by a law of nature, into trousered and the petticoat halves, and for Veblen nothing marked the essentially servile status of women so clearly as the fact that they were condemned to wear that hampering and hobbling device, the skirt.[125]

No doubt men have attempted to harness the force of fashion throughout history in order to train women to conform to a certain social mould and to utilize women as vehicles for the conspicuous display of male wealth,[126] but

---

120 Leigh Summers, *Bound to Please: A History of the Victorian Corset* (Oxford and New York: Berg, 2001), p.105.

121 'To be beautiful, one must suffer' (my translation).

122 George F. Watts, 'On Taste in Dress' *The Nineteenth Century: A Monthly Review* 13.71 (1883), pp.45–57, 54.

123 Summers, *Bound to Please*, p.81.

124 William Barry Lord, *The Corset and the Crinoline: A Book of Modes and Costumes from Remote Periods to the Present Time* (London: Ward, Lock and Tyler, 1865), p.210. Cited by Summers, *Bound to Please*.

125 Bell, *On Human Finery*, p.36, referring to Thorstein Veblen, *The Theory of the Leisure Class: An Economic Study of Institutions* (1899) (New York: The Macmillan Company, 1899).

126 Veblen, *The Theory of the Leisure Class*.

it would be naïve to deny that women have sometimes willingly submitted themselves to the force of fashion or to deny that they have sometimes sought to bring other women within its power. It would be equally short-sighted to suppose that men have escaped the domineering control of the dress code. Indeed, if we take a long view of European history, from ancient times until the present day, we must conclude that any male plan to dominate women has failed in grand style. Today it is the women who are free to wear the trousers, and the men who are not free to wear the skirts: David Beckham tried it once and was almost universally mocked for it, even though he wore his 'sarong' over a pair of trousers. If such a popular trendsetter as David Beckham cannot escape ridicule when wearing something approximating a skirt, there is little prospect that Western man will break free of the trousered mode any time soon. This, if one reflects on it, is all very strange and a most telling testament to the conforming power of dress codes in society, for in purely physiological terms, it is obvious that if either sex needs accommodating garments in the genital area, it is the man. Men in ancient civilizations, such as the Assyrian and the Egyptian, tended to do the sensible thing: they wore kilts, especially if they were members of the warrior class.[127] Nowadays Western man, the supposed master and maker of the modern world, is constrained in clothes better suited to women.

It is difficult to discern the mysterious forces of fashion that produced the state of affairs under which men have so passively conformed to ill-suited clothes. Sometimes, though, the source of the dress compulsion is obvious, for sometimes the law itself insists upon a certain dress code. Tudor England, dominated as it was by the flamboyant Henry VIII and his sartorially splendid daughter Elizabeth I, was notable for the revival of attempts to establish and enforce 'sumptuary laws' of the sort that had been prevalent in the Middle Ages. The label 'sumptuary' indicates that such laws purported to restrain luxurious expenditure, especially on sumptuous items imported from foreign (and therefore actually, or potentially, competitive) States. In fact, the express purpose of restraining consumption overshadowed a more subtle aim, which was to maintain reliable markers of social rank. Four 'acts of apparel' were passed in the reign of Henry VIII, the last of which, *An Act*

---

127   Hippocrates (c.460–c.370 BC) attributed the supposed impotence of Scythian cavalry to the fact that they rode horses and wore trousers. See part xxii of the essay 'Airs, Waters, Places', in John Chadwick and William N. Mann (trans.), *The Medical Works of Hippocrates* (Oxford: OUP, 1950), p.108.

for the Reformacyon of Excesse in Apparayle (1533),[128] aimed to establish 'good and politike ordre in knoweledge and distinccion of people according to their estates'.[129] Tudor sumptuary laws were not trying to invent a new form of 'appearential ordering',[130] but were attempting 'to freeze into place the signs that established status and social identity'.[131] Tudor sumptuary laws aimed 'to fix immutably, the exact signifying correspondences between the representations of clothing and socioeconomic status'.[132] In short, the sumptuary laws were an instance of the law's perennial project to reduce social change into a state of stasis and to reduce the fluidity of fashions to fossilized forms. Elizabeth B. Hurlock observes that '[w]here an aristocratic form of government prevailed, there seemed to be a strong tendency for fashions to remain stationary'.[133] The freedom of modern fashion, in stark contrast, allows frequent sartorial changes and therefore, in the words of Elizabeth Wilson, 'serves to fix the idea of *the body* as unchanging and eternal' (emphasis added).[134] Thus Wilson supplies a vision of the perpetuity of the physical being in the face of fashion which is compatible with Gilles Lipovetsky's metaphysical view of modern fashion as something that 'socializes human beings to change and prepares them for perpetual recycling'.[135]

Sumptuary laws have often proved unenforceable in practice. Staying in the context of Tudor England, we find Bishop Latimer complaining that '[t]here be laws made and certain statutes, how every one in his estate shall be apparelled, but God knoweth the statutes are not put in execution'.[136] What are we to read into this failure? One possibility is that the cultural forces which produce fashionable change are simply too powerful to be

128 Statute 24 Hen VIII c13.

129 Susan Vincent, *Dressing the Elite: Clothes in Early Modern England* (Oxford and New York: Berg, 2003), p.125. Maria Hayward, *Rich Apparel: Clothing and Law in Henry VIII's England* (Farnham: Ashgate, 2009).

130 Alan Hunt, *Governance of the Consuming Passions: History of Sumptuary Law* (Language, Discourse, Society) (Basingstoke: Palgrave Macmillan, 1996), p.137.

131 William C. Carroll, *Fat King, Lean Beggar: Representations of Poverty in the Age of Shakespeare* (Ithaca, NY: Cornell UP, 1996), p.5.

132 William C. Carroll, 'Semiotic Slippage: Identity and Authority in the English Renaissance' *The European Legacy* 2.2 (1997), pp.212–16, 212.

133 Elizabeth B. Hurlock, 'Sumptuary Law', in Mary E. Roach and Joanne B. Eicher (eds), *Dress, Adornment, and the Social Order* (New York and London: John Wiley & Sons, 1965), pp.295–301, 295.

134 Elizabeth Wilson, *Adorned in Dreams: Fashion and Modernity* (1985), rev. edn (London: I B Tauris & Co Ltd, 2009), p.58.

135 Lipovetsky, *L'Empire de l'éphémère*, p.149.

136 Hugh Latimer, *Sermon on the Epistle for the First Sunday in Advent*, 1552. Cited in Vincent, *Dressing the Elite*, p.139.

made to conform to the temporal and practical limits of any system of legal administration.

Formal laws do not have a monopoly on attempts to associate certain forms of attire with certain social ranks. Instead of statutes, a culture can produce stories to the same end. Hans Christian Andersen's *The Red Shoes* (1845),[137] for example, can be read as a lesson in obedience to social order defined by dress.[138] It is the story of a poor girl who was adopted by a lady who, having impaired vision, mistakenly bought the girl a pair of leather shoes not realizing that they were brilliant red. The shoes, we are told, had been made for the daughter of a count and were similar to those worn by the princess of that country. One day a strange soldier tapped the bright-red shoes on the poor girl's feet, commanding them never to come off when the girl danced, and cursing the girl to dance forever. The girl was powerless to resist, for it was 'as if the shoes controlled her'. It should not surprise us that dress should have such power (especially in the signal judicial colour red) and that a uniformed official (in this case a soldier, nowadays more likely a police officer) should be the instrument of such power. Like Cain, the marked girl found herself alone in the world. Like Adam and Eve, she was put under the curse of an angel of God armed with a broad sword. She was only released from the curse when she at last submitted her feet to an executioner's axe and lived out the short remainder of her life on wooden feet and crutches. She was then, at last, transported to heaven, where, in an Edenic state of freedom from the code of clothes, we are told that nobody made inquiry about the red shoes. One of the many morals that can be read into the story is the classic lesson of sumptuary law: you will be punished if you wear clothes that are worn by persons of higher status than you. If a cultural ghost of the sumptuary laws was still haunting creative imaginations in the early nineteenth century, it is nevertheless clear that the body of those laws was by this time truly dead and buried. In England, for example, the sumptuary laws were killed off in the very earliest years of colonialism at the start of the seventeenth century. The abolition of the sumptuary laws widened the way for the import of sumptuous products from the colonies, and facilitated the export of the English order

---

137   *Nye Eventyr. Første Bind. Tredie Samling* ('New Fairy Tales. First Volume. Third Collection') (Copenhagen: C A Reitzels Forlag, 1845). Andersen, who had been an apprentice weaver and tailor, is said to have attributed the inspiration for the story to an incident involving his father (a shoemaker) and a rich customer.

138   Andersen's *The Emperor's New Clothes* (1837) can be read the same way, but that is another story.

of dress alongside the order of law as part of the general dissemination of British civilization throughout the globe. From now on, law would not be a means of suppressing aspiration to a supposedly superior state of dress, but dress would be a means of securing adaptation to a supposedly superior state of law. It is a purpose that dress continued to serve throughout the period of British colonization. An example of that dress dynamic in operation is graphically demonstrated by Lieutenant-Governor George Arthur's pictorial proclamation to the 'aborigines' of 'Van Diemen's Land' (Tasmania), which dates to around 1830 (Figure 4.5).[139] The proclamation advertises equality under the law. If an indigenous person kills a European, he will be hung. If a European kills an indigenous person, he will be hung. The symmetry is perfectly played out, except in the banner panel at the top of the image. That panel depicts an imagined future in which both groups will live in harmony together, with the indigenous people dressed in European clothes. Here is an offer of equality under the law, but the law on offer is non-negotiably colonial law and it is inseparable from the European idea of civilization in which law and order are dressed in clothes.

The indigenous inhabitants of Tasmania were colonized by the European dress code in the early part of the nineteenth century, and by the latter part of that century the long arm of the European law of dress had reached Japan and taken hold. Not even Nippon, with its insular and self-confident culture, was immune to civilization by European sartorial power. In her fine essay on the legal regulation of nudity in nineteenth-century Japan, Satsuki Kawano observes how the Japanese ruling class began to suppress and regulate practices of public nudity in Japan.[140] The practice of going completely naked in public bathhouses had been acceptable, as had the practice widespread among labourers of wearing nothing but a loincloth, but the 1872 Misdemeanor Law (*ishiki kaii jorei*) outlawed nudity and partial dress in urban, public spaces.[141] Kawano notes that the Japanese regulations 'established a strict separation between public and private spaces' and 'aimed to transform homes into enclosed private spaces'.[142]

139   The date of 1816 and the attribution to Governor Davey which appear on this copy of the proclamation are incorrect.

140   Satsuki Kawano, 'Japanese Bodies and Western Ways of Seeing in the Late Nineteenth Century', in Adeline Masquelier (ed.), *Dirt, Undress and Difference: Critical Perspectives on the Body's Surface* (Bloomington and Indianapolis: Indiana University Press, 2005), pp.149–67.

141   Ibid., p.150.

142   Ibid., p.160.

Figure 4.5 'Governor Davey's Proclamation to the Aborigines, 1816'. (Erroneously ascribed when reproduced c.1866. The true author was Lieutenant-Governor George Arthur c.1828–30.)

Source: Reproduced courtesy of the National Library of Australia (BibID: 2134902; PIC U7547 NK458 LOC 4081-G).

The establishment of a formal regulatory face between public and private, accompanied by enclosure and exclusion of the private domain, is precisely in keeping with what we have learned about the character of law and dress throughout the present study. The Japanese law was administered with force: police took to assaulting workers seen out and about in traditional loincloth garb.[143] This did not stop workers from wearing the loincloth, but it did prompt them to put on clothes whenever they happened to spy a policeman in their vicinity.[144] Kawano relates an almost comical scene in which the police supervise those subject to the law and those subject to the law in turn supervise the police.

Law has attempted to harness forces of hierarchy, regulation, conformity and uniformity to assist in the effort of fabricating its public face and maintaining the authority of that face, but such forces, like unruly horses, are not easily harnessed. One problem with such forces is that they tend to the error of excess and from this it follows that our cultural habits of law and dress tend to their own destruction. This tendency to self-destructive excess has been attested to since ancient times. In his 163 BC play *Heauton Timorumenos* ('the self-tormentor'), the Roman comic dramatist 'Terence' (Publius Terentius Afer) refers to an established maxim on the point: *ius summum saepe summast militia* ('strictest law means greatest hardship') (4.4.796).[145] By the time Cicero repeated that maxim in *De Officiis* (44 BC), in its more familiar form *summum jus, summa injuria*, even the maxim was suffering from an excess of quotation and Cicero acknowledged that it was by then well worn.[146] The same tendency to suicidal surfeit can also be observed in dress. It was certainly the opinion of the fashion designer Paul Poiret that all fashions end in excess.[147] A parent will sometimes warn a child that if they pull a strange face it will stick that way. The warning for civil authorities is that the fixed face of the law makes itself a target for confrontation. For every routine of dress and law, there is always someone who refuses to follow suit. For every mask too rigidly imposed, there is always someone whom it will not fit, and who will therefore look to break the mould. With that in mind, the time has come to encounter the naked and the veiled.

---

143   Ibid., p.157.
144   Ibid., p.159.
145   (Trans. Betty Radice) (Harmondsworth: Penguin Classics, 1965).
146   *'tritum sermone proverbium'* I.33.
147   Paul Poiret, *En habillant l'époque* (Paris: Grasset, 1930), p.271.

CHAPTER FIVE

Addressing the Naked and Unfolding the Veil

Lives the man that can figure a naked Duke of Windlestraw addressing a naked House of Lords? . . . And yet why is the thing impossible?[1]

If we are to understand the reaction of civil authorities to public nudity and public face-covering, we will need to look beyond the usual analyses based on the balancing of individuals' civil rights and responsibilities. The balancing of rights provides one possible approach to resolving confrontations between individual dress codes and collective codes, but we need to look deeper if we are to appreciate the cultural causes that make such confrontations inevitable in the first place. What our inquiry will reveal is that the law demonstrates anxiety when individuals attempt to perform their own public face, through personal modes of dress and undress, in the liminal space of dress that the law takes to be a locus of its own dominion. Dress always represents order and control. When we choose to dress ourselves publicly in a particular way, we are exercising a form of self-government. We are taking control of our little state. This is most clear in the most careful and conscientious dressers, but even if our dress seems negligent we nevertheless make a state of ourselves. Even body modification through anorexia, though once attributed to excessive desire to conform to a social ideal of body type, is much better understood as a way of constituting a domain of private government in which the individual exercises 'resistance to social norms'.[2] We have seen that the law presents the face of civil order. Confronted with that face, the individual has three choices in cases of conflict: to conform, to contest or to compromise.

The pressure to conform is hard to resist. When women wore shoulder pads and masculine suits in the 1980s, was this really 'power-dressing' or was it

---

1   Thomas Carlyle, *Sartor Resartus: The Life and Opinions of Herr Teufelsdröckh* (1833–4) (Boston: James Munroe and Co, 1836), Book I, chapter 9.
2   Alexandra Warwick and Dani Cavallaro, *Fashioning the Frame: Boundaries, Dress and the Body* (Oxford and New York: Berg, 1998), p.14.

actually a case of being powerless to resist social forces of conformity?[3] (In this case, conformity to what was then the culturally encoded requirement that one should adopt the physical form of a man in order to gain admission into the world of business.) Quentin Bell asks some challenging questions about our seemingly docile compliance with the authority of dress and fashion:

> The case against fashion is always a strong one; why is it then that it never results in an effective verdict? Why is it that both public opinion and formal regulations are invariably set at nought while sartorial custom, which consists in laws that are imposed without formal sanctions, is obeyed with wonderful docility and this despite the fact that its laws are unreasonable, arbitrary and not infrequently cruel?[4]

More questions follow: could it be that, since the dawn of civil society, the ruling authorities have observed the dress compulsion at work and have sought to harness its force in order to encourage the civil habit of obedience to law? Is this one reason why dress and law became inseparable in so many of the foundational cultural orders of human civil society?

We obey the power of dress when others wear it, and we obey it when we wear it ourselves. The authors of a survey of several field studies carried out on the influence of dress concluded that 'dress had significant effects on the behavior of others in 85.3% of studies'.[5] This confirmed earlier studies which had shown that people wearing 'high status clothing' (such as a suit) 'were more successful in getting strangers to comply with requests than those wearing low status attire (e.g. work shirt and blue jeans)'.[6] We are sometimes obedient to the dress code even when no others are around to compel compliance. This is why we feel embarrassed when we realize that

---

3   On the imposition of workplace dress norms on women, see, for example, Jane M. Siegel, 'Thank You, Sarah Palin, for Reminding Us: It's Not about the Clothes' *Virginia Journal of Social Policy and the Law* 17 (2009), p.144; Katharine T. Bartlett, 'Only Girls Wear Barrettes: Dress and Appearance Standards, Community Norms, and Workplace Equality' *Mich Law Rev* 92 (1994), pp.2541–82; Mary Whiner, 'Gender-Specific Clothing Regulation: A Study in Patriarchy' *Harv Women's Law Jnl* 5.73 (1982).

4   Quentin Bell, *On Human Finery* (1947) (London: The Hogarth Press, 1976), p.24.

5   Kim K. P. Johnson, Jeong-Ju Yoo, Minjeong Kim and Sharron J. Lennon, 'Dress and Human Behavior: A Review and Critique' *Clothing and Textiles Research Journal* 26.1 (2008), pp.3–22, 15.

6   Ronald E. Bassett, Ann Q. Staton-Spicer and Jack L. Whitehead, 'Effects of Source Attire on Judgments of Credibility' *Central States Speech Journal* 30.3 (1979), pp.282–5, 285.

our flies are undone, or that we have tucked our skirt into our pants, even though nobody else has noticed. Quentin Bell observes that such dress faux pas 'are not incompatible with moral or theological teaching' and that 'the law takes no cognizance of such acts' and yet 'such behaviour will excite the strongest censure in "good society"'. This is so even where the offence occurs without witnesses and the offender is the only sufferer.[7]

There is a long-standing belief that we are obedient to the power and influence of our own dress; that the individual is fashioned by their dress even as the individual fashions their dress. Probably we have all at some time experienced the psychological shift that is induced by a change of clothing, especially where that change is from very casual to very formal clothing or from very formal to very casual. The physical constraint of a stiff collar and crisp cuffs, or the tautness of a tie, a belt and snug-fitting shoes, all combine to suit the mind to serious business.[8] The opposite effect, of relaxing the mind, can be achieved by 'slipping into something more comfortable'. The tendency of character to conform to clothing was contemplated by Eudoxus, one of the parties to the fictional dialogue in Edmund Spenser's *View of the Present State of Ireland*:

> [M]en's apparel is commonly made according to their conditions, and their conditions are oftentimes governed by their garments; for the person that is gowned, is by his gown put in mind of gravity, and also restrained from lightness, by the very unaptness of his weed . . . when Cyrus had overcome the Lydians, that were a warlike nation, and devised to bring them to a more peaceable life, he changed their apparel and music, and instead of their short warlike coat, clothed them in long garments like women . . . by which, in short space, their minds were so mollified and abated, that they forgot their former fierceness, and became most tender and effeminate. Whereby it appeareth, that there is not a little in the garment to the fashioning of the mind and conditions.[9]

7   Bell, *On Human Finery*, p.19.

8   See Paul Sweetman, 'Shop-Window Dummies? Fashion, the Body, and Emergent Socialities', in Joanne Entwistle and Elizabeth Wilson (eds), *Body Dressing* (Oxford, New York: Berg, 2001), pp.59–77, 66.

9   Edmund Spenser, *A View of the State of Ireland: Written Dialogue-Wise between Eudoxus and Ireneus* (1598, published 1633), reprinted in *The Works of Edmund Spenser* (London: Henry Washbourne, 1850), p.500. Spenser is alluding to a classical episode that is related in *Herodotus* (trans. Robin Waterfield) *Herodotus: The Histories* (Oxford University Press, 1998), p.69.

We are all incorporated into the political body by processes of conformity, including conformity to our clothes, but the military mind has appreciated better than most that clothes have the power to conform the individual to the ideals of the corps. As one military training manual puts it: 'It is good . . . to look the part, not only because of its effect on others, but because from out of the effort made to look it, one may in time come to be it.'[10]

Wendy Parkins acknowledges that dress has the capacity to 'reinforce existing arrangements of power', but that this also means that dress has the power to 'contest' them.[11] Parkins cites the example of the female legislators who in February 1999 wore denim jeans in the Italian parliament to protest against an Italian court which had decided that it is physically impossible to force non-consensual sex on a woman wearing jeans.[12] Nudity has also been used as a form of protest in political and public spaces. For example, IRA prisoners in Northern Ireland refused to wear prison uniform, preferring instead to live naked in their prison cells with only blankets for cover, in protest against the removal in 1976 of 'special category status'. Nowadays the news media frequently report street protests by topless women. In Nigeria, women (especially mothers) have traditionally employed genital exposure to their men in public as a form of curse. A revival of this tradition was threatened in 2002 when women protesting against ChevronTexaco barricaded hundreds of workers inside an oil terminal and committed to expose themselves if their demands were not met.[13]

Some forms of non-conforming dress (dress that does not conform to the majority custom) are challenging to the political State whether a challenge is intended or not. Probably very few Muslim women who wear a face-covering *niqab* in public do so deliberately intending to challenge the secular liberal States in which they live, but the majority of such States find extremely

<hr>

10   *The Armed Forces Officer* Department of the Army Pamphlet No 600–2 (United States Department of Defense, 1950), p.88. (Page references are to the online version published by the US Marine Corps Association.)

11   Wendy Parkins (ed.), *Fashioning the Body Politic: Dress, Gender, Citizenship* (Oxford and New York: Berg, 2002), p.4.

12   See Alessandra Stanley, 'Ruling on Tight Jeans and Rape Sets Off Anger in Italy', *New York Times*, 16 February 1999.

13   Terisa E. Turner and Leigh S. Brownhill, *Why Women Are at War with Chevron: Nigerian Subsistence Struggles against the International Oil Industry* (New York: International Oil Working Group, 2003); Misty L. Bastion, 'The Naked and the Nude: Historically Multiple Meanings of *Oto* (Undress) in Southeastern Nigeria', in Adeline Masquelier (ed.), *Dirt, Undress and Difference: Critical Perspectives on the Body's Surface* (Bloomington and Indianapolis: Indiana University Press, 2005), pp.34–60.

concealing modes of dress to be challenging in at least some contexts, for instance in court or at border control. We will consider the Islamic 'veil' in depth shortly. Staying with the unclothed subject, it will be informative to look closer at the case of the 'naked rambler', Stephen Gough. According to the Sexual Offences Act 2003, it is not a statutory offence to go naked in public in England, Wales and Northern Ireland unless it is done with the intention to cause 'alarm or distress'.[14] Unfortunately for Mr Gough, the preferred route of his naked walk takes him through Scotland. In Scotland, the 2003 statute has no application and a less lenient Common Law definition of indecent exposure is still applied, but that is not the crux of the problem for Mr Gough. The real problem is that breach of the peace is a criminal offence in Scots law, and, even though it has been narrowed to conduct that is 'genuinely alarming and disturbing' and threatens 'serious disturbance to the community',[15] the police presume that Mr Gough's conduct justifies bringing him to court. He then refuses to dress for the hearing and the result is that he is deemed to be in contempt of court; which is itself an imprisonable offence.[16] Mr Gough's continuing encounters with the civil authorities are very expensive for the taxpayer, and the police are for that reason, if none other, rather reluctant to arrest him. On one occasion, he was advised to modify his route so as to avoid passing a children's play park. He refused to do so, was arrested, and he was subsequently jailed for five months.[17] The upshot is that Mr Gough finds himself incarcerated for doing what he considers to be his right: to walk without clothes along a public path of his choosing.

Mr Gough expresses his philosophy in terms of 'Freedom to Be Yourself' (the slogan written on a white pennant that flies above his rucksack on his naked walks). He wants to live according to the mode of his choosing, and he wants to challenge social attitudes that would resist that, but arguably it is not his primary aim to challenge the State as such. The authorities nevertheless find his behaviour sufficiently challenging to justify the intervention of the power of the State against him. The Scottish authorities have been particularly strict. It is in Scotland that Mr Gough has been imprisoned

---

14   Sexual Offences Act 2003 s.66.

15   *Smith* v. *Donnelly* (Procurator Fiscal, Dumbarton) 2001 SLT 1007; 2002 JC 65 at para [17].

16   On contempt of court, see, further, below.

17   Hilary Duncanson, '"Naked Rambler" Stephen Gough jailed again', *The Independent*, 13 September 2012.

for long periods as a result of his persistent nudity. This is the country in which the men take pride in a military tradition of being totally naked under their kilts. How poignant to think that a few folds of cloth would transform Stephen Gough from the epitome of a naked menace to the epitome of a nation's manhood. A close reading of the report of one of his many court hearings reveals fascinating insights about the issues as he and the courts see them.

Gough v. *HM Advocate* was heard alongside another matter in the Scottish High Court of Justiciary on 7 November 2007.[18] The judgment of the court was delivered by Lord Gill (who has since been promoted to become head of the judiciary in Scotland). The judgment concerned Mr Gough's appeal against findings of contempt of court made against him in Edinburgh sheriff court. His lordship referred to Mr Gough's public nudity as 'incorrigible exhibitionism' and observed that he 'dresses on certain formal occasions, but these occasions do not include appearances in court' [10]. It would not be surprising if those exceptional occasions include wedding ceremonies and funerals. Such events are frequently exceptional to our dress codes, whatever they might be (even naturist brides have been known to wear a veil on their wedding day). Whenever Mr Gough appears in court, he appears naked. He is then found to be in contempt:

> Contempt of court is constituted by conduct that denotes wilful defiance of, or disrespect towards, the court or that wilfully challenges or affronts the authority of the court or the supremacy of the law itself. [29]

On the occasion of the first finding of contempt, Mr Gough indicated to the sheriff, via his solicitor, that he 'understood that the court was a public place where formal proceedings were conducted' but that he nevertheless 'considered nakedness to be natural and acceptable' [19].

The second finding of contempt occurred on 19 December 2005 at Edinburgh sheriff court before Sheriff Andrew Lothian. On that occasion, the sheriff 'considered that to allow Mr Gough to appear naked would be to invite him to repeat the offences with which he was charged' [15]. The offences he was charged with were breach of the peace and breach of bail

---

18   [2007] HCJAC 63 (2007) WL 3389577. Parenthetical references are to paragraph numbers in the report.

conditions that had accompanied his release from prison. The species of contempt with which the High Court of Justiciary was concerned was specifically 'contempt committed *in facie curiae* and directed at the administration of justice' [34]. Contempt '*in facie curiae*' is a most revealing description so far as it concerns our study of dress and law. In the previous chapter, we noted how the law makes a face in the world. Here we have juridical proof that confrontation results when a truly self-fashioned façade is presented in the face of the court. It seems that the courts are not only suspicious of the naked human form, but also deeply disturbed by it. In the present case, Lord Gill threw the proverbial book at Mr Gough. His lordship held that, by appearing in court naked, Mr Gough had 'committed the crime of public indecency', 'committed a breach of the peace' and 'disrupted the administration of justice'. His lordship added for good measure that in at least one of the cases under review Mr Gough had breached 'a bail condition that he should not appear in public in Scotland with his private parts exposed' [77]. His lordship took the view that Mr Gough would have been perfectly free to express his belief in the right 'to be naked at all times and in all places' provided he did so 'while remaining properly dressed' [76].

It was submitted on behalf of Mr Gough that his appearance naked in court was not 'an act calculated to offend the authority and dignity of the court' and that it was 'not an unjustifiable interference with the administration of justice' [71]. Lord Gill did not agree. His lordship held that 'the appearance of anyone in court naked, whatever crimes that may constitute, is unquestionably a contempt' [74]. But, with respect, whenever the word 'unquestionably' is employed without reasoned argument, we should take it as an invitation to ask questions, and even if we agree with the judge, we should at least ask what cultural causes produce the sense that a naked appearance in court is 'unquestionably' contempt. The judge went on to express his own opinion on the matter in the following terms: 'The court is entitled to enforce standards of decency and decorum in the dress and demeanour of those who appear before it, whether as witnesses, lawyers, jurors or accused' [74]. (The French artist and judge Pierre Cavellat appreciated that nothing would shock his judicial colleagues more than to be confronted by a naked person in court, see Figure 5.1.)[19] The judge

---

19   The image is reproduced from Ruth Herz, *The Art of Justice: The Judge's Perspective* (Oxford: Hart, 2012). Dr Herz explains that Cavellat was sent the picture as a gift and returned it after adding the nude figure (pp.35–6).

Figure 5.1 Pierre Cavellat (untitled, undated). Three judges confronted by a naked woman in court (caprice on a copy of 'Scandale au prétoire' by Gaston Hoffmann).

Source: Reproduced from Ruth Herz, *The Art of Justice: The Judge's Perspective* (Oxford: Hart Publishing Ltd, 2012), by kind permission of Ruth Herz, Hart Publishing and the family of Pierre Cavellat.

follows the usual habit of the law, according to which (to borrow a fitting phrase which Warwick and Cavallaro use in another context) 'the unclothed body is declared indecent and dress is invested with the ethical function of policing its frontiers'.[20] From the law's perspective his lordship is perfectly correct, of course, because it is in the very nature of a legal system to demand that society should assume a certain 'decency and decorum'. What I have endeavoured to show is that it is also in the very nature of the idea of dress to achieve a certain 'decency and decorum' in civil society; in fact I have argued that dress, no less than law, defines civil society in terms of an order that is decent and decorous.

Stephen Gough is both admirable and pitiable. Perhaps he consciously or unconsciously perceives that dress and law are inextricably intertwined and

20   Warwick and Cavallaro, *Fashioning the Frame*, p.138.

perhaps that is the inspiration for his philosophy of public nudity. However, if he understood just how inseparable is dress from civil order, he would realize that the wall of civil society is a wall of wool that cannot be unwound by him. He cannot win. If he goes naked, the civil authorities will cover him with prison walls. Mr Gough has an ally in Diogenes, the cynic philosopher of ancient Greece. Epictetus attributes to Diogenes the saying 'To go naked is better than any robe with the purple'.[21] It is doubtful that 'naked' meant as much (or as little) then as it does now, in terms of the precise degree of undress signified.[22] What we can say is that Diogenes suffered for his principles, and like Mr Gough spent much of his life confined alone in a cell. In Mr Gough's case, solitary confinement in a prison. In the case of Diogenes, a tub on a city street. Perhaps Mr Gough should heed the following words that Philip Stanhope, the 4th Earl of Chesterfield, wrote about dress customs in one of his *Letters to His Son*:

> [T]here are a thousand foolish customs of this kind, which, not being criminal, must be complied with, and even cheerfully, by men of sense. Diogenes the Cynic was a wise man for despising them, but a fool for showing it.[23]

One wonders if the 'naked rambler' might have more success if he were to claim a religious basis for going unclothed in public. He certainly might in the United States, for as the US case of *Wisconsin* v. *Yoder* says: 'A way of life, however virtuous and admirable, may not be interposed as a barrier to reasonable state regulation . . . if it is based on purely secular considerations.'[24] This brings us to the question of religious dress, and in particular to the so-called Islamic veil.

Headdress worn by Muslim women comes in a great many forms, but there is little consensus across Islamic communities regarding the type of headdress, if any, which ought to be worn, and neither is there consensus as to the terms by which various forms of headdress are described. For

---

21   Epictetus, *Discourses* 1.24.7. (Malcolm Schofield, 'Epictetus: Socratic, Cynic, Stoic' *The Philosophical Quarterly* 54.216 [2004], pp.449–56, 455.)

22   F. Gerald Downing, *Cynics, Paul and the Pauline Churches* (1988) (London: Routledge, 1998), p.151.

23   Dublin Castle, 29 November 1745. Quoted in Bell, *On Human Finery,* p.18. (Stanhope's advice should not be followed uncritically: in another letter he advises his son to smile often, but to laugh never [Bath, 9 March 1748]).

24   *Wisconsin* v. *Yoder*, 406 US 205 (1972), pp.215–16.

present purposes, the most pertinent forms of headdress are face-covering attire worn by females. We will not be concerned with headdress, such as *hijab*, which cover the hair but not the face.[25] Within the description 'Islamic veil', the extent of facial covering ranges from those which cover the face, but leave a narrow opening at the eyes to those which cover the entire face including the area of the eyes, the eyes being covered with thin cloth, a net, a grille or some similar covering which will allow the wearer to look out while obstructing onlookers' ability to see in. The former is generally called *niqab*. The latter is sometimes called *burqa*, although *burqa* more accurately describes the full-body covering and not merely the head-covering part. Throughout the remainder of this study, and where the context permits, I will use 'Islamic veil', 'veil' or '*niqab*' as generic descriptions of face-covering attire worn by Muslim women.

Modern commentators rightly point out that none of us can judge what the wearing of a veil by an individual signifies.[26] Thomas Carlyle made the same point almost 200 years ago, when he wrote that '[f]rom the veil can nothing be inferred'.[27] For every interpretation that the veil invites, an utterly opposite interpretation is opened up. For example, the veil might be read as a strong mode of self-fashioning, or it might be read as a means of relieving oneself of the pressure to present a public face. This is how Toby Fischer-Mirkin reads it where she writes that veils 'conceal your identity and relieve you of the obligation to be yourself'.[28] Examples can be cited of women who wear Islamic head coverings as a means of protest, but according to one survey the majority of veil-wearing women gave the impression that they were merely following fashion.[29] Despite the peril of inferring motives for veil wearing, courts have sometimes presumed to judge. On an international level, the European Court of Human Rights in its 2001 decision in *Dahlab*

---

25   Neither will we examine those exceptional cultures in which the men, rather than the women, wear forms of 'veil' (notably the nomadic Tuareg people of the Sahara) or those cultures in which the women do not show their faces even to their husbands or to their female relatives (examples of the latter are found in the Al-Jawf region of northern Saudi Arabia). I am grateful to Bayan Al Shabani for kindly elucidating the relevant Arabic-language sources.

26   See, for example, Katherine Bullock, *Rethinking Muslim Women and the Veil*, 2nd edn (London: The International Institute of Islamic Thought, 2007); Evan Darwin Winet, 'Face-Veil Bans and Anti-Mask Laws: State Interests and the Right to Cover the Face' *Hastings Int'l & Comp L Rev* 35 (2012), p.217.

27   Carlyle, *Sartor Resartus*, Book II, chapter 1.

28   *Dress Code: Understanding the Hidden Meanings of Women's Clothes* (New York: Clarkson Potter, 1995), p.242.

29   Liela Ahmed, *A Quiet Revolution: The Veil's Resurgence, from the Middle East to America* (New Haven and London: Yale UP, 2011), p.120.

v. *Switzerland* stated that the Islamic headscarf 'appears to be imposed on women by a precept which is laid down in the Koran and which . . . is hard to square with the principle of gender equality'.[30] This remains the position of that Court, as confirmed in subsequent decisions.[31]

None of us can confidently discern a person's motives for wearing any particular kind of dress, but we should be especially cautious to attempt an interpretation in the case of Islamic dress, where individual motives will frequently be a complex mix of cultural and religious concerns. Courts should be especially cautious in their efforts to scrutinize the religious basis for veil wearing. As the US Supreme Court held in *Thomas* v. *Review Board of Indiana Employment Security Division*: 'Courts are not arbiters of scriptural interpretation.'[32] That case concerned a Jehova's Witness who had been denied unemployment compensation after resigning from his work in a foundry in response to a requirement that he make military components. The court confirmed:

> The narrow function of a reviewing court in this context is to determine whether there was an appropriate finding that the petitioner terminated his work because of an honest conviction that such work was forbidden by his religion.[33]

Within that narrow function, the inquiry into the 'honesty' of a conviction is inevitably a fraught one.[34] It is, as lawyers phrase it, 'a question of fact'. It might as well be called a 'question of face', for it is determined only on the basis of what is evident, and that is hardly an adequate basis for reaching conclusions about the depth and integrity of an individual's religious convictions.

Although one cannot guess what an individual woman intends (if she intends anything) by wearing a veil, research into the motives of a great many veil-wearing Muslim women has apparently revealed a recurring range of

---

30 *Dahlab* v. *Switzerland* App No 42393/98, admissibility decision (2001) p.5.

31 For example, Şahin v. *Turkey* (44774/98) (2007) 44 EHRR 5 (ECHR [Grand Chamber]) and *Dogru* v. *France* [2008] ECHR 1579.

32 450 US 707 (1981), pp.715–16.

33 Ibid., p.716.

34 Gary Watt, 'Giving Unto Caesar: Rationality, Reciprocity, and Legal Recognition of Religion', in Richard O'Dair and Andrew Lewis (eds), *Law and Religion* (Oxford: Oxford University Press, 2001), pp.45–63.

motives that seem to persist 'across both time and space in the post-1970s era'.[35] These perennial meanings can often be understood to be 'implicitly invoking a notion of justice and deliberately signaling differences from the majority'.[36] Perhaps we can also say in a general way that '[t]he power of dress to threaten boundaries (between self and non-self, the individual and the collective, discipline and transgression) is emphasized by items of clothing such as masks and veils'.[37] Liela Ahmed states that the Islamic veil repeatedly remerges 'as a quintessential sign (among other things) of irresolvable tension and confrontation between Islam and the West'.[38] It might not be intended to act as such a sign: Ahmed acknowledges, quoting Macleod, that 'the idea of being Muslim has more to do with [a woman's] role as wife and mother in the family, rather than with expressions of nationalism or anti-Western feeling'.[39]

The Islamic veil has proved most controversial in democracies, such as France, Belgium and Turkey, which are constitutionally committed to political secularism.[40] On 14 September 2010, *Le Sénat français* passed a law (by 246 votes to 1) which prohibits the wearing in public spaces of clothing which covers the face. Article 1 states in stark terms that '*Nul ne peut, dans l'espace public, porter une tenue destinée à dissimuler son visage*' ('no one is permitted, in public spaces, to wear clothing designed to cover their face'). The penalty is a 150 Euro fine for the first offence.[41] The problem with the French law is that it is politically illogical to force someone to be free, and in practice the effect of such a ban must be to compel many women to remain hidden indoors who might otherwise have been free to venture out in public.[42]

35   Ahmed, *A Quiet Revolution*, p.211.
36   Ibid.
37   Warwick and Cavallaro, *Fashioning the Frame*, p.xxi.
38   Ahmed, *A Quiet Revolution*, pp.10–11.
39   Ahmed, *A Quiet Revolution*, p.123. Quoting Arlene Elowe Macleod, *Accommodating Protest: Working Women, the New Veiling, and Change in Cairo* (New York: Columbia University Press, 1991).
40   See Alev Çınar, *Modernity, Islam, and Secularism in Turkey: Bodies, Places, and Time* (Minneapolis: University of Minnesota Press, 2005), p.59; Valorie K. Vojdik, 'Politics of the Headscarf in Turkey: Masculinities, Feminism, and the Construction of Collective Identities' *Harv J L & Gender* 33 (2010), p.661.
41   '*La loi sur le voile intégral*', 14 September 2010 (Loi No. 2010–1192, le Sénat français).
42   Flügel makes the point that the Islamic veil can operate as a sort of architectural extension to the residential arrangement whereby some Muslim women are hidden from the outside world (that arrangement is sometimes called *purdah* [Persian: 'curtain']). (See John Carl Flügel, *Psychology of Clothes* [1930] [London: The Hogarth Press, 1950], 83fn.)

Forced unveiling is as politically objectionable as forced veiling (forced veiling, which is practiced in totalitarian Islamic States such as Iran and Somalia, is prohibited in most majority Muslim States, including, for example, Bangladesh[43]). Almost exactly one year after the French voted in favour of *'la loi sur le voile intégral'*, the lower chamber of the Swiss Parliament approved a similar law (by 101 votes to 77). The motion put to the Swiss Parliament not only prohibited full-face covering in certain public places, but (most telling in terms of concern for confrontation with the face of the State) it also required anyone addressing public authorities 'to present themselves with their faces uncovered'.[44] The French law was ratified in October 2010 by *Le Conseil Constitutionnel*,[45] and it came into force, despite some public opposition, on 11 April 2011.[46] This law is in the same spirit as the 2008 decision of the French *Conseil d'Etat* in which a Muslim woman was refused French citizenship, despite being married to a French citizen, because of her failure to integrate (*défaut d'assimilation*). She was said to have adopted radical religious practices, notably the wearing of a *niqab*, which were deemed to be incompatible with the essential values of French society, in particular the principles of gender equality and laïcité.[47] Cases like this have generally received scholarly analysis in terms of competing human rights.[48] I wish to set the issues on a wider cultural canvas by suggesting that the Islamic veil is controversial because it occupies the regulatory space between self and society which the law takes to be the plane of its own dominion. The thin interface between the inner private being and the outer public scene is a border that the law by its nature as dress must define and control if it is to have a distinct identity and role. By wearing the veil, the religious believer is appropriating the power to regulate her own relations between her private (including her religious) life and the public, civil sphere. The law is threatened by such an assertion of regulatory authority over the precise interstitial or liminal space – the space of dress – in which the law

---

43   *Agence France Presse*, 16 September 2010.
44   Ibid., 28 September 2010.
45   *'La loi sur le voile intégal'* (Décision n° 2010–613 DC, le Conseil Constitutionnel, 7 October 2010).
46   Steven Erlanger, 'France Enforces Ban on Full-Face Veils in Public', *The New York Times*, 11 April 2011.
47   Laïcité is the formal political separation of religion from the secular State. See Anastasia Vakulenko, 'Gender Equality as an Essential French Value: The Case of *Mme M' H R L Rev* 9.1 (2009), pp.143–50.
48   For example, Tom Lewis, 'What Not to Wear: Religious Rights, the European Court, and the Margin of Appreciation' *Int'l & Comp LQ* 56.2 (2007), pp.395–414; Nicholas Gibson, 'Faith in the Courts: Religious Dress and Human Rights' *Cambridge LJ* 66.3 (2007), pp.657–97.

claims dominion. The veil thus becomes a means of (if I might mix another sartorial metaphor) throwing down the gauntlet to secular law's regulatory monopoly over the border between private and public, inner and outer. Even if there was no intention to 'throw down the gauntlet', the civil authorities sometimes take up the challenge as if the veil were a personal affront.

If some might object that the religious believer's choice is antagonistic to the secular State in which she finds herself, her defence might be that the State 'started it'. Reflecting on French and Spanish suspicion of the Islamic veil, Martha Nussbaum observes:

> It gets very cold in Chicago – as, indeed, in many parts of Europe. Along the streets we walk, hats pulled down over ears and brows, scarves wound tightly around noses and mouths. No problem of either transparency or security is thought to exist, nor are we forbidden to enter public buildings so insulated. Moreover, many beloved and trusted professionals cover their faces all year round: surgeons, dentists, (American) football players, skiers and skaters. What inspires fear and mistrust in Europe, clearly, is not covering per se, but Muslim covering.[49]

The French law that prohibits the wearing of the Islamic veils in public does not in fact mention Islam anywhere in the text, but this rather goes to support Professor Nussbaum's suggestion that we ought to be suspicious of the terms in which such laws are expressed. Having said that, the issue is in other respects and in other places not as 'clear' as Professor Nussbaum claims. For example, Islam was quite irrelevant when, in the aftermath of a week of riots in English cities in August 2011, British prime minister David Cameron announced that he would 'give the police the discretion to remove face coverings under any circumstances where there is reasonable suspicion that they are related to criminal activity'.[50] The source of confrontation between the veil and civil authorities really is 'covering per se', albeit that this concern is sometimes expressed in terms, such as 'security', 'identification', 'sincerity' and 'liberty', which might cause us to doubt the reliability of the justifications expressed. Civil authorities' concern with covering is not

---

49 Martha Nussbaum, 'Veiled Threats?', *New York Times*, 11 July 2010. See, also, Joan Wallach Scott, *The Politics of the Veil* (Princeton, NJ: Princeton University Press, 2010). I am grateful to Professor Reina Lewis for alerting me to this, and to other books that have helped inform this chapter.

50 Prime minister's statement on disorder in England on 11 August 2011. (The Criminal Justice and Public Order Act 1994 s.60AA authorizes police officers to remove items worn 'for the purpose of concealing identity'.)

trivial, or merely incidental to more overt concerns. On the contrary, I have demonstrated that dress has always been a defining concern of civil order. That this concern has not been made overt in the official reasoning of politicians, courts and other statements of civil authority should hardly surprise us. Had it been made overt, its cover would have been blown.

Here is not the place to rehearse the competing human rights that are at stake in the State supervision of veil wearing,[51] not least because a debate framed in the secular language of rights predetermines, at least in general terms, the outcome of the debate. We will consider, instead, the long cultural history which shows that State prohibition of veils is nothing new and which indicates that in 'Western' societies in the not-too-distant past the wearing of veils and masks, of somewhat different design to the Islamic variety, was a personal choice which women made for their own pleasure and protection and occasionally in the face of social pressure – sometimes legal, sometimes male – to reveal themselves. In all of the examples that follow, the veil or mask not only performs a practical function such as disguise or protection from the elements, but was also, in its time, considered fashionable.

We will start in the nineteenth century and proceed backwards, a century at a time, to the fifteenth. Ironically, given what we have already seen of current official attitudes to the Islamic veil in France, it is in France in the late nineteenth century that we find some of the strongest indicators of the veil as status symbol and fashion statement. The veil was worn partly as protection from the dust thrown up by Haussmann's radical architectural reordering of the Parisian cityscape and partly as a badge of bourgeois respectability. It was, admittedly, a rather thin and revealing affair quite unlike a *niqab*, as one can see, for example, from the key female figure in Gustave Caillebotte's 1877 oil painting 'Paris Street: Rainy Day',[52] but it gestures to the fact that the complex semiotics of female face-covering do not always lead to the implication of female oppression. Nevertheless, in some contexts that implication is irresistible. Earlier in the same century, Charles Dickens produced a deeply nuanced study of a fashionable English lady, Lady Dedlock, in his novel *Bleak House*[53] which was set around

---

51 For a summary of the European debate from a US perspective, see Jennifer M. Westerfield, 'Behind the Veil: An American Legal Perspective on the European Headscarf Debate' *Am J Comp L* 54.3 (2006), pp.637–78.

52 See, generally, M. R. Kessler, *Sheer Presence: The Veil in Manet's Paris* (Minneapolis: The University of Minnesota Press, 2006).

53 Quotations are taken from Charles Dickens, *Bleak House* (serialized 1852–3) (Harmondsworth: Penguin English Classics, 1971).

1827.[54] The first chapter of the novel, 'In Chancery', introduces the main legal theme, which is the fog or obfuscation (one might say the 'veil') of law. The second chapter introduces the socially circumscribed existence of Lady Dedlock under the title 'In Fashion', in which Dickens observes at the outset that '[b]oth the world of fashion and the Court of Chancery are things of precedent and usage'. Pertinent for present purposes is that 'the figure of the veil is repeatedly associated in *Bleak House* with Lady Dedlock'.[55] The text subtly hints at resemblance between Lady Dedlock, the terrified creature of fashion, and Mr Tulkinghorn, the terrible creature of law. Tulkinghorn lives as a legal mask; Lady Dedlock lives under a fashionable one. As she says to her daughter: 'If you hear of Lady Dedlock, brilliant, prosperous, and flattered, think of your wretched mother, conscience-stricken, underneath that mask!' (36). Tulkinghorn's 'dress is like himself' (2); Lady Dedlock's dress is a part of her: 'the traces of her dresses and her ornaments, even the mirrors accustomed to reflect them when they were a portion of herself, have a desolate and vacant air' (58).

Lady Dedlock's veil is open to a range of interpretations, many of which would regard it negatively, but it must also be acknowledged that the veil was part of the wardrobe of a fashionable lady and a useful disguise, which, even as it confined her features, freed her to walk the streets of a crowded and dangerous city.[56] That interpretation is supported by the Franco-Peruvian feminist Flora Tristan, whose knowledge of the '*Tapadas*' ('covered') women of Lima led her to claim in 1837 that 'there is no place on Earth where women are more free'.[57]

This capacity of the veil simultaneously to fetter the wearer and to free her evokes a related form of female facial covering that was in vogue in London

54   William S. Holdsworth, *Charles Dickens as a Legal Historian* (New Haven: YUP, 1928), p.79.

55   K. McLaughlin, 'Losing One's Place: Displacement and Domesticity in Dickens's *Bleak House*' MLN, *Comparative Literature* 108.5 (1993), pp.875–90.

56   For an argument that alternative ('male' or mixed 'male-female') clothing worn by marginal women in the period might have operated as non-verbal resistance, see Diana Crane, 'Clothing Behavior as Non-Verbal Resistance: Marginal Women and Alternative Dress in the Nineteenth Century' *Fashion Theory: The Journal of Dress, Body & Culture* 3.2 (1999), pp.241–68.

57   Flora Tristan, *Peregrinations d'une Paria* (*Peregrinations of a Pariah*) (Paris: L'advocat, 1838) (my translation). The *Tapadas* wore a headscarf which they held in place by hand in such a way that it covered almost the entire face, frequently leaving only one eye revealed. It has been noted, likewise, that in Egypt at the turn of the twentieth century, 'Some women of the new middle class, who began to enjoy an unprecedented degree of mobility, actually considered the veil as a form of protection as they ventured out more into public'. Yedida K. Stillman, *Arab Dress: A Short History: from the Dawn of Islam to Modern Times* (Norman A. Stillman ed.) (Leiden: Brill, 2000), p.155. Compare the experience of a female Muslim student on a US college campus who felt 'liberated' by wearing *hijab* in the period immediately following 9/11 (Ahmed, *A Quiet Revolution*, p.208).

a century before Lady Dedlock's time. In the early eighteenth century, it was a female fashion to wear a full-face velvet mask for the purpose of promenading in public parks. Christoph Heyl observes that such 'masks both obscure their wearers and attract attention at the same time'.[58] Heyl locates the veil in the regulatory or legal plane that separates the private from the public: 'protected by a mask, an element of privacy could be maintained while frequenting public spaces'.[59] The female fashion of the black mask goes even further back, to the middle of the seventeenth century. Bohemian by birth, but a naturalized Englishman, Wenceslaus Hollar (1607–77) produced numerous etchings of London's fashionable women, including one which shows a lady in the winter dress of c.1644 (Figure 5.2). Her black mask covers the upper part of her face in a style reminiscent of a Venetian carnival mask to produce an effect of concealment and disguise which is comparable to that produced by the *niqab* – with this notable difference: that the *niqab* covers the mouth.

We can be confident that it was masks of the sort depicted by Hollar that were worn by the women who reportedly interrupted the trial of Charles I in January 1649. At the close of the trial, Bradshaw announced that the King had been 'brought before the Court to make answer to a charge of treason and other high crimes exhibited against him in the name of the people of England'. Whereupon

> there was a stir in one of the galleries where two masked ladies sat side by side, and one of them called out: 'Not half, not a quarter of the people of England. Oliver Cromwell is a traitor.' Colonel Axtell, who was in charge of security in the Hall, ordered his men to level their muskets at her. Some say they heard him shout 'Down with the whores.' . . . she was hustled out, and Bradshaw resumed his interrupted speech.[60]

According to C. V. Wedgwood, 'the masked interrupter was Lady Fairfax, who had come, accompanied by her friend Mrs. Nelson, to relieve her conscience, and perhaps also to relieve her husband's'.[61]

58   Christoph Heyl, 'When They Are Veyl'd on Purpose to Be Seene: The Metamorphosis of the Mask in Seventeenth- and Eighteenth-Century England', in Entwistle and Wilson, *Body Dressing*, pp.121–42, 127.
59   Ibid., p.132.
60   Quotations are from Cicely V. Wedgwood, *The Trial of Charles I* (London: Collins, 1964), pp.154–5.
61   Ibid., p.155. (Lady Fairfax's husband, Lord Fairfax, was parliamentary commander-in-chief during the English Civil War.)

Figure 5.2 Wenceslaus Hollar, 'Winter' (etching), c.1644.

Source: Reproduced courtesy of the Thomas Fisher Rare Book Library, University of Toronto.

Another century earlier, facial coverings of various sorts were a common feature of female dress. Masks were used in revels,[62] and formal veils were used to indicate special status, for instance that a woman had entered religious orders or taken a vow of chastity.[63] Attire for the brow and thin veils or nets for the face were a commonplace component of fashionable apparel, as appears, for instance, from the following dialogue in John Heywood's *The Four P's* (c.1545):

Pardoner: I pray you tell me what causeth this:
                That women, after their arising,
                Be so long in their apparelling?
Pedlar: Forsooth, women have many lets,
                And they be masked in many nets,
                As frontlets, fillets, partlets, and bracelets:
                And then their bonnets and their poinets.[64]

The description 'lets' is highly apposite shorthand for the range of facial attire which adorned women in this period, for the word 'lets' invites two directly contrary interpretations: 'lets' in the sense of 'allows' and 'lets' in the sense of 'hinders'. The word efficiently summarizes the way in which facial coverings have consistently performed in an ambiguous fashion – at once freeing the female to participate in public life while fencing her off from it.[65] The same equivocation has been observed in the wearing of Islamic headdress today. Liela Ahmed, summarizing Macleod's research,[66] observes that to fulfil their own sense of freedom in the face of such factors as the jealous supervision of male partners, donning *hijab* (the headdress that covers the hair but not the face)

allowed women to go about their lives and keep their jobs while affirming their identities as Muslim women and presenting themselves as

---

62   Maria Hayward, *Rich Apparel: Clothing and Law in Henry VIII's England* (Farnham: Ashgate, 2009), p.293.
63   Ibid., pp.248–9.
64   (London: William Middleton, 1547). This extract is my own modernization of the text appearing in the first volume of *A Select Collection of Old Plays in Twelve Volumes*, 2nd edn (London: J Nichols, 1780), pp.47–98, 64.
65   The word 'let' has what Empson called the seventh type of ambiguity, that is, the ambiguity of a word which carries directly opposite meanings: William Empson, *Seven Types of Ambiguity* (London: Chatto and Windus, 1930).
66   Macleod, *Accommodating Protest*.

women who were conforming to conservative Islamic notions of women's roles.[67]

Yet another century further back in time, we find that female facial concealment was already disconcerting the ruling powers to the extent of legislation. Thus a law of James II of Scotland (1430–60) laid down a stern prohibition against female face-covering in church: 'na woman cum to Kirk nor mercat with her face mussled or covered that she may nocht be kenn'd under the pain of escheat of the curchie'.[68] It is somewhat ironic that this prohibition should apply in a religious setting, for to 'take the veil' was at that time standard metonymical shorthand for a woman's entry into holy orders. No matter how far back we go, the fashion for facial covering has been a feature of the female sartorial landscape. Even in Old Testament times, it was known that veils could as easily be attention-grabbing and ostentatious as modest. When the prophet Isaiah prophesized against the 'haughty' women of Zion, his complaint concerned such features of their dress as 'veils', 'headdresses' and 'shawls' and their habit of 'flirting with their eyes' (Isaiah 3:16–23).

Returning to Europe, it was not until the twentieth and twenty-first centuries that the veil and other forms of face-covering attire finally lost their place in the wardrobe of fashionable women. Outside of religious usage, the veil is nowadays almost wholly reserved for use in wedding ceremonies. In that context, as so often, it speaks simultaneously of innocence and seduction. Throughout its long history, the veil or mask worn by females has challenged and disconcerted predominantly male authority. This alone must cast some doubt on the claim, made now by the authorities in France and elsewhere, that the veil is oppressive to women.

The courtroom is a domain of dress and a key site of confrontation with the face of the law. Among those accused of crimes there is a long tradition of dressing up to give the appearance of respectability. As far back as Tudor times, it was said that so-called Egyptians ('Gypsies') appear 'at every assize, sessions, and assembly of justices, and . . . so clothe themselves for that time, as any should deem him to be an honest husbandman'.[69] The practice is an

---

67   Ahmed, *A Quiet Revolution*, p.122.

68   6 March 1457. Thomas Murray, *The Laws and Acts of Parliament Made by King James The First, and His Royal Successors, Kings and Queens of Scotland* (In Two Volumes), Vol. I (Edinburgh: David Lindsey and His Co-Partners, 1682), p.79.

69   Richard H. Tawney and Eileen Power, *Tudor Economic Documents* (London: Longmans, Green & Co, 1924), II, p.345.

acknowledgement that defendants expect to be judged, not merely on the evidence of the case, but on their own evident external appearance.

The appearance in court of a veil-wearing woman calls for especially considered judgment. Natasha Bakht observes that judicial opposition to the wearing of the *niqab* in courtrooms is usually a 'knee-jerk response'.[70] A number of instances suggest that this is, indeed, true. For example, the case of a magistrate in Manchester who walked out of a hearing when the female defendant refused to remove her veil.[71] The defendant, who had committed criminal damage when she was evicted from her State-owned residence, made an official complaint against the magistrate and he was subsequently given a formal reprimand and required to undergo further training.[72] As so often happens, the knee that jerks at first instance is put back in line on appeal. The authors of 'Freedom in Dress: Legal Sanctions' note that in their sample of American cases, sanctions which at first instance were threatened or imposed for breach of various sartorial codes, were subsequently disapproved by higher-ranking judges on review or appeal on 61 per cent of occasions.[73] We can compare this to the case of the woman who refused to remove her headscarf when she accompanied her nephew into a municipal court in the State of Georgia in 2008. She was arrested and, after protesting, briefly jailed for contempt of court, but Georgia has since recommended that religious head coverings should be permitted in State courthouses.[74]

Bakht explains that there is no justification for the instinctive negative response to the wearing of an Islamic veil in court (pointing out that a thin cloth, covering the face, does not prevent factual evidence from being submitted),[75] but what she does not seek to explain is the sense that causes

70   Natasha Bakht, 'Objection, Your Honour! Accommodating *Niqab*-Wearing Women in Courtrooms', in Ralph Grillo, Ralph Grillo, Roger Ballard, Alessandro Ferrari, André Hoekema, Marcel Maussen and Prakash Shah (eds), *Legal Practice and Cultural Diversity* (Farnham: Ashgate, 2009), pp.115–34. See, also, Natasha Bakht, 'Veiled Objections: Facing Public Opposition to the Niqab', in Lori Beaman (ed.), *Defining Reasonable Accommodation* (Vancouver: UBC Press, 2010), pp.70–108.

71   *The Guardian*, 29 June 2007.

72   'Veil row magistrate reprimanded', BBC News (online), 8 January 2008.

73   Pat Marie Maher and Ann C. Slocum, 'Freedom in Dress: Legal Sanctions' *Clothing and Textiles Research Journal* 5.14 (1987), p.21.

74   Laurie Goodstein, 'Georgia: Lawsuit Over Muslim Woman's Head Scarf', *New York Times*, 15 December 2010, p.A20.

75   There is a debate around the possibility that the veil might infringe an accused's ancient right to have their accuser brought before their face. See, for example, Daniel H. Pollitt, 'The Right to Confrontation: Its History and Modern Dress' *Journal of Public Law* 8 (1959), pp.381–413; Ian Dennis, 'The Right to Confront Witnesses: Meanings, Myths and Human Rights' *Crim L R* 4 (2010), p.255; Brian M. Murray, 'Confronting Religion: Veiled Muslim Witnesses and the Confrontation Clause' *Notre Dame L Rev* 85 (2010), p.1727.

Figure 5.3 Pierre Cavellat (untitled, 13 April 1992), a Muslim woman in veil emerging from the sea.

Source: Reproduced from Ruth Herz, *The Art of Justice: The Judge's Perspective* (Oxford: Hart Publishing Ltd, 2012), by kind permission of Ruth Herz, Hart Publishing and the family of Pierre Cavellat.

the knee to jerk in the first place. The relevant stimulus may be non-rational, but it might also be culturally ingrained and deeply and sincerely felt. (The French artist and judge Pierre Cavellat produced a watercolour image late on in his life which expresses his appreciation of the cultural significance of the veiled Muslim woman and which perhaps reveals a degree of personal – and perhaps juridical – unease concerning her potential to confront French cultural traditions, see Figure 5.3.)[76] In short, it may have a good deal in common with religious sensibility. It is not my purpose here to attempt to put another spin on the endlessly turning debate regarding the rights and wrongs of the Islamic veil in a secular society. My interest is in the law's cultural commitment to the fabrication of a certain idea of the civil face and

76   See Ruth Herz, *The Art of Justice: The Judge's Perspective* (Oxford: Hart, 2012).

the force with which it seeks to fashion that face for itself and to enforce it on (and perform it for) society at large. It is the cultural commitment of the civil authorities, combined with the force of fashion, that tends to produce confrontation and conflict (knee-jerk or otherwise) when the Islamic veil is presented in *facie curia*. So far as the dull currency of justiciable rights and wrongs is concerned, it must be the case that neither side is wholly right or wholly wrong. All that is required, legally speaking, is to find a workable compromise in particular cases of conflict. The practice adopted in the New Zealand case *Police* v. *Razamjoo*[77] shows what can be achieved if the knee-jerk reaction is appropriately inhibited. In the case, two *niqab*-wearing female witnesses were required to remove the *niqab* but were permitted to wear headscarves covering their hair and to give evidence from behind screens so that only the male judge (Justice Lindsay Moore), counsel and female court staff were able to see their faces. A leading scholar of law and religion has called this an 'elegant compromise'.[78] The current guidance for UK courts is equally nuanced. According to the section on 'Religious dress' in the *Equal Treatment Bench Book*, the current guidance, as amended by the Judicial Studies Board in February 2007, is as follows:

> While there are a range of different possible approaches, depending on the circumstances of the particular case and the individual concerned, the interests of justice remain paramount. In essence, it is for the judge, in any set of circumstances, to consider what difference, if any, would be made to those interests by the niqab being worn. It may well be, that after consideration, there is no necessity to take any steps at all.

The guidance goes on to state that '[a]s with all practices, the response must be thoughtful and sensitive'. No knee-jerking here. There is, though, a most revealing paragraph in which the guidance questions whether a veil-wearing judge would be compatible with the official face of the law:

> It is where the woman concerned is providing the 'face' of justice – as a judge, magistrate or tribunal member – that the question of the

---

77   [2005] DCR 408. Discussed in David Griffiths, 'Pluralism and the Law: New Zealand Accommodates the *Burqa*' *Otago L Rev* 11 (2006), p.281; Rex J. Ahdar, 'Reflections on the Path of Religion-State Relations in New Zealand' *Brigham Young University Law Review* (2006), pp.619–959.

78   Ahdar, 'Reflections on the Path of Religion-State Relations'.

'transparency of justice' might be said most obviously to come into play. Is the constituency which is served by the courts entitled to see the person dispensing justice?

The guidance covers almost every conceivable category of case, from veil-wearing judges, to veiled witnesses, counsel, jury members, court staff and people in the public gallery. Cases of conflict have arisen in relation to each of these groups and will no doubt continue to do so. Examples include the magistrates in Leicester, England, who ordered a *niqab*-wearing woman to reveal her face but allowed her to give evidence behind a screen in a 2010 case that had been brought against her partner;[79] the decision of the Ontario Court of Appeal to uphold a rape victim's right to testify in court while wearing a veil provided it does not impede a fair trial;[80] in France, the day after the veil law was ratified,[81] the expulsion of a woman from the public gallery because she was wearing a face-covering veil;[82] the Muslim woman who, on the point of being sworn in to a jury in a criminal trial in England, confirmed her preference to continue wearing her *niqab* and was therefore required by the judge to stand down.[83]

If any location rivals the courtroom as a potential site of confrontation between the face of law and the fashioned face of an individual, it is the point of entry into the territorial jurisdiction of a nation State. The border is equivalent to the gate of the ancient polis. It is something like the skin of the State. As such, it is a defining locus for the demonstration of civil order through dress. No wonder, then, that uniformed guards police the border and that people passing through the threshold are scrutinized in every aspect of their physical appearance. Sometimes the response of the civil authorities is extreme. Liela Ahmed cites the example of a teenage girl at the security checkpoint at Baltimore airport, who reported that she 'experienced a distinct sense of menace when . . . asked to remove her *hijab*' (not even a veil, it should be said). She queried the request 'and tried to explain that it was a religious symbol', but acceded when 'she was surrounded by military

---

79   Andy Bloxham, 'Magistrates Order Pregnant Muslim to Remove Veil', *The Telegraph*, 8 October 2010.
80   *The Queen* v. *NS* (2010) Court of Appeal for Ontario, Court File C50534.
81   '*La loi sur le voile intégral*' (Décision n° 2010–613 DC, le Conseil Constitutionnel, 7 October 2010).
82   Agence France Presse, 8 October 2010.
83   Owen Bowcott, 'When a Veiled Woman Had to Leave Court', *The Guardian* (Features), 21 March 2012.

personnel carrying rifles'.[84] Such an incident might shock us, but it should not surprise us given what we now know about the place of dress in the fabrication of the façade of State. The phenomenon is not restricted to States with a Muslim minority. Algeria has a 99 per cent Muslim population, but it has imposed a ban on the wearing of Islamic veils and Islamic styles of beard for the purposes of passport photographs.[85] A cultural appreciation of the veil is essential to understanding what is at stake for the wearer when they present themselves at the international border of a State. Susan Ireland makes the point that when people 'migrate from one country to another, they are faced with the question of how to fit in and must decide which aspects of their culture of origin to keep'.[86]

Dress codes are culturally contextual. If someone flees semi-naked into a public street to escape a house fire, no right-thinking person would consider that any customary code of dress has been infringed. Laws are likewise truly meaningful only within the culture that produces them.[87] We do not expect to export our national laws when we travel to foreign jurisdictions, why should we expect to export our domestic dress code? When a Saudi woman living in France asked a leading Muslim cleric how women should respond to local laws in countries that ban the veil, his ruling (*fatwa*) that they could obey such laws, confirms the culturally contextual nature of the practice.[88] If veiling had been a strict requirement of Islamic law (which most Muslim clerics agree it is not), he would have ruled that women must defy the ban or depart the country. At least one leading Islamic jurist has gone even further and has said that Muslim women should positively abide by local rules if the removal of the veil poses no threat to their well-being. In a lecture delivered in New Zealand, Dr Muhammad Tahir-ul-Qadr stated that '[f]or women living here, it's not a Koranic obligation. They should follow the law of the land'.[89]

84   Ahmed, *A Quiet Revolution*, p.204 (quoting Anny Bakalian and Medhi Bozorgmehr, *Backlash 9/11 Middle Eastern and Muslim Americans Respond* [Berkeley: University of California Press, 2009], pp.145–6).

85   For an interesting global survey of controversies involving the male beard, see 'Hair, Beards and Power: Taking It on the Chin', *The Economist*, 5 August 2010.

86   Susan Ireland, 'Writing the Body in Marlène Amar's *La Femme sans tête*' *The French Review* 71.3 (1998), pp.454–67, 454.

87   Gary Watt, 'Comparison as Deep Appreciation', in P. G. Monateri (ed.), *Methods of Comparative Law* (Cheltenham: Edward Elgar, 2012), pp.82–103.

88   'Fatwa on Veil Ban', *Dominion Post*, 26 July 2010.

89   Ian Steward, 'Take Off Face Veils, Says Leading Muslim Scholar', *Fairfax NZ News*, 6 August 2011.

The challenge for the wearer of Islamic dress is an example of the challenge we all face when confronted with codes of dress and codes of law. The challenge is to respect the prescriptions and proscriptions that others place on us publicly while endeavouring to respect the pressures that are imposed on us, and the principles that we adopt for ourselves, privately. The challenge is to find a way to live with others while being able to live with ourselves. In short, the challenge is to fit in.

CHAPTER SIX

Something More Comfortable: A Fitting Conclusion

That the Thought-forms, Space and Time, wherein, once for all, we are sent into this Earth to live, should condition and determine our whole Practical reasonings, conceptions, and imagings – seems altogether fit, just, and unavoidable.[1]

Carlyle accepts that the formal frames of the world are bound to condition our image of the world and to determine the practical ways in which we imagine ourselves in it. Those formal frames include dress and law. What Carlyle does not accept is that such forms should usurp 'pure spiritual Meditation' on 'the wonder everywhere'. As he writes elsewhere in *Sartor Resartus*:

> . . . a Cause-and-Effect Philosophy of Clothes, as of Laws, were probably a comfortable winter-evening entertainment: nevertheless . . . Let any Cause-and-Effect Philosopher explain, not why I wear such and such a Garment, obey such and such a Law; but even why *I* am *here*, to wear and obey any thing![2]

Carlyle anticipates one of the major challenges facing law and dress today, which is how we can accommodate an individual's deeply held philosophical or spiritual principles within the workaday practices of the world. Of course, it is not a new problem. Socrates died for it. Probably the most famous instruction on the subject is Jesus' counsel that we should 'give to Caesar what is Caesar's, and to God what is God's'.[3] How shall we know what is Caesar's and what is God's? Jesus' advice is to look to the matter at hand and to consider what face appears in it. Caesar's image is on the coin, so

---

1   Thomas Carlyle, *Sartor Resartus: The Life and Opinions of Herr Teufelsdröckh* (1833–4) (Boston: James Munroe and Co, 1836), Book III, chapter 8.

2   Ibid., Book I, chapter 5.

3   Mt. 22.21.

that belongs to Caesar. God's image is on the human heart, so that belongs to God. How, then, should we respond when the State requires us to dress or undress in a certain way? Which face do we see in the fabric of the State's command? Carlyle identifies the problem of accommodation, but he offers little in the way of advice, except that we should seek to look through all artificial fabrications in order to see spiritual reality. In this concluding chapter, I will consider how in practice it might look and feel if we were to attempt to achieve, and if we were actually to achieve, a 'comfortable fit'.

The first thing is to correct our understanding of the notion of 'comfortable fit'. There can hardly be a phrase in the English language that is so diametrically opposed to its original etymological sense. For most of us a comfortable fit denotes clothing that is so much like a second skin that we are almost wholly unaware that we are wearing it. On that understanding, a comfortable fit is something that makes us feel relaxed. The actual etymological sense of 'comfort' is that it should strengthen us (to comfort is to supply 'with strength': '*con-fortis*'), and when something is 'fit' for us it should present us with a well-matched struggle (as in the phrase 'a fitting opponent'). A comfortable fit, in the etymological sense, is a struggle that strengthens. When clothes are a comfortable fit, they are not so loose that they accommodate us effortlessly and neither are they so tight that they constrain us unhealthily. Clothes that are a comfortable fit, such as a bespoke pair of shoes, suit us so well that we are improved by wearing them and they are improved by being worn by us. It is nevertheless a struggle to find such clothes, and very often it is a struggle to squeeze into them at first. This is a metaphor for our struggle to fit into society and to find accommodation in the formal frames that such cultural orders as language, architecture, dress and law impose on us. If we feel no struggle in society, it cannot be that the shape of society fits us perfectly. It can only be that we have lost our own sense of shape or, which is much the same thing, that we have become desensitized at those points where we ought to be feeling the squeeze that comes from pressure to conform. It is to criticize the type of self-indulgent person who feels no struggle in the effort to accommodate themself within society, that the novelist Mr Popular Sentiment (a character in Trollope's *The Warden*) depicts the villain of one of his populist novels as someone who wears 'huge loose shoes' to accommodate his deformed feet.[4]

---

4   Anthony Trollope, *The Warden* (London: Longman, Brown, Green and Longmans, 1855), chapter 15. (Trollope's 'Mr Popular Sentiment' was intended to parody Charles Dickens.)

The problem of finding a fit is exacerbated by the difficulty of finding the form of the civil face that confronts us and the contours to which civil authority requires us to conform. Accordingly, the first task of this book has been to reveal the cultural connections between law and dress that surround us everywhere but are concealed, camouflaged or otherwise invisible to us. Before I became a legal academic, I qualified as a practicing lawyer. In the first week or two of my training period with the law firm, one of the partners kindly drew me aside to offer a friendly word of advice. He had noticed that in my dealings with the partners of the firm I had been 'rather overfamiliar', by which he meant 'insufficiently deferential'. That this was his actual meaning was made clear in the peculiar turn of phrase with which he cautioned me. Smiling, still kindly, he informed me that 'we are not in the army . . .'; then, slowly and deliberately, he tapped his left shoulder with the fingers of his right hand, 'but there is invisible braid on these shoulders'. I hadn't signed up for this, but I struggled on, continually alert to the forces that are always seeking to compel conformity to concealed codes. I wonder if that partner in the law firm ever struggled within the skin of his professional suit.

We should be swift to judge ourselves and slow to judge others.[5] The architectural threshold was an ancient site of judicial judgment and the personal threshold of dress is the site at which we judge others and at which we ourselves are judged, whether or not we offer ourselves up for judgment. Emmanuel Levinas has written a great deal on the ethical dimension of face-to-face encounter. I read him to say that when we are presented with the face of another we should not oppose it and impose upon it, but that we should attempt to appreciate it. He writes that 'the face presents itself and calls for justice' (*'le visage se presente et reclame justice'*),[6] and, even more dramatically, that the 'face of the other is the first expression and its first word is "thou shalt not kill"' (*'son visage, est l'expression originelle, est le premier mot: "Tu ne commettras pas de meurtre"'*).[7] It is interesting in this regard that Liela Ahmed's survey of Muslim women's reasons for wearing the veil revealed that for some of them it 'functioned as a way of signaling a

---

5   On the relation between time and the process of judgment, see Julen Etxabe, *The Experience of Tragic Judgment* (Abingdon: Routledge, 2012).

6   *Totalité et Infini: essai sur l'extériorité* (1961), 4th edn (The Hague: Martinus Nijhoff, 1984), p.270.

7   Ibid., p.173. See, further, Steven Hendley, *From Communicative Action to the Face of the Other: Levinas and Habermas on Language, Obligation and Community* (Landham, MD: Lexington Books, 2000). Jeffrey Bloechl (ed.), *The Face of the Other and the Trace of God: Essays on the Philosophy of Emmanuel Levinas* (New York: Fordham University Press, 2000).

call for justice'.[8] The legal philosopher John Rawls argues that the exercise of just judgment requires that we should imaginatively conceal ourselves from ourselves behind a 'veil of ignorance' through which we are unable to discern the extent to which others share our gender, our race, our creed or any of our other particular qualities and interests.[9] Putting an interesting spin on this, I. Bennett Capers proposes '[s]omething akin to Rawls in drag',[10] when he argues that judges (including all of us) should imaginatively cross-dress others in other clothes, and ask how our appreciation of a person might change if they were of a different gender, race, creed and so forth.[11] Cross-dressing was prohibited in ancient Israel.[12] Perhaps cross-dressing, judicially imagined, is the justice to supplement that law.

We might accept that civilized social life requires that we should judge others as if they were other than they are, or judge others as if they were ourselves. We might be less ready to accept that we have a duty to judge ourselves. We might subscribe to the Millsian view that we are all sovereign and free to do as we like, provided that our conduct does no harm to others. If we think that way, what kind of a society are we imagining for ourselves? Is it one in which each is free to indulge himself or herself right up to the point at which the law can prove harm to others? Would the sense of respect in such a society extend at all beyond respect for the face of law? Should an individual's freedom to fashion themselves be absolute within the bounds of legality, or does freedom entail direct responsibility to respect each other?

Consider, again, the example of the female who insists on presenting herself topless in public in a modern city. In most jurisdictions, the reasonable onlooker would disapprove of such behaviour. Not, perhaps, out of any personal objection or prudish outlook, but because of the sense that in a society which recognizes great freedom to self-fashion, it is down to each one of us to govern (i.e. to 'dress' or 'order') ourselves appropriately. This state of affairs can be contrasted with England in the late sixteenth

---

8   Liela Ahmed, *Quiet Revolution: The Veil's Resurgence, from the Middle East to America* (New Haven and London: Yale UP, 2011), p.211.

9   John Rawls, *A Theory of Justice* (Cambridge, MA: Harvard University Press, 1971), chapter 3, part 24.

10   I. Bennett Capers, 'Cross Dressing and the Criminal' *Yale Journal of Law & the Humanities* 20.1 (2008), p.23.

11   Jimmy McGovern's' television drama *Accused* tells the story of a transvestite who appeared in the dock 'in drag' with a view to presenting a more true face to the court. (Series 2 Episode 1 'Tracie's Story' [Dir: Ashley Pearce], BBC television, 2012). I am grateful to Catherine Wooldridge, one of my students, for bringing this scene to my attention.

12   See Deut. 22.5.

century, when, despite contemporary puritanism, contemporary reports identify a fashion among women to go topless in public.[13] Arguably, it was the very fact that dress was officially governed by laws which made people feel so free to liberate themselves within the letter of those laws (a law that prohibits a woman from wearing fine furs cannot, on a strict reading, touch her freedom to wear nothing at all). Today, choice of dress is not restricted by formal rules. If we wish to adorn ourselves in nothing but purple silk, nothing but our purse and peer pressure can stop us. In terms of modes of dress, we are all monarchs now. It is therefore incumbent upon us to govern ourselves with respect for others. A monarch's freedom should not be turned to tyranny.

Recall how King Gilgamesh grew tyrannical because he had all the rights and freedoms of a king, but lacked all restraint. Enkidu, who was the king's equal in strength, was sent to be his adversary. He provided a fitting match for the king and thereby rendered the king fit to rule. It is written that 'they that wear soft clothing are in kings' houses'.[14] Enkidu can be said to have fitted Gilgamesh to a dress more suitable for a king – a suit of struggle. Enkidu provided the comfortable fit that the king required. He resisted and restrained Gilgamesh where the king could not resist and restrain himself. Gilgamesh and his kingdom were strengthened as a result. The notion that struggle (especially with wild or 'uncivilized' nature) produces moral growth was taken up in Greek philosophical thought and recurs as a theme in Greek art. For example, part of the ornamentation on the Parthenon of the Acropolis depicts civilized nature struggling with untamed wildness in the form of Lapiths wrestling with Centaurs.[15] The theme also emerges in other areas of Greek endeavour, including sport. In ancient Greece when two men wrestled, as Gilgamesh and Enkidu wrestled, they wrestled naked. Why they did so is not clear, but perhaps there was a sense that the restraining, civilizing order of dress was otiose where the civil project was being so perfectly progressed through the fitting match of sporting adversaries.

What each of us wants as an individual citizen of the State is for the laws of the State to accommodate us as carefully as they can. If a rule is too strict

---

13   For a useful discussion, see Valerie Traub, *The Renaissance of Lesbianism in Early Modern England* (Ann Arbor: University of Michigan, 2002), chapter 3.

14   Mt. 11.8 (King James Version).

15   It is strangely fitting that the struggle for those stones – the so-called Elgin marbles – is ongoing to this day, although it remains to be seen if progress will proceed from the realization that there is something of the civil and the Centaur on both sides.

and rigid to accommodate the contours of our particular person, we hope that the rule might be modified and moulded a little, so that we can live with it without having to break the law or break ourselves. When we talk about desiring law that is modified or moderate in this sense, what we are requesting, in fact, is that individual agents of the law – those who make it and enforce it and facilitate it – will acknowledge their own humanity and in so doing acknowledge ours. We are asking them to question the routines they follow – we are asking them to sit uncomfortably in their suits. If we have such hopes of the individuals who make up the face of the law, would it not be hypocritical to have no similar aspiration for ourselves? At the time of writing, the BBC website carries a page on the status of the Islamic veil in European countries. The first line makes the point that European States 'have wrestled with the issue of the Muslim veil'. The least we can ask of ourselves, if we wish to go veiled or naked, is that we should wrestle with the problem of fitting in and consider the challenge in terms of individual responsibilities as well as individual rights. Instead of standing on our right to wear such and such and demanding that the face of the law should be made to accommodate us, should we not struggle to squeeze ourselves, as far as we may, to the shape of the society that surrounds us? There will come a point beyond which we cannot bend our principles without breaking them, and we should not press beyond that point: 'Everyone knows where his own shoe pinches.'[16] We should, though, feel the pain of approaching that point. This is the true meaning of a comfortable fit.

'No symbolic code can fully cover something so infinitely malleable and changeful as the human being.'[17] That statement was made in the context of dress, but it applies just as well to law. Indeed, the problem of how to fit or fashion general rules to the particular form of a human individual and to the facts of their particular case has been a recognized feature of law since ancient times.[18] Georg Simmel sees the same essential struggle in dress and in law:

The whole history of society is reflected in the striking conflicts, the compromises, slowly won and quickly lost, between socialistic adaptation

---

16   Trollope, *The Warden*, chapter 13.

17   William J. F. Keenan, 'Introduction', *Dressed to Impress: Looking the Part* (Dress, Body, Culture) (Oxford and New York: Berg, 2001), p.26.

18   So far as law is concerned, that effort has the name of 'equity'. See Gary Watt, *Equity Stirring: The Story of Justice Beyond Law* (Oxford: Hart, 2009).

to society and individual departure from its demands . . . It becomes self-evident that there is no institution, no law, no estate of life, which can uniformly satisfy the full demands of the two opposing principles. The only realization of this condition possible for humanity finds expression in constantly changing approximations, in ever retracted attempts and ever revived hopes.[19]

The truth we are searching for to make sense of our social life is not a naked truth hidden from our gaze, or the shows of truth that civil authority thrusts before our eyes. The truth we seek resides rather in the fact that law and dress will always confront us so long as we are social and civil beings; more than this, the truth resides in the struggle which must be our constant response to that confrontation.

19   Georg Simmel, 'Fashion' *International Quarterly* 10 (1904), pp.130–55, 131.

Select Bibliography

Agamben, Giorgio, *Homo Sacer: Sovereign Power and Bare Life* (trans. Daniel Heller-Roazen) (Stanford: Stanford University Press, 1998).

Ahmed, Liela, *A Quiet Revolution: The Veil's Resurgence, from the Middle East to America* (New Haven and London: Yale UP, 2011).

Alexandre, Arsène, *Honoré Daumier, l'homme et l'oeuvre* (Paris: H Laurens, 1888).

Ashelford, Jane, *The Art of Dress: Clothes and Society, 1500–1914* (London: National Trust, 1999).

Beaman, Lori (ed.), *Defining Reasonable Accommodation* (Vancouver: UBC Press, 2010).

Bell, Quentin, *On Human Finery* (1947) (London: The Hogarth Press, 1976).

Bloechl, Jeffrey (ed.), *The Face of the Other and the Trace of God. Essays on the Philosophy of Emmanuel Levinas* (New York: Fordham University Press, 2000).

Bourdieu, Pierre, *Outline of a Theory of Practice (Esquisse d'une théorie de la pratique*, 1972) (Cambridge: CUP, 1977).

Bruzzi, Stella, *Undressing Cinema: Clothing and Identity in the Movies* (Abingdon: Routledge, 1997).

Burroughs, Catherine B. and Ehrenreich, Jeffrey (eds), *Reading the Social Body* (Iowa City: University of Iowa Press, 1993).

Cain, Julien, *Daumier: Les Gens de Justice* (New York: Tudor Publishing Co., 1959).

Cardona, George, Henry M. Hoenigswald and Alfred Senn (eds), *Indo-European and Indo-Europeans: Papers Presented at the Third Indo-European Conference at the University of Pennsylvania* (Philadelphia: University of Pennsylvania Press, 1970).

Carlyle, Thomas, *Sartor Resartus: The Life and Opinions of Herr Teufelsdröckh* (Boston: James Munroe and Co., 1836).

Carter, Michael, *Fashion Classics from Carlyle to Barthes* (Oxford and New York: Berg, 2003).

Certeau, Michel de, *The Practice of Everyday Life* (trans. Steven F. Rendall) (Berkeley: University of California Press, 2002).

Çinar, Alev, *Modernity, Islam, and Secularism in Turkey: Bodies, Places, and Time* (Minneapolis: University of Minnesota Press, 2005).

Clark, Kenneth, *The Nude: A Study in Ideal Form* (London: John Murray, 1956).

Craik, Jennifer, *Uniforms Exposed: From Conformity to Transgression* (Oxford and New York: Berg, 2005).

Derriman, James Parkyns, *Pageantry of the Law* (London: Eyre & Spottiswoode, 1955).

Douzinas, Costas and Nead, Lynda (eds), *Law and the Image: The Authority of Art and the Aesthetics of Law* (Chicago: University of Chicago Press, 1999).

Edmondson, Jonathan and Keith, Alison (eds), *Roman Dress and the Fabrics of Roman Culture* (Toronto: University of Toronto Press, 2008).

Eicher, Joanne B., Evenson, Sandra L. and Lutz, Hazel A. (eds), *The Visible Self: Global Perspectives of Dress, Culture, and Society* (2nd edn) (New York: Fairchild, 2000).

Elias, Norbert, *Über den Prozess der Zivilisation* (1939); (trans. Edmund Jephcott) *The Civilizing Process* (Oxford: Blackwell, 1978).

Entwistle, Joanne and Wilson, Elizabeth (eds), *Body Dressing* (Oxford and New York: Berg, 2001).

Feher, Michel and Ramona Naddaff (eds), *Fragments for a History of the Human Body* Vol. II (New York: Zone Books, 1989).

Ffoulkes, Charles, *The Armourer and His Craft* (London: Methuen, 1912).

Fischer-Mirkin, Toby, *Dress Code: Understanding the Hidden Meanings of Women's Clothes* (New York: Clarkson Potter, 1995).

Flügel, John Carl, *Psychology of Clothes* (1930) (London: The Hogarth Press, 1950).

Foucault, Michel, *Discipline and Punish: The Birth of the Prison* (London: Penguin, 1977).

Fox, Kate, *Watching the English* (London: Hodder & Staughton, 2004).

Foyer, Jean le, *Daumier au Palais de Justice* (Paris: La Colombe, 1958).

George, Andrew, *The Epic of Gilgamesh* (Penguin Classics) Rev. edn (London: Penguin Books, 2003).

Göle, Nilüfer, *The Forbidden Modern: Civilization and Veiling* (Ann Arbor: University of Michigan Press, 1997).

Hargreaves-Mawdsley, William Norman, *A History of Legal Dress in Europe Until the End of the Eighteenth Century* (Oxford: Clarendon Press, 1963).

Hart, Herbert L. A., *The Concept of Law* (Oxford: Clarendon Press, 1961).

Hayward, Maria, *Rich Apparel: Clothing and Law in Henry VIII's England* (Farnham: Ashgate, 2009).

Hendley, Steven, *From Communicative Action to the Face of the Other: Levinas and Habermas on Language, Obligation and Community* (Landham, MD: Lexington Books, 2000).

Herz, Ruth, *The Art of Justice: The Judge's Perspective* (Oxford: Hart, 2012).

Horn, Marilyn J. and Gurel, Lois M., *The Second Skin: An Interdisciplinary Study of Clothing* 3rd edn (Boston: Houghton Mifflin & Co, 1981).

Hunt, Alan, *Governance of the Consuming Passions: History of Sumptuary Law* (Language, Discourse, Society) (Basingstoke: Palgrave Macmillan, 1996).

Hutson, Lorna, *The Invention of Suspicion: Law and Mimesis in Shakespeare and Renaissance Drama* (Oxford: Oxford University Press, 2007).

Keenan, William J. F. (ed.), *Dressed to Impress: Looking the Part* (Dress, Body, Culture) (Oxford and New York: Berg, 2001).

Kessler, Marni R., *Sheer Presence: The Veil in Manet's Paris* (Minneapolis: The University of Minnesota Press, 2006).

Kuhn, Cynthia and Carlson, Cindy (eds), *Styling Texts: Dress and Fashion in Literature* (Youngstown, NY: Cambria, 2007).

Langner, Lawrence, *The Importance of Wearing Clothes* (New York: Hastings House Publishers, 1959).

Laver, James, *Taste and Fashion: From the French Revolution Until Today* (London: George Harrap, 1937).

— *Costume in Antiquity* (London: Thames and Hudson, 1964).

— *Modesty in Dress* (London: William Heinemann Ltd, 1969).

Levinas, Emmanuel, *Totalité et Infini: essai sur l'extériorité* (1961) 4th edn (The Hague: Martinus Nijhoff, 1984).

Lévi-Strauss, Claude, *Structural Anthropology* (New York: Basic Books, 1963).

Lindley, David (ed.), *The Court Masque* (Manchester: MUP, 1984).

Lipovetsky, Gilles, *L'Empire de l'éphémère: la mode et son destin dans les sociétés modernes* (Paris: Gallimard, 1987); (trans. Catherine Porter), *The Empire of Fashion: Dressing Modern Democracy* (Princeton, NJ: Princeton University Press, 2002).

Lurie, Alison, *The Language of Clothes* (London: Bloomsbury, 1992).

MacDonald, William L., *The Architecture of the Roman Empire II: An Urban Appraisal* (New Haven and London: Yale University Press, 1986).

MacLeod, Arlene Elowe, *Accommodating Protest: Working Women, the New Veiling, and Change in Cairo* (New York: Columbia University Press, 1991).

Mahmood, Saba, *Politics of Piety: The Islamic Revival and the Feminist Subject* (Princeton, NJ: Princeton University Press, 2004).

Mallory, James Patrick and Adams, Douglas Quentin, *The Oxford Introduction to Proto-Indo-European and the Proto-Indo-European World* (Oxford: OUP, 2006).

Marmor, Andrei, *Social Conventions* (Princeton, NJ: Princeton University Press, 2009).

Masquelier, Adeline (ed.), *Dirt, Undress and Difference: Critical Perspectives on the Body's Surface* (Bloomington and Indianapolis: Indiana University Press, 2005).

Mulcahy, Linda, *Legal Architecture: Justice, Due Process and the Place of Law* (Abingdon: Routledge, 2010).

Norton-Kyshe, James W., *The Law and Customs Relating to Gloves* (London: Stevens and Haynes, 1901).

Parkins, Wendy (ed.), *Fashioning the Body Politic: Dress, Gender, Citizenship* (Oxford and New York: Berg, 2002).

Pastoureau, Michel, *Etoffe du diable: Une Histoire Des Rayures et des Tissus Rayés* (Paris: éditions du Seuil, 1991); (English trans. Jody Gladding) *The Devil's Cloth: A History of Stripes and Striped Fabric* (New York: Columbia University Press, 2001).

Poiret, Paul, *En habillant l'époque* (Paris: Grasset, 1930).

Raffield, Paul, *Images and Cultures of Law in Early Modern England: Justice and Political Power, 1558–1660* (Cambridge: CUP, 2004).

Roach, Mary E. and Eicher, Joanne B. (eds), *Dress, Adornment, and the Social Order* (New York and London: John Wiley & Sons, 1965).

Rosen, Lawrence, *Law as Culture: An Invitation* (Princeton, NJ: Princeton University Press, 2006).

Saggs, Henry W. F., *The Babylonians* (1962) (London: The Folio Society, 2002).

Scott, Joan Wallach, *The Politics of the Veil* (Princeton, NJ: Princeton University Press, 2010).

Shapiro, Barbara J., *'Beyond Reasonable Doubt' and 'Probable Cause': Historical Perspectives on the Anglo-American Law of Evidence* (Berkeley: University of California Press, 1991).

Stallybrass, Peter and Jones, Ann Rosalind, *Renaissance Clothing and the Materials of Memory* (Cambridge: Cambridge University Press, 2000).

Stillman, Yedida K., *Arab Dress: A Short History: from the Dawn of Islam to Modern Times* (ed. Norman A. Stillman) (Leiden: Brill, 2000).

Stubbs, Phillip, *Anatomy of Abuses in England* (London: Richard Jones, 1583).

Summers, Leigh, *Bound To Please: A History of the Victorian Corset* (Oxford and New York: Berg, 2001).

Tristan, Flora, *Peregrinations d'une Paria* (*Peregrinations of a Pariah*) (Paris: L'advocat, 1838).

Turner, Victor W., *The Forest of Symbols: Aspects of Ndembu Ritual* (Ithaca: Cornell University Press, 1967).

Veblen, Thorstein, *The Theory of the Leisure Class* Oxford World's Classics (1899) (Oxford: OUP, 2007).

Vincent, Susan, *Dressing the Elite: Clothes in Early Modern England* (Oxford and New York: Berg, 2003).

Warwick, Alexandra and Cavallaro, Dani, *Fashioning the Frame: Boundaries, Dress and the Body* (Oxford and New York: Berg, 1998).

Welton, Donn (ed.), *The Body* (Oxford: Blackwell Publishers, 1999).

White, James Boyd, *The Legal Imagination* (Boston: Little, Brown and Co, 1973).

Wilson, Elizabeth, *Adorned in Dreams: Fashion and Modernity* (1985) Rev. edn (London: I B Tauris & Co Ltd, 2009).

Woodcock, Thomas, *Legal Habits: A Brief Sartorial History of Wig, Robe and Gown* (London: Ede and Ravenscroft, 2003).

Zito, Angela and Barlow, Tani E. (eds), *Body, Subject, and Power in China* (Chicago: University of Chicago Press, 1994).

Index